THE POLITICS OF THEATRE AND DRAMA

INSIGHTS

General Editor: Clive Bloom, Senior Lecturer in English, Middlesex Polytechnic

Editorial Board: Clive Bloom, Brian Docherty, Gary Day, Lesley Bloom and Hazel Day

Insights brings to academics, students and general readers the very best contemporary criticism on neglected literary and cultural areas. It consists of anthologies, each containing original contributions by advanced scholars and experts. Each contribution concentrates on a study of a particular work, author or genre in its artistic, historical and cultural context.

Published titles

Clive Bloom (*editor*)
JACOBEAN POETRY AND PROSE: Rhetoric, Representation and the Popular
              Imagination

TWENTIETH-CENTURY SUSPENSE: The Thriller Comes of Age
SPY THRILLERS: From Buchan to le Carré

Clive Bloom, Brian Docherty, Jane Gibb and Keith Shand (*editors*)
NINETEENTH-CENTURY SUSPENSE: From Poe to Conan Doyle

Gary Day (*editor*)
READINGS IN POPULAR CULTURE: Trivial Pursuits?

Gary Day and Clive Bloom (*editors*)
PERSPECTIVES ON PORNOGRAPHY: Sexuality in Film and Literature

Brian Docherty (*editor*)
AMERICAN CRIME FICTION: Studies in the Genre
AMERICAN HORROR FICTION: From Brockden Brown to Stephen King

Rhys Garnett and R. J. Ellis (*editors*)
SCIENCE FICTION ROOTS AND BRANCHES: Contemporary Critical Approaches

Robert Giddings (*editor*)
LITERATURE AND IMPERIALISM

Robert Giddings, Keith Selby and Chris Wensley
SCREENING THE NOVEL: The Theory and Practice of Literary Dramatization

Graham Holderness (*editor*)
THE POLITICS OF THEATRE AND DRAMA

Paul Hyland and Neil Sammells (*editors*)
IRISH WRITING: Exile and Subversion

Maxim Jakubowski and Edward James (*editors*)
THE PROFESSION OF SCIENCE FICTION: SF Writers on their Craft and Ideas

Mark Lilly (*editor*)
LESBIAN AND GAY WRITING: An Anthology of Critical Essays

Christopher Mulvey and John Simons (*editors*)
NEW YORK: City as Text

Adrian Page (*editor*)
DEATH OF THE PLAYWRIGHT? Modern British Drama and Literary Theory

Jeffrey Walsh and James Aulich (*editors*)
VIETNAM IMAGES: War and Representation

Further titles in preparation

The Politics of Theatre and Drama

Edited by

Graham Holderness
Head of Drama, Roehampton Institute
London

MACMILLAN

First published 1992 by
THE MACMILLAN PRESS LTD
Houndmills, Basingstoke, Hampshire RG21 2XS
and London
Companies and representatives
throughout the world

ISBN 0–333–51932–9 hardcover
ISBN 0–333–51933–7 paperback

A catalogue record for this book is available
from the British Library.

Printed in Hong Kong

Reprinted 1993

Series Standing Order

If you would like to receive future titles in this series as they are published, you can make use of our standing order facility. To place a standing order please contact your bookseller or, in case of difficulty,write to us at the address below with your name and address and the name of the series. Please state with which title you wish to begin your standing order. (If you live outside the United Kingdom we may not have the rights for your area, in which case we will forward your order to the publisher concerned.)

Customer Services Department, Macmillan Distribution Ltd
Houndmills, Basingstoke, Hampshire RG21 2XS, England

Contents

v

Notes on the Contributors

Clive Barker is Senior Lecturer in the Joint School of Theatre Studies at the University of Warwick. He is author of *Theatre Games* (1977) and joint editor of *New Theatre Quarterly*.

Jill Dolan is Assistant Professor in the Department of Theatre and Drama, University of Wisconsin-Madison. She is author of *The Feminist Spectator as Critic* (1988), and co-editor of *'The Drama Review'*: *thirty years of commentary on the avant-garde* (1986).

Richard Fotheringham is Lecturer in Drama at the University of Queensland. He is editor of *Community Theatre in Australia* (1987).

Graham Holderness is Head of Drama at Roehampton Institute, London. He is author of *D. H. Lawrence: history, ideology and fiction* (1982), *Shakespeare's History* (1985), *Wuthering Heights* (1985), *Women in Love* (1986), *Hamlet* (1987), *Shakespeare in Performance: 'The Taming of the Shrew'* (1989), *'Richard II': a critical study* (1989), *'Romeo and Juliet': a critical study* (1991); co-author of *Shakespeare: the play of history* (1987), and *Shakespeare: out of court* (1990); and editor of *The Shakespeare Myth* (1988).

Javed Malick teaches English in Khalsa College, University of Delhi.

Christopher J. McCullough is Lecturer in Drama at the University of Exeter.

Derek Paget is Senior Lecturer in English and Drama at Worcester College of Higher Education. He is author of *True Stories? documentary drama on radio, screen and stage (1990)*.

Peter Reynolds is Principal Lecturer in Drama at Roehampton Institute, and author of *Drama: Text into Performance* (1986), *As You Like It: a dramatic commentary* (1988), *Practical Approaches to Teaching Shakespeare* (1990) and *Shakespeare: Text into Performance* (1991).

Jeremy Ridgman is Senior Lecturer in Drama at Roehampton Institute, London.

Val Taylor is Lecturer in Drama at Roehampton Institute, London, and a freelance theatre director.

1

Introduction

GRAHAM HOLDERNESS

> Is political theatre a dead duck?
> (Michael Billington, *Guardian*, 10 May 1980)

When work on this book began in 1989, the Soviet Union was a one-party state, as it had been since 1917. The 'Berlin Wall' still divided East and West Germanies, standing as an obstructive monument to the Cold War, as it had stood for almost half a century. Nelson Mandela was in his twenty-sixth year of political imprisonment. Now as the project nears completion, all these familiar landmarks of my own generation's political world, each a great symbolic focus for political emotion and a framework for political organisation (anti-Stalinism, 'Eurocommunism', anti-apartheid), have vanished, apparently for good. Symptomatically these alterations testify to shifting configurations of circumstance and event which can induce a vertiginous dizziness, if we try to seek a firm foothold on such a rapidly-spinning globe. If these potent symbols of political oppression can evaporate so swiftly, then all that is solid may truly melt into air, and the clearing of these and other obstacles to human emancipation may signal a huge resurgence of political liberation.

Yet the contradictory quality of contemporary developments forbids any premature utopian celebration. Muscovites, still queuing for food, now wait patiently outside McDonald's. Bertolt Brecht's grave in Berlin has been desecrated by neo-Nazis, encouraged by hopes of German re-unification.[1] The South African government is still routinely shooting black workers in the streets. The definitive and vigorous popular rejection of centralised, bureaucratic state Communism in Eastern Europe seems accompanied there by no clear conception of what is likely to follow that collapse; by a hopelessly naïve reverence for the virtues of free-market capitalism; and by an alarming resurgence of nationalism, religious fundamentalism, reactionary political ideologies of all kinds. Some

1

commentators see a global bourgeois revolution sweeping through the East, and a Europe now ironically haunted by the spectre of capitalism.

Certainly the term from which this book's title was adapted – 'political theatre' – can hardly be expected to remain unaffected by such developments: if a term so much debated could ever have held coherent meaning as a theoretical concept, such meaning can scarcely now remain uninterrogated, undisturbed, unchanged. What does 'political theatre' mean today? The linking of the two terms immediately identifies a context of cultural difference, perhaps even a binary opposition: political theatre is not the same as ordinary theatre because it displays a different kind of relationship with something other than itself – 'politics'. What then is 'politics'? Politics is normally understood to be concerned with systems of government, the processes by means of which such systems are changed, and the nature of social participation in those changes; with relations between those systems of government, in co-operation and competition, peace and war; and with the individuals, parties and ideas which sustain, develop, defend and overthrow governments and the ideological formations by which their power is maintained. So to identify theatre as 'political' is to define a certain type of drama, but also to suggest a certain habitual relationship between theatre and politics: that they are *normally* very different areas of experience, which happen to become, in the activity of political theatre, interconnected.

What are the possibilities of this relationship? Theatre may be 'political' without becoming 'political theatre', in the sense that a play may represent political matters or address political issues, in exactly the same way as a play can represent love, or old age, or poverty, or madness; if, that is, the play performs that representation of politics in an *objective* way, without taking sides. Such drama is in a sense political by accident. Politics proper is surely, however, incompatible with a detached, objective perspective: politics is about making choices, taking sides, getting things done in order to re-shape the world along particular lines of development. If 'political theatre' is understood as theatre engaging in a different sort of relationship with politics, that process must entail theatre's becoming partisan, splitting along the lines of party conflict, lining up with one particular political group, or cause, or ideology, and offering articulate opposition to another group, or cause, or ideology.

So we could theoretically, and should in logic, have types of political theatre corresponding to divisions within the political life of a society. But in practical usage the concept 'political theatre' is almost exclusively synonymous with left-wing theatre, socialist theatre of various types. The concept can, within that limitation, cover a broad spectrum of dramatic activities and forms: it can relate to the major socialist dramatists who choose to work 'oppositionally' within mainstream institutions – Edward Bond, Howard Brenton, David Edgar, David Hare, Trevor Griffiths – or it can refer to a broad range of 'alternative' theatre groups that have operated on the 'fringe' of the mainstream, and often see themselves as politically active in a direct, agitational way. These activities span a broad spectrum, using different institutional spaces, different cultural forms, different technical conventions, to speak to different audiences. What they have had in common is a clear and overt commitment to socialist ideas, which in turn colours the form and content of their cultural production. But where is there a political theatre of the right? It seems that political theatre can be progressive, but not regressive; socialist but not conservative; subversive but not conformist or radically reactionary.

Earlier I distinguished between drama that merely represents the political as an aspect of life, and drama that is fundamentally shaped by political commitment and conviction. If we pursue that second definition in opposition to the first, 'symptomatic' concept of political theatre, we also have to acknowledge that the politics of a truly political theatre must be a matter of conscious choice and deliberate intention. If a political tendency is only a matter of unconscious predilection or instinctive preference, then that would seem to belong to the symptomatic definition of political theatre, where the realm of the political is merely an object of representation, and does not otherwise form a central or constitutive part of the cultural product itself. There is much more drama of this instinctively conservative type than there is polemically right-wing drama: the example of the stridently pro-Thatcher dramatist Ian Curteis, whose *Falklands Play* is discussed in Chapter 8, is unusual enough to stimulate curiosity. In the accepted use of the word, Ian Curteis is, oddly, a right-wing political dramatist, where writers who only convey an implicit or unconscious preference for (say) capitalism over socialism, the free market over the planned economy, competition over equality, bourgeois over proletarian culture – say Tom Stoppard – are not. As Derek Paget suggests in his essay on drama of the Falklands war, overtly political, reactionary agit-prop such as *The Falklands Play* appears if anything to be an embarrassment to the very Establishment it sycophantically supports. Such open disclosure is not the preferred means by which right-wing politics chooses to operate.

The various descriptive and analytical accounts of political theatre tend rather to ratify and endorse a generic class-distinction, whereby the term 'political' is appropriated as description and identification for drama of the left. Books about political theatre, essays on political drama, concern themselves wholly with left-wing production, largely with socialist, Communist and revolutionary Marxist work. If we postulate a tradition of political theatre, it goes back to Communist dramatists like Brecht. The term itself derives from *The Political Theatre*,[2] the Communist director Erwin Piscator's book about his own struggle to establish and develop revolutionary forms of progressive political drama in the Weimar Republic. When in 1960 Eric Bentley wrote about 'The Pro and Con of Political Theatre',[3] his pantheon of political dramatists consisted of Brecht, Shaw, and Clifford Odets. John Bull's *New British Political Dramatists*[4] deals with the socialist 'entrists' mentioned above, Brenton, Edgar, Hare, Griffiths.

 Catherine Itzin's *Stages in the Revolution: political theatre in Britain since 1968*[5] professes a concern with 'writers who were not just socially committed, but committed to a socialist society' (p. x). Her book covers the early, fringe work of Brenton–Edgar–Griffiths–Hare, and a host of socialist and socialist–feminist agit-prop groups and radical community theatre organisations active through the 1970s, some still alive today – Red Ladder, Inter-Action, Welfare State, 7:84, Belt and Braces, Joint Stock, Monstrous Regiment. These groups have varied in the particular form of their political engagement: some being (or having been) agit-prop groups, trying to relate drama and working-class politics very closely by direct engagement in trade union struggles, political campaigns, and so on; some drawing on older popular dramatic traditions and linking them with contemporary involvement; some concentrating on taking theatre to the people by touring; some settling in building-based companies aiming to relate to a specific working-class community, like the Half Moon Theatre or Theatre Workshop in Stratford East; some concerned with the development of political support for particular oppressed groups such as women or gays. All have been linked by a common commitment to an alternative, oppositional politics.

Sandy Craig, a founder-member of 7:84, included in his critical anthology *Dreams and Deconstructions* an essay called 'Unmasking the Lie: Political Theatre',[6] which covers exactly the same alternative ground as Itzin – Red Ladder, Inter-Action, Welfare State, 7:84, Belt and Braces, Joint Stock, Monstrous Regiment – though with some attempt to trace a historical tradition of popular political theatre from suggested roots in the proletarian theatre (Workers' Theatre Movement, Unity Theatre) of the 1930s. Andrew Davies in *Other Theatres*[7] deals with both these periods, with a chapter on 'Political Theatre Groups Between the Wars' – Workers' Theatre Movement, Unity Theatre – and another on 'Political Theatre in Britain since the 1960s' – which again goes over the same Craig-Itzin ground, with Red Ladder, Inter-Action, Welfare State, 7:84, Belt and Braces, Joint Stock, Monstrous Regiment.

Now this automatic identification of 'political' drama with 'left-wing' drama presents many problems of a theoretical kind. These problems are thrown into particularly sharp relief by those recent developments in cultural theory which insist, as a matter of course, that all drama, all theatre, all art, all culture, is in some fundamental sense, necessarily political. Post-structuralist theories of art, Marxist theories of ideology, deconstructionist theories of language and the sign, may differ one from another in many emphases, but all concur in recognising the political character of all culture. Alan Sinfield writes:

> Culture does not transcend the material forces and relations of production. Culture is not simply a reflection of the economic and political system, but nor can it be independent of it. Texts are inseparable from the conditions of their production and reception in history; and involved, necessarily, in the making of cultural meanings which are always, finally, political meanings.[8]

All culture, that is, contains or expresses or implies a political view: all art, whether consciously or unconsciously, is tendentious, polemical, partisan; all literature and drama speak on behalf of an admitted or unacknowledged belief that one order of things, one set of social arrangements, one structure of political relations, is better or worse than another.

Sinfield's position is a Marxist one, a philosophical allegiance indicated by the use of Marx's own key concepts 'forces and relations of production'. But in its definition of the relations between 'culture' and 'the economic and political system' it is quite different from the arguments many have found in Marx's own writings, and certainly different from what was the dominant Marxist understanding of culture prior to the 1970s. Earlier Marxist theories of art tended to assume that culture is very much a second-order activity, less important and less 'real' than the economic (and perhaps the political)[9] organisation of a society. To argue in those original Marxist terms that culture is dependent on the 'forces and relations of production' usually entailed the assertion that culture could only reflect and represent the primacy of economic and social activities. Sinfield is arguing for the very different view that culture is a material activity in its own right, and that it is one of the indispensable and constitutive ways in which a society's struggles, contradictions and developments are fought out, disclosed and advanced or thrown back.

Marx himself argued, in the passage from which Sinfield draws his philosophical vocabulary,[10] that a society's culture was a 'reflection' of its social and economic structure, a 'superstructure' automatically determined by changes and developments in the economic 'base'. Early Marxist work on literature and drama generally accepted this model, and regarded art as a passive reflector of reality. Aesthetic criticism was merely a matter of distinguishing between those works of art that reflected society accurately, and those that 'distorted' it. The former were then judged to be politically 'progressive', since they provided a means by which the working class could better understand the nature of the world, and the latter 'reactionary', since their distorted images of society would be likely to confuse and subvert the revolutionary political will.[11]

Although any socialist culture in Britain is likely to have been formed in part by the largely non-Marxist socialism of the indigenous Labour movement, that culture can be seen as strongly influenced by Marxism, and responding to changes in the nature of Marxist philosophy itself. Thus the rudimentary Marxist position outlined above, in which culture passively reflects the character of a society's economic and political structure, requires of artistic productions that they should manifest an overt 'politics of *content*', being unmistakably addressed to matters of political 'reality' – governments, administrative and legal systems, revolutions and reactions, economic oppression and militant proletarian organisation, war and class struggle. Much modern socialist drama does indeed exhibit this politics of content, and its radical credentials are affirmed by the accuracy and directness of its representation of the 'political'.

This emphasis on the politics of content is not without its theoretical difficulties. It coincides for example with what I have called the 'symptomatic' definition of political theatre, in which the matter of the play is simply the matter of 'politics' as conventionally understood, irrespective of any political intention the play may manifest, any political programme it may be designed to advance. The consequent representational emphasis of both content and form may transcend fundamental political divisions: Robert Bolt's *The State of Revolution* (1977), and Trevor Griffiths' *Occupations* (1970), though written from virtually opposite political perspectives, are indistinguishable as to either content or form.[12] A piece of reactionary agit-prop such as Ian Curteis' *The Falklands Play* occupies the same thematic and formal territory, offering a realistic account of the decisive actions of prominent politicians on the direction and development of the political process. These comparisons also raise a third category by means of which the 'political' quality of drama may be defined, which I shall call 'the politics of *function*'. A play by a dramatist like David Hare, clearly definable as a political play on the basis of these criteria, may be a conventional drama of high naturalism, performed in the Royal National Theatre, before an audience composed entirely of middle-class Londoners. The 'politics' of the play are confined exclusively to its content, and have no bearing on either its form, or its function within the institutional process of dramatic production.

There is evidence that Marx himself was dissatisfied with the 'base/superstructure' model as an explanation of culture, and his collaborator Friedrich Engels attempted in some important Marxist texts[13] some influential revisions. Engels argued that Marx and himself had been stressing the primacy of the economic base for justifiable reasons of emphasis and polemic, and that they had never intended to suggest that culture merely or mechanistically reflects social activity. The various spheres of institutional, ideological and cultural production are in reality, Engels proposed, relatively autonomous and to some degree independent of the primary material basis of a society; their nature is determined only 'in the last instance' by economic and social factors. This argument has been profoundly influential, but it remains by no means clear just how 'autonomous' these cultural spheres can be, if they are determined in the last instance by the economic base. The argument has been used to push Marxist cultural theory in opposite directions, towards the view that culture is in fact extremely autonomous, and towards a re-affirmation of the earlier Marxist position that social reality is the real foundation on which relatively independent cultural superstructures arise, only to be determined ultimately by the over-riding primacy of the economic process.

If culture is relatively (to whatever degree) autonomous, then the implication for our concept of political theatre is clear: drama would not need to provide any direct reflection of social reality, or to address directly the world of 'politics', in order to be considered political. A play could choose as its subject an apparently 'non-political' area of experience, and use it to explore political ideas and themes at some distance from the conventional 'reality' of political and economic process. Trevor Griffiths' play *Comedians* (1975), which explores political issues through the 'non-political' arena of stand-up comedy, would be a good example.

Engels' theory of 'relative autonomy' exercised an important influence on the development of structuralism, and was applied directly to cultural analysis by the French Marxist theoretician Louis Althusser.[14] In his work, and in that of many other seminal Marxist and Marxist-influenced thinkers, this revised Marxist position justified, from the late 1960s onwards, a shift of emphasis away from the direct analysis of society as economic and political organisation, and towards the analysis of a society's *ideology*. Again Marx's original formulations had appeared to suggest a very simple concept of ideology as 'false consciousness', a mystified representation of reality. Ideology gave only blurred and distorted visions of reality, while 'science' (that is, the Marxist philosophy of historical materialism) could provide a true representation. The new Marxist theories (which had in any case been anticipated by work initiated in the USSR in the 1920s)[15] began to acknowledge ideology as a much more substantial and concrete element of social organisation and development, and to conceive the task of Marxist philosophy as the critique of ideology as much as (or even rather than) the analysis of social, economic and political organisation.

This shift has profound implications for all theories of culture, and in particular for any conception of the politics of theatre and drama. The function of ideology is to endorse and naturalise a particular form of social organisation. Ideology may accomplish this task in complex, mediated, even distorted ways. One of its strategies is to shape and define the conception of a society's 'reality', closing off certain possible perspectives of interpretation: so that people will be able to experience and understand their society only in certain ways – as natural, inevitable, flawed but unalterable – and not in others – as constructed, arbitrary, powerful but subject to change. A drama which addresses what is conventionally accepted as the political 'reality' of a society may in fact be collusive with that society's ideology: a play might propose that a society's politicians are corrupt, without looking beyond the existing political system to alternative forms of government, administration and political morality. Thus a politics of content cannot guarantee political efficacy, if both form and function are simultaneously collaborating with a dominant ideology.

The critique of ideology has entailed more than anything else a politics of form. The progressive political role of art becomes that of exposing and interrogating ideology: and since ideology is rooted in the structures of culture and in artistic forms, the pressing and priority task is to expose structure and form, to open cultural artefacts up to investigation and challenge. The kind of theatre (such as that of Brecht) which 'lays bare the device', exposes the mechanisms of its own construction, encourages in the spectator a critical and questioning alertness towards all ideological naturalisation, can be regarded, whatever its ostensible political content, as *politically more progressive* – because it targets the most powerful weapon of social control, ideology – than a theatre which collaborates in form and function with a hegemonic ideology and with dominant cultural forms.

This recognition that the 'political' character of a drama may be contained within it as form rather than content has been profoundly influential in contemporary cultural analysis; but it is not without its theoretical difficulties. In the following chapter on developments in American feminist theatre, Jill Dolan compares a naturalistic play about feminism, Wendy Wasserstein's *The Heidi Chronicles*, with a Brechtian 'entertainment' performed by Spiderwoman Theatre. The former is clearly more overtly 'political' in terms of the politics of content: but it is through the politics of form that the latter is shown to be the more radical and creative intervention. On the other hand, as Christopher McCullough shows in his essay on Brecht, the formal devices of political drama can be readily assimilated into a theatre with a very different political inflection; and although Brecht's drama obviously developed the politics of theatre on all three fronts, it is in those types of drama offering a radical politics of *function* that the real political effectivity of Brechtian drama can be said to reside.

A concern with a politics of function, sometimes but not necessarily associated with radical form and progressive content, could be identified as the underlying theme of this book, the common preoccupation of a diversified body of contributors. Just as the world of contemporary political event and situation is characterised by extraordinary structural and institutional change, so our focus on the politics of theatre and drama discloses a singular emphasis on the emergence of new forces and relations of cultural production. This issue can be confronted by problematising the relationship between 'theatre' and 'drama'. Often used interchangeably, these terms are also periodically thrown into theoretical antagonism and binary opposition. Writing in the 1950s, Raymond Williams proposed that 'drama' – dramatic literature analysed in terms of its performance in specific historical theatre spaces – should not be identified with contemporary 'theatre', which was operating as an institution of cultural oppression.[16] Williams was to some degree concerned with drama as a literary form: but starting from very different theoretical premises, a powerful pedagogic theory of 'educational drama', in which drama is conceived as self-development, therapeutic play and spiritual healing, developed in Britain in direct opposition to the professional and institutional structures of 'theatre'.[17] Today this unsettled marriage is enjoying a period of reconciliation, and the study of drama – as dramatic literature, practical activity and experiment, dramatic theory – is recognised as inseparable from the study of 'theatre' – as the domain of public performance, professional expertise, institutional organisation. 'Drama' is usually known in educational contexts as 'theatre studies'.

If by 'theatre' we mean simply professional companies performing in buildings, then it must be accepted that we are referring to a minority cultural form. Only 5 per cent of the UK population attends the theatre, opera or ballet; only 2 per cent of the UK working class attends either these institutions or museums and art galleries. Apart from students, only 2 per cent of all young people in the UK attends the theatre, a percentage which includes none of the young unemployed. Ninety-eight per cent of the UK population watches television on average for over twenty-five hours per week.[18] Terry Hawkes once observed that television is the only truly 'national theatre' we are ever likely to have.[19]

If we think of 'drama' and 'theatre' as primarily descriptive terms, then these matters are not especially difficult to resolve. Certain types of dramatic production such as television and film have historically associated themselves with theatre: cinemas were once called 'theatres', and drama on television routinely referred to as 'armchair' or 'masterpiece' theatre. If that relationship no longer holds, as a consequence of these relatively new cultural technologies coming of age and achieving independence, and the term 'theatre' can no longer be stretched to contain them, let the broader and more comprehensive term 'drama' substitute for 'theatre' as the dominant form.

This proposed semantic revision however takes no account of the cultural power of the theatre as an institution, influential far beyond its evidently minority domain. Practical attempts to liberate 'drama' from 'theatre' are unlikely to be as simple as an exchange of words. Peter Reynolds proposes that the contemporary community theatre movement could be considered as a 'potentially revolutionary' cultural force (in Augusto Boal's sense of drama as a 'rehearsal for revolution'),[20] since it rejects the exclusive minority form of traditional theatre, returns the means of cultural production into popular control, and operates to empower groups and individuals with a practical and theoretical grasp of their own destiny. But far from abolishing the traditional theatre, community theatre engages – through the participation of theatre professionals in community events – in a complex relationship of distance and deference, rejection and return. The case of David Edgar's *Entertaining Strangers*, written for performance as a community play in Dorchester, and subsequently transferred as a professional production to the National Theatre, traces in its institutional transition a striking new cultural configuration. From one point of view a means of democratic participation and popular empowerment, community theatre can be seen from another standpoint as the means by which an increasingly moribund professional theatre revitalises itself by plundering the energies and resources of the people.

Both elements, theatre and drama, have thus been retained in this book's title, not as stable descriptive formulae or distinctive theoretical definitions, but rather as linked terms in a complex and

continual process of interaction and interdependence, opposition
and intimacy, sundering and reconciliation. It is, however, recognised that 'drama' as a formal category cannot be contained within
'theatre', and that film, television and other kinds of performance
belong appropriately within this cultural field. It is equally clear
that the concern with a politics of function returns us continually to
this theoretical problem of the relationship between drama – all
that is written, produced and performed – and theatre – a hegemonic space of institutional and ideological control, as well as an
enabling mechanism of significant cultural production.

Having linked these changing conceptions of political drama
with developments in Marxist philosophy, it is finally necessary to
register the crisis in Marxism (and in cultural theory generally)
precipitated by theories of 'post-modernism'.[21] The post-modern
critique of Marxism identifies it as one of the great ideological
'master-narratives', like Religion and Progress, which subsume
and dissipate the heterogeneous and contradictory needs and
aspirations of specific groups of people into a spurious but powerful coherence and unity. Post-modernism requires a theoretical
destruction of such 'macro-narratives', and the re-instatement of
cultural diversity and pluralistic perception through the development of 'micro-narratives' witnessing to the discrete and unassim-
ilable experience of particular oppressed groups – women, racial
and ethnic minorities, lesbians and gay men, people with disabilities. Politically this theory points away from, for example, the
model of centralised state socialism, held in place by a macro-
narrative of party dominance and national progress, and towards
the 'forum politics' of loosely co-ordinated separate interest groups
that we see developing today in Eastern Europe.

Superficially this theoretical model seems akin to Engels' formu-
lation of the relative autonomy of separable cultural and economic
spheres of activity. In fact it is radically different. In Engels'
proposition each relatively independent sphere nonetheless bears
the identifying stamp of its determinant origin, the economic base;
each cultural activity combines, like a child, its own individuality
with an over-riding similarity to the parent. Thus in that method of
Marxist cultural analysis, the individual shape of a culture may be
appreciated for its own sake, but it remains possible (and is usually
considered more important) to read the character of the social basis
through the distorted images of its cultural superstructures. In
post-modernist terms, by contrast, the political radicalism of a

cultural activity depends on the extent to which it refuses that relationship with the master-narrative, resists its paternal power, fights to liberate and occupy a free space independent of its authoritarian claims. In this sense a politics of content can be read as a collusion with the dominant ideology, and the political character of a cultural form should be sought only in its politics of form – estranging, alienating, self-reflexive – and its politics of function – de-stabilising the conventional relation between spectator and performance, disrupting traditional expectations of narrative and aesthetic coherence, de-familiarising and interrogating the oppressive power of naturalised cultural forms.

In one sense, this emphasis is not new to the politics of theatre and drama. The inescapably political character of culture prescribed by modern cultural theory, and the post-modern privileging of oppressed and minority perspectives, was arrived at in the political theatre by more directly experiential routes. One chapter in the anthology *Dreams and Deconstructions*, by feminist Micheline Wandor, is called 'The Personal is Political: feminism and the theatre'. It is particularly in the experience of feminist women, of gay women and men, of oppressed colonial peoples, of ethnic minorities, that the sense of being an individual person (what we term 'experience') and that will towards active engagement in the practical processes of changing society (what we call 'politics') have come to seem inseparable. If the 'experience' of a woman, a homosexual man, a black person, is one of oppression, victimisation, then that can either be explained psychologically – there's something wrong with them – or politically – they are subjected to structures of injustice and exploitation built into the practical arrangements of society, built into political systems, built into cultural apparatuses like education and language.

If that is the case, then only by political action can that negative experience of the individual be redeemed. So while in a sense this perception points towards forms of political action and organisation that are analogous to those of formal politics, it points on the other hand away from that specialised domain of the 'political', towards individual and collective experiences formerly considered 'private' or 'personal'. If the domains of culture and language are saturated with political meaning, then wherever we live or act or feel through them, we are potentially at a point of political confrontation. Against the traditional notion that 'political' drama has to be about revolutions, strikes, demonstrations, pickets, factory occupations and police brutality, we can set the modern recognition that plays about sexism in language, or male prostitution, or the personal experience of racism, have just as much claim to the status of 'political theatre'. Today the same concern to start from the particular experience of individuals and social groups, rather than from dramatic tradition, artistic convention and professionalised theatre, gives rise (especially in an international context) to 'liberation theatre' and 'theatre for development'.[22] The political content of such work is determined absolutely by the specific consciousness of the group concerned in producing it.

Where then does this leave the descriptive concept of a *political* theatre and drama, as distinct from the analytical method of a *politics of theatre and drama*? Does it remain possible and rationally justifiable to use the former strategically, in order to distinguish, not between political and non-political drama, but between those forms of theatre whose political sympathies lie with the status quo and with the dominant social classes, and those which are oppositional in their politics? The theatre of the status quo can imply political meanings unself-consciously, precisely because the political perspective on which it rests is the dominant one. The principal aim would be to make the ruling order seem a 'natural' condition ('there is no alternative') rather than a system requiring justification by political argument. The principal responsibility of a progressive drama would then be the legitimate and necessary task of challenging that dominance, by showing that the existing order is not 'natural' but politically constructed and fundamentally unjust. 'It is not our *disorder*,' said Bernard Shaw, 'but our *order* that is horrible.' And Edward Bond: 'Come with me into the open air, and I will show you something unforgivable.'

There is a danger, however, that this strategic opportunism may leave things very much where they stood, and may permit and even encourage the oppositional argument, that drama of a rightist or centrist persuasion does not need to bring 'politics' onto its agenda, because it rests satisfied with the status quo, not necessarily as a perfect, but certainly as a 'natural' condition. In terms of this polemic it is left-wing drama that for its own propagandist purposes brings politics in where they are not needed, confuses art with propaganda, entertainment with political argument. Rightist and centrist forms of theatre can simply take 'life' as their subject, where socialist theatre is overwhelmingly concerned to bully its audience into acceptance of a certain political creed.

In the complex and changing cultural conjuncture that gives shape to this book, it was from the outset unlikely that such work would produce any unified and consistent theory of the politics of drama, and accordingly no such unity has been imposed or developed. Some of the essays contained here to some extent retain the older notion of a political theatre, while others move outwards towards the kind of 'cultural materialism' which recognises the essentially political nature of all drama. The centrifugal tendencies of such pluralistic theoretical explorations could well result in 'political' theatre ceasing to be a specialised area of dramatic practice, approachable by particular methods and assumptions, and being collapsed into a general body of performance work, conceived as always and at every point (though often in complex, indirect and mediated ways) susceptible to a political analysis. The theoretical problems then of course take on a very different shape and require different methods of resolution. How are different political perspectives articulated in different artistic forms? How do we distinguish between the 'political' character of a theatre which is self-consciously political, and one which denies its own political orientation? Are certain dramatic and theatrical forms inherently inflected towards a different political ideology – is the assimilation of popular cultural forms potentially radical, or naturally conformist? Are post-modernism and the avant-garde progressive or reactionary?

Just as the range of theoretical questions becomes broader and more complex, so the critical and theoretical agenda opened up by this book becomes intimidating in its scope and scale. *The Politics of Theatre and Drama* has no pretensions therefore to be inclusive or comprehensive, but rather exploratory, provisional, incomplete, indicative and facilitating. There is no address here to the work of the major left-wing dramatists whose work negotiates with the professional theatre; though since their writing is a familiar and fully-recognised element of traditional 'political theatre', that absence is not particularly significant or damaging. Neither is there any sustained examination of gay and lesbian drama. There is no discussion of the position of black and Asian theatre in 'multicultural' Britain, or of the relation between these forms and the international politics of, for example, the 'Commonwealth'. There is no extensive treatment of the new forms of 'development theatre' initiated by practitioners like Augusto Boal, and which have been found particularly appropriate and liberating for cultural work in Africa and Latin America. Areas of cultural debate which are very interestingly inserting themselves into the political arena, such as the issues of access and representation for people with disabilities, are not directly addressed, though adumbrated by Val Taylor's discussion of *Tumbledown* and *Born on the Fourth of July*.[23] In short, the transformation of 'political drama' (as an object of enquiry), into 'the politics of drama' (as a method of analysis) calls for large-scale theoretical revaluation and extensive detailed practical investigation of a much larger field of cultural production. If this book can help to clarify that theoretical transition, and offer some exploratory work in a bewildering and exciting new field, it will have achieved its object.

Notes

1. Brecht's gravestone has been decorated with the graffiti inscription 'Jewish pig', presumably a reference to his Jewish wife Helene Weigel. The desecration of Jewish cemeteries by neo-Nazis is becoming commonplace, having occurred to date in France, Italy and Canada as well as Germany.
2. E. Piscator, *The Political Theatre*, 1929, trans. H. Rorrison (London: Methuen, 1980).
3. E. Bentley, 'The Pro and Con of Political Theatre' (1960), in his *The Theatre of Commitment* (London: Methuen, 1968).
4. J. Bull, *New British Political Dramatists* (London: Macmillan, 1984).
5. C. Itzin, *Stages in the Revolution: political theatre in Britain since 1968* (London: Eyre Methuen, 1980).
6. S. Craig, 'Unmasking the Lie: Political Theatre', in his edition *Dreams and Deconstructions* (Ambergate: Amber Lane Press, 1980).
7. A. Davies, *Other Theatres* (London: Macmillan, 1987).
8. A. Sinfield, 'Cultural Materialism', Foreword to the *Cultural Politics* series (Manchester: Manchester University Press, 1988–).
9. See J. Bull, *Stage Right: the recovery of the mainstream*, (London: Macmillan 1984), which acknowledges this point, but by evading the term 'political' adroitly evades the theoretical difficulty entailed in Bull's earlier definition of 'political dramatists' (see Note 3).
10. From Marx's *Contribution to the Critique of Political Economy* (1859); see *Marx/Engels: On Literature and Art* (Moscow: Progress Publishers, 1976) pp. 41–2.
11. See particularly the work of Georg Lukács: e.g. *Studies in European Realism*, trans. E. Bone (London: Hillway Publishing, 1950).
12. R. Bolt, *The State of Revolution* (London: Heinemann/National Theatre, 1977), and T. Griffiths, *Occupations* (Calder and Boyars, 1972).
13. F. Engels' letter to J. Bloch, in K. Marx and F. Engels, *Selected Corre-*

spondence, 1846–95 (London: Lawrence and Wishart, 1934, reprinted 1943) pp. 475–7.

14. L. Althusser, *For Marx*, trans. B. Brewster (Harmondsworth: Penguin, 1969) pp. 117–128.
15. See. T. Bennett, *Formalism and Marxism* (London: Methuen, 1979).
16. See R. Williams, *Drama in Performance* (1954), ed. G. Holderness (Milton Keynes Open University Press, 1991).
17. The theory of 'educational drama' is interrogated, and its chief practitioners discussed, in D. Hornbrook, *Education and Dramatic Art* (Oxford: Blackwell, 1989).
18. These statistics, taken from various information sources, are quoted in P. Willis, *Common Culture* (Milton Keynes: Open University Press, 1990), between p. viii and p. 1.
19. T. Hawkes, *Shakespeare's Talking Animals* (London: Methuen, 1973).
20. A. Boal, *Theatre of the Oppressed* (London: Pluto, 1979).
21. See particularly J-F. Lyotard, *The Postmodern Condition*, trans. Geoff Bennington and Brian Massumi (Manchester: Manchester University Press, 1984).
22. See C. Barker, Chapter 1 of this volume, p. 36.
23. The debate initiated by disabled actors over the film *My Left Foot*, in which paraplegic writer Christy Brown was played by able-bodied actor Daniel Day-Lewis, gives some indication of the theoretical contradictions involved. The demand that a disabled actor should have been cast instead cuts sharply across the normal left-wing acceptance of a Brechtian separation between actor and role.

2

Alternative Theatre/ Political Theatre

CLIVE BARKER

Since the subject under discussion is theatre the title of this chapter is not to be taken literally as an equating of these two terms. Both sides of the equation would not necessarily balance exactly in any quantitative sense. Linking them is rather a device to focus attention on the relationship between the two terms and some aspects of the theatrical reality which lies behind them. Both terms arise from a particular historical context although the sense of either term has loosened with the passage of time to encompass a wide range of possible meanings, some of which would be mutually contradictory. The relationship between the terms has also varied in time. In the early 1970s in Britain a good argument could be made that the Alternative Theatre, which was at that time in its early years, had political significance across the spectrum of its performance styles. Simply by existing it posed critical alternatives to the dominant culture of the time, that of the Establishment to which it defined itself as alternative. At the start of the 1990s it would be difficult to make that argument and, disillusioned by what has happened in the intervening years, some writers who would have promulgated the earlier argument would probably now support an opposing view. The Alternative Theatre has lost direction and political significance.[1]

Without wishing to take up and champion either assessment it is necessary for me to establish what I mean by Alternative and Political Theatre and what range of relationships are possible between the terms. What do we mean by the terms *Alternative* Theatre and *Political* Theatre?

POLITICAL THEATRE

The term grows out of and in counter-distinction to other terms –
People's Theatre, in France *Théâtre Populaire*, in Germany *Volksbühne*.
The distinctions between the terms have ideological significance.
In the years before the French Revolution of 1789, the philosophers
Diderot and Rousseau deliberated on the theatre. Drawing on
what they saw as the supreme example of a socially potent theatre
– the theatre of fifth-century BC Athens – they proposed two
possible paths for restoring the theatre to its former glory. They
proposed mass festivals in which the people or nation celebrated
the victories and values of democracy, and a stage on which the
great issues of the day would be dramatised and debated. When
the Revolution came both these proposals were implemented. A
building existed with *Le Théâtre du Peuple* inscribed on its portico
and several mass Fêtes were held.

The high ideals of Diderot and Rousseau and their followers,
Chenier and Mercier, were never fully realised. As events revealed
the hollowness of *Liberté, Égalité, Fraternité*, the middle class pros-
pered and the revolutionary spirit was damped down. The theatres
were closed and the Fêtes discontinued. The revolutionary stage
had failed to find the dramatists willing or capable to take on the
great themes and, through correspondence, it was the German
Schiller who took on the task. With Schiller the nature of the task
changed and the basis of *bourgeois* morality and *bourgeois* supremacy became the object of scrutiny and the subject for
promotion.[2] The concept of a People's Theatre was thus shang-
haied and exploited by the bourgeoisie throughout the nineteenth
century. When Michelet returned to the idea in the 1850s the term
'nation' or 'people' meant something different from what it had
signified in the years of the Revolution. The class-structured nature
of French society was well known and the task of the People's
Theatre was re-defined to overcome class divisions and to unite all
sections of society in promoting the interests of the bourgeoisie.
Like it or not, we live today in the aftermath of the rise of the
European bourgeoisie. The theatrical forms and structures we have
inherited were built out of the need of that class to consolidate its
social position, to propagate its values and to suppress class
antagonisms through concessions and alliances. The theatres we
have and the cultural policies pursued all reflect this. The great
instrument of bourgeois drama is the National Theatre. In those

countries where bourgeois cultural interests coincided with movements for national liberation, such as Czechoslovakia and Hun-
gary, the term National Theatre has a direct political meaning. In
the countries of Western Europe the term *National* masks class
interest and the political intent is implicit. It is in this sense that it is
often said that all theatre is political, although the arguments
behind this are rarely made clear. The normal sense given is that
that which does not promote the cause of the working class and
social revolution automatically and by default reinforces the status
quo. Can such a vague notion adequately cover the complexities
and power of the current situation, not only in Britain but also in
the rest of Europe?

A variety of questions needs to be asked in this area. Does the
National Theatre in Britain (and by extension in other Western
European countries) still promote middle-class values and interests
and, if so, in what ways? Is this through the repertoire it presents,
the organisation of the theatre, the way in which it contacts and
attracts the public, the pressure it exerts upon artists to conform to
certain 'standards of excellence'? To what extent does the policy of
the National Theatre (or theatres if we include the Royal Shakespeare
Company) measure up to the title *National* and reflect the value
and interests of the whole *nation*? If this line of questioning is
pursued, the political ramifications of adding the distinction of
'Royal' to the title are manifold.

One possible effect of using the term Royal National Theatre,
which is historically a contradiction in terms, might be to presume
to lift the theatre above class interests and above class politics. This
might be construed as reflecting that the political scene in Britain
(or perhaps we ought more properly to use the term England) no
longer reflects any clear class struggle but a division of opinion
between opposing sections of the petit-bourgeoisie. In France a
succession of policies has been pursued since the great revival of
interest in People's Theatre in the last decade of the last century to
broaden the base of the audience. To this end they have set up
institutions called *Théâtre National Populaire* and instituted policies
of de-centralisation. The dialectics of this course of action pose the
questions: If you make the theatre more widely available does this
process liberate or indoctrinate the people to whom it extends
theatrical literacy? Do you animate people or anaesthetise them?[3]
Nominally the Arts Council of Great Britain has within its charter
the duty to make the arts available as widely as possible. However,

there has been little change in audience composition over the period of the Arts Council's existence and it is questionable whether the policy of supporting 'centres of excellence' and maintaining 'high standards' has not served simply to perpetuate the form and content of theatre which is supported by middle-class audiences. Subjective ideological judgements are masked behind considerations of 'good taste' and 'aesthetic standards'. What is supported by middle-class audiences becomes accepted as the norm upon which standards are set.[4] Administrators are chosen because they have a sense of what audiences will support and applaud, and reactionary commercial manipulation is raised to the level of fine critical judgement.[5] Lip service is paid to the duty to facilitate access to the theatre for all classes but the terms of entry make this difficult.

These arguments can all be seen laid out quite clearly in the history of the *Volksbühne* movement in Germany from 1890 to 1930.[6] The *Volksbühne* movement intended originally to create audiences for theatres but the ultimate intention was to build and run its own theatre(s). It followed a parallel course to the French People's Theatre movement in looking for its audiences amongst the working class. Through a series of strategies, which included block-booking to reduce the price of seats and commissioning performances at times when working-class audiences could attend, the *Volksbühne* supported productions of plays which were socially critical and reformist in nature.[7] These plays were of course written by bourgeois writers with social consciences. It is fair to ask how this could be any different. Movements which have sought to confine themselves to working-class audiences have invariably run up against the problem of repertoire from their inception. In a middle-class theatre, playwrights of quality are almost without exception from that same class. From what other sources could the repertoire come? Very early in the existence of the *Volksbühne* a split occurred between those who saw the movement as educating the working class *in* theatre and those who saw themselves as educating the working class *through* theatre; between those who wanted to promote performances which could be appreciated by the working-class audiences, and those who wished to promote performances which advanced the cause of the working class. It is worth reflecting on the rise of Social Democratic parties in Europe during the same period and the ways in which their policies also showed this split and the controlling and patronising positions which were adopted towards the working class. Official cultural policies in Western Europe have never fully escaped from these ideological attitudes and it is against the pervasiveness of these attitudes that most western political theatre has struggled in the years since 1968.[8]

ALTERNATIVE THEATRE INTO NATIONAL THEATRE

It is important to realise that the institutions and policies described above did not spring up fully realised, but developed as an alternative or in opposition to what was the dominant form of theatre. Before the 1960s the term Alternative Theatre was not specifically in use but, as with Political Theatre, it has several forerunners which set the ground for its arrival. In some sense or other it could be said that there has always been an alternative theatre. The theatre of the travelling players existed side by side with the Court theatres. Not all of these forms of theatre were politically oppositional, but it is remarkable how often by their very existence they were seen by authority to be prejudicial to good order and civil obedience. Whenever the theatre is outside the immediate control of authority it is seen to be subversive to a degree which does not apply to the other art forms. Regardless of the intention or orientation of the theatrical venture, authority seems always to perceive alternative theatre as a political threat.

Frequently the implicit political threat has been actualised as explicit political opposition. In order to establish the People's Theatre of the French Revolution the revolutionaries suppressed the theatre of the *ancien régime*, the *Comédie Française*. Napoleon, consolidating the rule of the bourgeoisie, restored the *Comédie Française* in a changed form and suppressed or placed under heavy restrictions the popular theatres of the boulevards. In England, at the same time, the end of the eighteenth and early nineteenth centuries, the monopoly of the patent houses was challenged by the *Minor Theatres* which grew up to cater for the growing middle-class audiences and by the *Saloon Theatres* and *Penny Gaffs* which catered for the growing working-class audiences. The work of all of these theatres was scarcely overtly political but, by their existence, they constituted an attack on the law and they expressed theatrically the political movement for enfranchisement that gave rise to the 1832 Reform Act and the

Chartist movement.[9] The Theatres Act of 1843 gave England a free stage but the existence of the Lord Chamberlain's Office controlled the direction of the theatre through strict censorship which, among other things, prohibited political issues being dramatised.[10]

The Minor Theatres set the basis for the commercial theatre we have in England today. The working-class theatres were easily suppressed through a judicious use of building and safety requirements, re-building and police activity. The most successful in any case took advantage of the new freedom in the theatre and became music-halls or joined with the Minors to create the commercial theatre. Andrew Davies, using the term *Other Theatres* to cover this activity, finds political significance in the existence of the working-class theatres.[11] There is also an argument that the music-halls promoted a form of popular culture that is in itself oppositional, an alternative way of seeing the world and accomodating to it, if not controlling it.[12] The movements to create National Theatres which I have described earlier, and which I see as now being the dominant and repressive form of theatre, began as alternative theatre or *other theatre* movements. In Eastern Europe they championed the cause of nationalism against foreign oppression. In Western Europe two strands of opposition to the gross materialism of the preceding generations emerged in the 1890s. Having established its material dominance in society the mercantile and manufacturing middle class turned to culture. Building on the pioneer work of Ibsen, one strand of this opposition turned critically on the evils arising out of capitalism and the late industrial revolution.

Following Ibsen came Shaw and Hauptmann and others. The other strand rejected materialism and sought to establish a counter-aesthetic, a more spiritual and metaphysical theatre. To this movement belong Edward Gordon Craig and Adolphe Appia. The first strand of this movement created the *Théâtre Libre*, the *Freie Bühne*; the second strand, the Art Theatre. Together they form the Independent Theatre movement. From this, in England, springs the Repertory Theatre movement and the campaign to found the National Theatre.[13]

Because this movement throughout Western Europe sprang from within the dominant class it has not been seen as a political movement but essentially as an aesthetic one. But this should surely not be seen as anything other than a political strategy to maintain and perpetuate hegemonic dominance. In opposition to the purely commercial theatre, which is how its justification is usually presented, the National and Art Theatre movement now dominates the developed world and has been imposed on large sections of the under-developed and developing world.[14]

In a world where inflation and rising costs make theatres expensive to run and some level of government subsidy necessary, these theatres assume a level of importance as flagships of a nation's culture. Whether they do present the most important or even the most accomplished theatre in a country is at least open to critical doubt. Nevertheless, the Royal National Theatre and the Royal Shakespeare Theatre between them take the lion's share of available subsidy, which consolidates their power and facilitates empire building, to the detriment of other theatres and companies. Size is often equated with quality and these theatres attract the tourist audiences and are able to devote large budgets to publicising themselves. Quantity of publicity is often mistaken for prestige. In these cases subsidy becomes a selective instrument of political control. National must be best and anything other is relatively less than best.[15]

The external and internal politics of National Theatres provoke interesting questions. Why does this form of theatre dominate *all* of Europe, East and West? Why did the Soviet government choose to give supremacy to the Moscow Art Theatre of Stanislavsky and the Bolshoi and Kirov Ballets after the Revolution, rejecting many revolutionary and innovative forms of theatre? Why have socialist states chosen to promote bourgeois art? There is a National Theatre movement right across Europe in which theatres are remarkable for their resemblance rather than their differences. The late Zygmunt Hübner, director of the Powszechny Theatre in Warsaw, complained not of overt censorship but of having to serve two masters. His audience and his paymasters were not looking for the same return for their money. Hübner saw this as a problem in East and West with directors and actors being steadily turned into civil servants.

> It is true that socialistic bureaucracy has a deserved ill name, but I presume that the dead hand of bureaucracy appears wherever the state subsidizes theatre, whatever the political system. Thus, we are caught in a vicious circle: there is no professional theatre without state subsidy, but subsidy creates an unacceptable theatre. Few like it, but it costs a lot.[16]

Hübner in his article looks wistfully at an idealised concept of an 'alternative' theatre in which artists work because of an inward need to create, regardless of whether they find an audience or not; but he himself went on working in a state theatre. Why? Is it only financial security which keeps so many talented artists working in National Theatres?

Hübner says: 'For many years, and despite serious difficulties, I have been trying to create a theatre which questions the principles of our political reality.' If the National Theatres are such a powerful instrument of hegemonic control, can they be left unhindered to get on with this work? Or should the struggle to combat the hegemony be carried into the heart of these institutions? Can politically conscious and radical artists subvert these institutions from within? The obverse question has to be asked, will not the institution overpower the radical artist and render him or her sterile? Some dialectical process will always be at work in which the artist compromises and the institution changes to accommodate the work of the artist. Zygmunt Hübner, along with a mass of other artists in Eastern Europe, considered himself a master in the art of concealed allusion and veiled comment; but his ultimate verdict was that working this way constricted artistic horizons and created bad theatre. However worthy the cause, the theatre was being used politically rather than political theatre being created. It is worth considering if this is the case in our own institutions at this time. Are David Hare, Howard Brenton and David Edgar effective in their work with the National Theatre and the RSC?[17]

THE POLITICAL THEATRE

Historically there are two sources for an overt Political Theatre and they both belong to the same period of time, the early 1920s. In Germany, Erwin Piscator created first the *Proletarian Theatre* which departed from both the wings of the *Volksbühne* movement by not being a theatre to provide the proletariat with art, nor a theatre for the proletariat but a theatre which would make conscious propaganda and serve the revolutionary movement. Piscator saw *The Political Theatre*, as he called his book, as representing the interests of the most advanced arm of the proletariat, the revolutionary party; and although the Communist Party was never wholehearted in its trust in Piscator or its support for his work, he built a considerable support for his first Proletarian Theatre among the trades unions of Berlin. He also ran foul of the police and his theatre was prohibited. The important features of Piscator's work were' . . . simplicity of expression, lucidity of structure, and a clear effect on the feelings of a working-class audience. Subordination of all artistic aims to the revolutionary goal: conscious emphasis on and cultivation of the idea of class struggle.'[18] This is not to say that Piscator's work was crude. The two large-scale revues he mounted for the Communist Party in 1924 and 1925 were characterised by a very sophisticated use of popular entertainment forms. In *Trotz Alledem* (1925) Piscator combined film with stage action for the first time and, since the revue included the portrayal of real political figures and the film included censored footage of the First World War in all its horrors, actuality became incorporated into stage fiction. Piscator's other major achievements were these. He saw that a proletarian form would have to break the authority of the playwright and/or director.

> The show was a collective effort. The separate tasks of writer, director, musical director, designer and actor, constantly over-lapped. The scenery was built and the music composed as we wrote the script, and the script emerged gradually as the director worked with the group. Different scenes were put together simultaneously in different parts of the theatre, sometimes even before a definite script had been worked out.[19]

Piscator took this co-operative structure further. Workers were on the organising committee. Since no one playwright was capable of comprehending the full political and economic complexity of the late capitalist world, a dramaturgical collective was set up to construct texts. This collective included politicos and economists as well as dramaturgs and directors. Piscator's other great contribution was to establish the *epic* form, against the prevailing *dramatic* form of the bourgeois theatre, as the basic necessity for a political theatre. In order to deal with political issues, let alone take part in political action, the theatre must break free from domestic settings and conflicting representative characters and must be able to use montage and juxtaposed scenes; to utilise a wide range of locales and to fragment character. It must also be able to break the proscenium frame and to address the audience directly. In assessing the political viability of the theatre at any time, these criteria are useful to consider.[20] Which is not to say that all theatre based on these considerations is in itself radical or even political. A great deal of avant-garde experimental theatre has been built upon the structural emancipation from presenting consistent characters, linear action and localised settings.

The great master of the 'epic theatre' was, of course, Bertolt Brecht, who freely acknowledged his debt to the pioneering work of Piscator, with whom he worked. In one sense, Brecht took Piscator's work backwards. Piscator's work was performed during a period of political and revolutionary struggle, a time of direct confrontation and contestation between mass political parties. In spite of his problems with the Communist Party, Piscator could relate his theatrical work directly to a viable and powerful political programme. Piscator could create revolutionary political theatre in a way which very few have been able to do since. Is it necessary, as John Arden and Margaretta D'Arcy would argue, to link theatre work directly to a party programme in order to be politically effective? And if so, what would that party be in a specific situation?

In the early 1930s Brecht drew upon this political confrontation to create the *Lehrstücke* or teaching works. The great plays of the exile belong to the school of critical realism: that is, they attack the middle class from inside its own theatre traditions. In his essay 'On Experimental Theatre' Brecht acknowledges the basis of his theatre is to unite the two traditions of the bourgeois revolt, the reformist and the aesthetic, the didactic and the entertaining.[21] Perhaps it is this feature of his work which has made it easy for it to be absorbed, as a 'classic' within the National Theatre circuit, and for certain critics to dismiss his political convictions as irrelevant to his theatrical aesthetic.

Concurrent with Piscator's work in Germany, the Russian theatre, following the 1917 Revolution, re-interpreted early forms. In the early 1920s the mass Fête of the French Revolution was employed to celebrate the Revolution and to re-enact its triumphant events. The most famous of these events was *The Storming of the Winter Palace* (1924) directed by Nicolas Evreinov. In the early Soviet society these events served a similar purpose to those in the French Revolution, to instil a sense of a united nation. In the USSR they did not last long. The Spartakiade based on athletic and gymnastic competition has since replaced dramatic representation as the main type of national spectacle. This is more potent and less dangerous than re-enacting the Revolution. The mass spectacle is a politically unifying instrument best used sparingly. The bicentenary of the American Declaration of Independence and the Los Angeles Olympics, among other instances, utilised this form recently.

The post-Revolution years were characterised by many exciting forms of theatrical innovation and experimentation. Almost all of these were suppressed by Stalin, who established a version of the bourgeois dramatic form, *Socialist Realism*, typical figures presented against a typical ground, as the repressive form of Soviet theatre. One of these new forms, similar in many ways to Piscator's proletarian work, set the pattern for most later political theatre. The early years of the Revolution saw the Bolsheviks faced with the necessity of attracting the mass support of the peasantry and proletariat to shore up their weakness as a minority party. Methods had to be found to indoctrinate the masses and arouse their support. Since there was widespread illiteracy more direct, non-literary forms had to be formed. The programme was termed *agitational-propaganda* or, more usually, *agit prop*. On the theatrical side of agit-prop, two features are worth stressing. The *Living Newspaper* began as simple dramatisation of news items presented in a range of styles, sometimes satirical, sometimes exhortatory. Out of the early work a movement arose which between 1924 and 1928 spread from one professional group in Moscow to 484 professional groups and around 8000 amateur groups throughout the Soviet Union. This was the Blue Blouse movement.[22] The basic structure through which the Blue Blouse companies worked was a montage of popular forms. Behind this was a theory derived from Eisenstein of the *montage of attraction*.

> An attraction (in relation to the theatre) is any aggressive aspect, that is, any element of it which subjects the spectator to a sensual or psychological impact, experimentally regulated and mathematically calculated to produce in him certain emotional shocks, which, when placed in their proper sequence within the totality, are the only means whereby he is enabled to perceive the ideological side of what is being demonstrated – the ultimate ideological conclusion.[23]

The theory thus expressed shows its origins in futurist performance and owes something to behaviourist theories of psychology.

It can be related to Russian formalist theories, from which Theatre Semiotics has developed. Perhaps, in the end, it amounts to 'get out and grab an audience and get the message across in an effective way.' It is worth considering, though, the thought expressed in the quotation that agit-prop is not simply a question of saying the right things or having the right ideological attitudes. Political theatre has to work as theatre. Bad theatre makes bad politics.[24] The Blue Blouses made effective politics through striking theatre. In 1928 they were disbanded by Stalin largely because of the satirical and corrective view they presented of Soviet society and in particular its bureaucracy. They were presenting a view of Soviet society which was at odds with the official interpretation.

This attempt to be alternative within the dominant structure raises some interesting points. On a simple level, why should a government financially support its critics? The policy in the US during the 1930s under the Federal Theatre Project was designed to alleviate unemployment. Paradoxically it enabled the most refined development of the Soviet form of the *Living Newspaper* and gave a public voice to artists who criticised the capitalist system and government policies for creating unemployment in the first place. Consequently the Federal Theatre Project was stopped, ostensibly because it had been infiltrated by Communists.[25] Alternative political theatre voices were stifled by both capitalists and Communists. The issue was taken up in a more sophisticated manner in the German Democratic Republic in the 1960s. Bequeathed the heritage of Bertolt Brecht, theatre in the GDR initiated a debate about the role of a critical theatre in a socialist state. Should the ideas of Brecht now be considered *passé* and a more exhortatory and positivist form of theatre employed? This form would be the Stalinist Socialist Realism which had been imposed on most of the Europe which fell under Soviet influence after 1945. In the end, it was decided that there was a place for Brecht. As the state moved towards perfection (and in Marx this is reckoned to take a very long time) through resolving successive contradictions, critical reasoning could be seen to be part of this process. In practice this did not work out so well. One of the assumptions behind aggressive or critical political theatre is that what is hidden or obscured in politics should be made manifest on the stage.[26] In a country under single-party rule this is difficult: under a dictatorship it can be positively fatal. Vaclav Havel suffered great hardship in Czechoslovakia. To discuss the existence of torture by secret police in Chile or Romania before 1989 would have been to invite murder.[27] When a dramatist or a theatre company takes up a critical role within a political system they are basically sympathetic towards, another set of problems arise. The presumption (though not the reality, of course) is that nothing is hidden in politics. If the stage makes manifest what is already presented in the press, there will be no possible interest for the audience. If it makes manifest what is not shown in the official press the presumption will be that it is idealistic and immature and counter-productive and it will be censored. The state decides the rate of improvement and the level and direction of criticism. Since the state is the arbiter of political policy and political viability, anything which diverges from this must be politically incorrect. The GDR did not solve this problem. Its theatre, once so vital, became duller and duller. One solution was to present more plays which were politically innocuous. The revelation that the state was neither politically correct nor omniscient may now lead to a revival in the theatre. In Britain, which is not a one-party rule country, it is worth looking at the tactics by which the Thatcher government has attempted (and managed) to stifle artistic and media opinion and revelation of hidden material over the years 1988–89.

THE WORKERS' THEATRE MOVEMENT

In 1927 the original Blue Blouse troupe were sent to Germany as part of the celebrations of ten years of Russian Revolution, ironically one year before Stalin disbanded them. The troupe toured twenty-five cities but the most important feature of their tour was that it coincided with a congress of International Workers' Aid with delegates from all parts of the world. This organisation which was ostensibly to collect and transmit aid to the Soviet Union also fulfilled a number of other covert political functions. The presence of the international visitors and the Blue Blouse performances sparked off an international growth of agit-prop groups.[28]

The political situations in which agit-prop has been used have varied. In Korea, for example, fly-by-night agit-prop groups were instrumental in arousing resistance to Japanese occupation. Groups undertook a similar function against the American forces in the Vietnam war. In Europe street theatre became the dominant mode and the sketch and mass declamations were its usual forms.

In Germany the theatre attacked a specific enemy, the fascists. In England the targets were less specific and because of this the theatre was also less effective. In a non-revolutionary situation it is futile to call for armed revolution and many WTM pieces could find nothing more powerful than 'Demonstrate!' as their climactic call. Where agit-prop scored in England was in specific local situations, such as the Becontree Rent Strike where the issues were tight and the course of action clear – 'Withhold Your Rent!' Whereas in Germany many professionals were involved in agit-prop work, in England professionals were rigidly excluded and the movement proudly proclaimed its policy under the headline 'Their Theatre and Ours'.[29] The amateur policy was taken further into a policy which placed the political message paramount and regarded aesthetic considerations as irrelevant. By extension, this could be seen as the major question at the heart of a great deal of alternative political theatre. It is based on a belief that if you say the right words the world will change.[30] There is a talismanic belief in messages which has led some critics (and some activists during the 1930s) to condemn agit-prop for creating an illusion of activity in place of effective political action.

The involvement of professionals in agit-prop work is also problematic. The further the performer is removed from identification with the cause being promoted the less convincing the message becomes. The Alternative Theatre in England during the early 1970s had too many examples of groups of students explaining to car-workers how the car-workers were being exploited, a subject on which the car-workers were experts and the students were not. The same period (the 1970s) was marked by a whole range of struggles to create a potent political theatre in Britain against the centralised and compartmentalised culture prevailing. Based in London and working in a theatre which traditionally is not expected to be politically aware or to play to working-class audiences the work of these groups was not easy.[31] Augusto Boal, working in Brazil, recalls a performance in which the actors exhorted the peasants to rise and seize the land by force. After the performance a peasant told Boal that they agreed with the message and invited the actors to go with them. When the actors explained that their guns were only imitation, the peasant said that didn't matter. They, the peasants, had enough real ones to go round. It is essential for the actors in political theatre to be part of the action they prescribe and for all involved to understand quite clearly the

exact function and limits of theatre in any situation. In commercial
theatre it does not much matter if you put on a rotten play or
performance. In political theatre that which does no good does not
necessarily do no harm. It may be art, but political theatre im-
pinges on real life, and is a part of real life, in a more influential
and direct way than non- or a-political theatre.

When the Alternative Theatre movement arose in Britain in the
late 1960s, as in other parts of the developed world, it arose out of a
particular set of circumstances. A succession of governments had
failed to deliver their election promises, which peaked with the
failure of the Wilson administrations of 1964 and 1966 to deliver the
anticipated socialist revolution. The 1970 General Election had the
lowest poll turn-out in history as voters had difficulty in distinguishing one party from another, and trusted none of them.
Drawing in ideas from the anti-Vietnam movement in the US and
from the Prague Spring, where there was direct confrontation with
repressive authority, and from France, where popular revolt was
seen as being politically potent, a series of responses attempted to
transform the nebulous British situation into something much
more dynamic and meaningful.[32]

Underlying the activity of the 1960s was a subtle transformation
of the need for social revolution into the politics of personal
liberation. When theatrical censorship was removed in 1968 the
anticipated politicisation of the British stage did not take place.
Instead the stage was flooded with nude display. What was at first
called fringe theatre arose as a response to the failure of the Labour
government to create positive cultural and political change and to
the continued triviality and sterility of the established stage. The
political theatre did not arise in any strength until the early 1970s,
when there was a rise in working-class militancy, notably the
miners' strike of 1972, and there seemed a chance that industrial
action might bypass parliamentary prevarication and force the
introduction of socialism. At this point, John McGrath and others
rejected the term fringe, declaring their work had never been on
any fringe, and the term Alternative Theatre came more into use.
The fragmentary nature of working-class militancy at that time and
its failure to go beyond replacing a Conservative government with
an even less effective Labour one and Heath, as Prime Minister,
with an even less sympathetic Callaghan, left the political theatre
in Britain struggling for support and credibility. What has followed
is a process typical of English politics, as it is of nowhere else.

Oppositional movements are absorbed through a process of temporisation, compromise and patronisation, tactics which led Lenin to give the opinion that the British revolution would be the last to happen and that it would be the easiest, because all the required institutions would be, by that time, in place and formed. Whether we can accept Lenin's opinion these days is open to debate.

During the 1970s and into the early 1980s, the Alternative Theatre became gradually absorbed into the Establishment by subsidy. What characterises this period is a remarkable display of skill and ingenuity as playwrights and companies tried to subvert the system and exploit its advantages to create theatre which had political potency and to break through to non-theatregoing audiences. That the theatre created by Trevor Griffiths, John McGrath, David Edgar, Joint Stock, Foco Novo, Belt and Braces, Monstrous Regiment and many many others was marvellous theatre is beyond doubt. Whether it had any political effect is a question to be asked, particularly in view of the drift into Thatcherite policies, supported by a substantial working-class vote, and the ease with which the political theatre was dismantled by the removal of subsidy when government pressure on the Arts Council was more reactionary. Overall, the question has to be asked, can any effective political theatre be constructed and exist within a government system?

Particularly, can theatre exist in these times, without subsidy and can it be politically effective if it receives it? The bigger question which has to be asked in the British context is, if the context for political theatre arises naturally out of political confrontation, how can we have political theatre, or what forms can we construct in a political system which is so skilled at de-fusing conflict and avoiding direct confrontation?[33]

CONSCIENTISATION

John McGrath criticised both Piscator and Brecht in his book *A Good Night Out*. He saw the political principles and ideas of both as compromised and restricted because they continued to work within the bourgeois theatre. John Arden gave his opinion after a visit to West Bengal in 1971 that, in the context of West Bengal, even a British left-wing revolutionary was a bourgeois imperialist. Arden gradually dropped out of mainstream theatre after that and has chosen to work in Ireland in community theatre and small-scale political theatre since then.[34] Augusto Boal, in a trenchant critique of the traditions of European theatre from Aristotle to Brecht, acknowledged his debt to the latter but criticised him for working through performance-oriented theatre at all.[35] We might ask what price we pay for having such a defined tradition of theatre in Britain in which we automatically assume the paramount importance of performance. Should we abandon discussion of direction, style, intent, content of performance and discuss theatre in totally different terms? For Boal, in order that theatre be politically effective, the distinction between audience and performers has to be broken down. Any process whereby the (political) educational project is devised outside the community and then imposed upon it is doomed at best to fail and at worst to continue the oppression of individuals and the community in a changed form only.[36] For Boal theatre becomes a process through which a community objectivises the forms of its oppression and the internalised attitudes that follow from this and devises ways of overcoming these. A considerable body of work through the developing world has now grown up, variously called conscientisation theatre, liberation theatre or theatre for development.[37]

A lot of experimentation and thought has gone into finding the ways whereby intellectuals, educationalists and extension workers can initiate or participate in projects which must inevitably be self-help, grass roots actions if they are to be politically effective. The temptation to patronise the oppressed is great and the process is open to perversion. Ross Kidd, in his introductory essay to the bibliography *The Popular Performing Arts* (see note 37), finds it necessary to revive the old terminology and to make a clear distinction between what is liberating and what is continuing oppression in changed forms:

> A distinction . . . must be made between:
> a) *people's culture* – the autonomous expression, values, customs, etc. of the people which has imbedded within it ruling class ideology and
> b) *popular culture* – which is built out of selective aspects of people's culture that reflect their true interests, for example, elements of protest and resistance against the structures of domination.[38]

Can those of us who have been brought up, educated and imper-
meated by the forms and values of the residual and dominant
theatres in this country liberate ourselves sufficiently to reject our
conditioning and move into entirely new forms of theatrical activity? Can forms of theatre devised and applied in developing
countries where the forms of oppression are naked and daily
present be utilised in developed Western countries? Here the
forms of oppression are restricted by or concealed behind the
processes of law; and institutions, such as the trade unions and the
political parties left of centre, exist to protect the individual
against blatant exploitation and oppression beyond the legally
allowable limit. The grounds for a close examination of these
questions exist. Over the last ten years there has been a steady
build-up of a large section of the population who are largely
marginal to the main concerns of government. The long-term
unemployed and large numbers of homeless and dispossessed
people who populate the cities of Britain exist in social conditions
not that far removed in experience from the street beggars of South
(and North) American cities. The political songwriter and playwright Ewan MacColl considered that one of the major problems of
our theatre lay in the individuality of the writer:

> What most writers do is to start from a preconceived notion of
> what language is, of how men and women express ideas and
> how they express emotion. This concept they usually arrive at
> during the very earliest period of their decision to be a
> writer . . . They start off with a concept of what language is that
> lasts them through their life. Very rarely do they say, 'Does this
> concept bear any relation to the truth?' . . . But the fact is that
> language, and concepts of language, are constantly changing,
> with each new generation . . .[39]

And, of course, with each new set of social circumstances and
experiences. Some engagement with the homeless of Waterloo
Bridge, on their terms; some going to them to learn rather than to
teach or preach might result in the development of new and
relevant forms of theatrical activity, *which cannot be foreseen*. It
should certainly seek to eradicate the present obscenity whereby the
Royal National Theatre slants its productions towards relevance to
the homeless and includes pictures of Cardboard City in its pro-

grammes, whilst using stage-settings which display conspicuous waste of time and material resources.

Theatre used in this way in isolation would be a hopeless, altruistic and missionary activity: but as part of an overall pro-gramme of education and self-help organisation could prove effec-tive. The model exists in the work which Boal and Freire did in Peru. There are other leads to follow (or being followed). The Ayni Ruway theatre movement in Bolivia works entirely with Indians. It has no direct political aims. The reasoning is that the Indians are well aware of how they are exploited and oppressed but lack the means to protect themselves. The Ayni Ruway move-ment has concentrated on strengthening the sense of cultural identity among the Indians. If this can be strengthened, self-confidence will result and the Indians themselves will produce the political cultural institutions and actions to protect themselves. Something of this order can be seen in the work of John McGrath. 7:84 (Scotland) and other Scottish theatre companies have made a consistent policy of utilising and strengthening the forms of Scot-tish popular culture in the style of their work.[40] But this work has all been done within the concept of performance for an audience. Perhaps it is asking too much for the Ayni Ruway model of work to be applied in this country, although the principle deserves atten-tion. Perhaps we should consider the example set by Teatro Escambray in Cuba, and other companies, who have begun as agitational groups coming in from outside the community, at-tempting to raise political consciousness, progressing towards direct participation, through critical discussion and re-structuring of the performance, and into the formation of local theatrical activity based on problem-solving workshops.[41]

What makes this activity possible is the revival in regional culture. In terms of Wales, Scotland and Northern Ireland discrimi-natory political measures and economic exploitation have long helped forge a sense of separateness and have preserved and strengthened national cultural forms making it difficult for theatre in these countries to disengage from political concerns. The major metropolitan areas and large cities of England are witnessing a new situation in which the overwhelming central influence of London is weakening and theatre companies, as one example, are forming as a purely regional activity with little or no ambition of moving on to the capital.[42]

A great deal of the political theatre discussed earlier has been formulated on the principle that it should in some way or other contribute to the overthrow of the capitalist system and the furtherance of socialism. In view of recent events at the end of the 1980s and the start of the 1990s, it is doubtful if such a programme would elicit much widespread support and such a programme has usually been predicated on the assumption of mass support. Without suggesting or accepting recent events as presaging the demise of socialism or socialist ideas, should we not, at this time, be looking at different forms of political activity?[43] Regional rather than national or international? What balance or dialectic can be struck between the specific and realisable against the trivial and parochial? The repressive measures of the Conservative Party and the Labour Party policy of abolishing the trade union block vote both serve to diminish the political role of the trades union movement in Britain. The base of working-class political action is shifting. What should be done about this? Does this invalidate areas of political theatre which have existed previously? Does it open up the way for new alliances? And quite clearly the implications of European unity must be taken into account in any discussions. Most political theatre in the past has taken for granted a society structured upon class interests and motivated by class allegiances. In Western Europe this has given an oppositional role to any theatre wishing to be politically effective. In Eastern Europe, curiously, the same process has also taken place. There appears to be a middle ground of dissident artists combating capitalism on one side and Stalinist ideas and governments on the other. Will they share a common role as the drive is on to create a free market economy throughout Europe, East and West? And what will be, or can be, the basis of their common concerns? What will Vaclav Havel do next, now that he is inside the system? Can Western intellectuals and artists continue to posit socialism as the alternative to the free market economy which is clearly embraced so enthusiastically by the majority of all Europeans? Or, when theatre ceases to be oppositional, on what basis does its politics rest? The political map of Europe is changing and, in spite of the first nationalist reaction to the break-up of collectivisation in the East and the intransigence of the British government in the West, European unity must come, and this will create a new and complex set of political problems and opportunities which go way beyond the simplistic dream of the West imposing capitalism on the East. New allegiances and alliances will emerge. What direction or responsibility should a historically committed theatre take in all this?

What are the alternatives open in this new situation? Brecht advised that there is only one world and that is the one we are living in. Can we resist the temptation to go on believing in and re-creating the past or some utopian ideal of the future? In the pluralist world, which is our immediate future, can we find the sophistication to ditch grand plans and to utilise a pluralism of means directed at specific, if limited, objectives? If political gains and objectives through theatre are limited does this mean that they should be dismissed or that they cannot be politically correct in the circumstances? Can we afford at this point to jettison *any* of the forms of political action through theatre which have been the subject of this enquiry? Even such a crude, limited and old-fashioned form as agit-prop street theatre can have its uses, as, for instance, in the recent ambulance workers' strike, putting the case across pithily and dramatically. What would be wrong would be to persist in a widespread use of agit-prop in situations where it is no longer valid or effective. The purpose in posing all the foregoing questions has not been to diminish or destroy the case for political theatre but to make a case for greater sophistication in its use. As never before we need to be clear about objectives and to be able to apply effective means to achieve these. One way forward is to turn our backs on alternative worlds, to accept this one world and to have a plurality of alternative strategies to employ in it. If times become hard and repressive in the short term then there is value in bearing witness. Whatever is happening in Britain and in the rest of Europe, people are starving and oppressed, and the dis-possessed are being abused. In this world the theatre still has a role. The minimal role in protest is to stand up and be counted. In Romania, sufficient people standing up to be counted toppled a régime.

There is one last possibility to be discussed. In John McGrath's play *Trees in the Wind*, one of the characters, musing on 'boring, old politics', comes up with the thought that the only reason for being in politics is to get rid of them. Piscator claimed that politics should be kept out of the theatre but, unfortunately, that wasn't yet possible. Zygmunt Hübner, after many years of trying to subvert Polish bureaucracy, yearned to create theatre which sprang from some aesthetic need and impulse. In an essay entitled 'Theater-Culture', Eugenio Barba asks: 'What sort of theater does today's society need?' He qualifies the question by saying: 'Often, latching on to a Political Theater means escaping from the problem of pursuing, with theater, a policy.' The argument throughout this chapter has been against this happening but Barba is prepared to argue that: 'It is illusory to believe that only big organisms provoke big changes.' In Barba's concept of the Third Theatre, theatre is not a means to political ends or a way of earning a living. It becomes a way of life. Its value lies not in its performances alone but in the social relationships built up inside the company and between the company and the world outside. He takes further Brecht's injunction to remain a 'foreigner' in one's own society, creating an a-social situation in which people pursue socially, through theatre, the dream of building their own lives. Barba is careful to point out that this can only be pursued in the real world we live in but it is an escape from the control and categorisation which a serialist world imposes upon you. As such, it is a distinct alternative to theatre which supports the status quo and to that which directly opposes it. Both theatres are defined and categorised. In a world in which the human being is becoming increasingly marginalised, if not surplus to requirements, Third Theatre presents a way of escape but not escapism. If sufficient companies, or Floating Islands, to use Barba's term, develop, the world will change. It will change during the process of this happening.[44]

Notes

1. See E. van Erven, *Radical Popular Theatre* (Indiana: Indiana University Press, 1988) and A. Davies, *Other Theatres* (London: Macmillan, 1987).
2. See B. Brecht, 'Theatre for Pleasure or Theatre for Instruction', translated from 'Vergnügunstheater oder Lehrtheater', *Schriften zum Theater* (1957) included in *Brecht on Theatre* ed. and trans. J. Willett (London: Eyre Methuen, 1964).
3. The history and theory of French People's Theatre is in R. Rolland, *The People's Theatre* (London: Allen and Unwin 1919) and Bradby and McCormick, *People's Theatre* (London: Croom Helm, 1978). See also *Theatre Quarterly* V, 23, 1976 (French Theatre Issue).
4. The arguments for this are articulated in J. McGrath, *A Good Night Out* (London: Methuen, 1981).
5. See J. Pick, 'The "Arts Industry"' in *The Journal of Arts Policy and Management*, 3, 1 (March, 1988).
6. See C. Davies, *The Theatre for the People* (Manchester: Manchester University Press, 1977).
7. This question is explored in P. Szondi, *The Theory of the Modern Drama* (Cambridge: Polity Press, 1987). See especially pp. 50–52.

8. The term 'hegemony', taken from Gramsci, figures in much discussion of the politics of culture as denoting the process by which one class imposes its values on the whole.
9. See C. Barker, 'A Theatre for the People' in Richards and Thompson (eds) *Nineteenth Century British Theatre* (London: Eyre Methuen, 1971), and C. Barker, 'The Chartists, Theatre, Reform and Research', *Theatre Quarterly*, 1, 4 (Oct–Dec 1971).
10. There is some reason to view the powers of the censor as being increased by the 1843 Act, since the Lord Chamberlain took a much more active role in overseeing the respectability of all aspects of the theatre. See J. Davis, 'Cleaning-up the East London Theatres' in *New Theatre Quarterly*, VI, 23 (August 1990).
11. See Davies, *Theatre for the People*.
12. P. Davison, *Songs of the British Music Hall* (New York: Oak Publications, 1971) advances some argument for this. Robert Tressell's working-class classic *The Ragged-Trousered Philanthropists* depicts the music-hall as a corrupting influence. Trevor Griffiths explores something of the dialectics in *Comedians*.
13. The strength of the commercial theatre in England was such that it took longer to establish a National Theatre in England than elsewhere, although prototypes existed in the Old Vic and in the Shakespeare Memorial Theatre. It is worth noting that the original campaign for a National Theatre in England was tied up with finding a home for England's greatest dramatist. The hegemonic function of Shakespeare, both historically and today, is another political question worth pursuing. Can the oppositional theatre afford to cede the area of the national heritage to the bourgeoisie?
14. It is not unusual to find National Theatres in African and Arab countries, where the process of de-colonisation has left an ethnic middle-class in power. The Kenyan National Theatre was the subject of a bitter oppositional campaign led by Ngugi wa Thiong'o. See: Ngugi wa Thiong'o, 'The Making of a Rebel', *Index on Censorship*, 9(3) pp. 20–24.
15. The influence of the National Theatre on the repertory theatres has been considerable, although there is some evidence that this is lessening. Regional theatres have fed off the publicity put out by the National companies. If the Royal National Theatre presents *The Beaux Stratagem* this year, and it is successful, the other theatres will mount it next year. The set examination texts for GCSE and 'A' level have a similar standardising and stultifying effect.
16. See Z. Hübner, 'The Professional's Guilty Conscience', in *New Theatre Quarterly*, IV, 15 (August 1988).
17. Looking at this question from the other side would raise the complementary question of whether a theatre company playing in a building can ever escape the charge of being in pawn to the bourgeoisie. The *Théâtre de l'Est Parisien*, a radical theatre in the environs of Paris, when accused of attracting a middle-class audience, asked whether this meant that they should give up the theatre and the

organisation which had taken up many years of work. They reasoned that, if and when the political situation changed, the apparatus would be there to be utilised for revolutionary purposes.

18. E. Piscator, *The Political Theatre*, ed. and trans. H. Rorrison (New York: Avon Publications, 1978) p. 45. Graham Holderness discusses Piscator's work at length in Chapter 5.

19. Piscator, p. 92.

20. The argument for this forms the basis for Piscator's book, as it did for his theatre work. For the 'epic theatre' of Piscator or Brecht, see below Chapters 5 and 6.

21. B. Brecht, 'On Experimental Theatre' translated from 'Über experimentelles Theater' in *Theater der Zeit*, 4 (1959). Included in *Brecht on Theatre* ed. J. Willett, (London: Eyre Methuen, 1964). See also Chapter 6 of this volume.

22. See McCreery and Stourac, *Theatre as a Weapon* (London: RKP, 1986). For the mass spectacles see F. Deak 'Russian Mass Spectacles', *The Drama Review*, 19, 2 (*T66*) (June, 1975) pp. 7–22.

23. Quoted in F. Deak, 'Blue Blouse', *The Drama Review*, 17, 1 (*T57*) (March, 1973) p. 42.

24. It was Brecht's opinion that if a pamphlet would serve to get the message across, a pamphlet should be written. In a different part of the field, Eugenio Barba has pointed out that theatre groups which begin with some centre to the work which is other than theatre *per se* fail to sustain themselves and disappear.

25. See J. de H. Mathews, *The Federal Theatre 1935–1939* (Princeton: Princeton University Press, 1967).

26. One example of this occurred in McGrath's work for 7:84 (Scotland), *The Cheviot, the Stag and the Black, Black, Oil*. No public register exists of all land-holdings in Scotland. Drawing on a register constructed privately by an individual, the show was able to make public in each performance exact details of who owned what land and in what amount in the area in which the company were playing.

27. In Colombia the political theatre directors Enrique Buenaventura and Santiago Garcia have been placed on a hit-list by right-wing death squads and warned to leave the country. In India, Safdar Hashmi, director of a political street theatre group was beaten to death by thugs supporting a right-wing politician.

28. See McCreery and Stourac, *Theatre as a Weapon*.

29. The manifesto proclaiming this is reprinted in Samuel, MacColl and Cosgrove, *Theatres of the Left 1880–1935* (London: RKP, 1985) pp. 138–148. This book also contains more material on the Workers' Theatre Movement in Britain and America. The personal memoire by Ewan MacColl is particularly important.

30. I am indebted for this idea to Paul Bayes who extends it as far as Brecht. In this case the thesis would run 'If you say the right words, people will change the world.' Bayes, who has never published his ideas, considers that most oppositional or critical political theatre so far has been hung up on the words. Theatre which is celebratory has

been mistrusted and considered reactionary. Bayes argues eloquently against this, asking that we should consider what we are celebrating and how.

31. At present several of the more important of these groups, 7:84 (England), Belt and Braces, Foco Novo, Joint Stock, have, for a variety of reasons, disappeared. Several, like Red Ladder, have modified their political line.

32. I do not propose to detail the history of the political Alternative Theatre in Britain. This can be found in C. Itzin, *Stages in the Revolution* (London: Eyre Methuen, 1980) and S. Craig (ed.), *Dreams and Deconstructions* (Ambergate: Amber Lane Press, 1980). See also, C. Barker, 'From Fringe to Alternative Theatre', *Zeitschrift für Anglistik und Amerikanistik*, 1 (1978) pp. 48–62.

33. The work of John McGrath has been hampered in these ways. The 7:84 (England) company had its Arts Council funding terminated and no reason was given. The quality of the work of the company was undoubted and all political bias was denied. McGrath was forced to resign from the directorship of 7:84 (Scotland) when conditions which went counter to the stated policy of the company made contingent on the renewal of the grant .

34. See Arden's preface to *Two Autobiographical Plays* (London: Eyre Methuen, 1971), and J. Arden, *To Present the Pretence* (London: Eyre Methuen, 1977). In the latter he discusses the difficulties of working in the established theatres.

35. A Boal, *Theatre of the Oppressed* (London: Pluto, 1979).

36. The educational theory and practice on which Boal's work draws is in P. Freire, *Pedagogy of the Oppressed* (London: Penguin Educational, 1972).

37. An excellent and succinct survey of this theatre is in the introductory essay to R. Kidd (ed.), *The Popular Performing Arts, Non-Formal Education and Social Change in the Third World: a bibliography and review essay*, Centre for the Study of Education in Developing Countries, Bibliography no. 7 (The Hague: CESO, February 1982). Also Kidd and Colletta (eds) *Cultivating Indigenous and Traditional Media for Non-Formal Education and Development*, (Bonn: German Foundation for International Development, 1981).

38. Kidd, p. 23.

39. Conversation recorded on tape and held by the editors of *New Theatre Quarterly*.

40. It is interesting that McGrath has found it necessary in *Border Warfare* (1989) and *John Brown's Body* (1990) to mount a re-examination of the history of Scotland. A study deserves to be made of the uses of history in political theatre throughout Europe.

41. The Jamaican Women's Theatre company Sistren work across the whole range from consciousness-raising to performances. See Kidd and Colletta (eds) *Cultivating Indigenous and Traditional Media for Non-Formal Education and Development*, pp. 541–49.

42. An interesting project planned by the Everyman Theatre, Liverpool, which will combine the professional functions of the theatre with the

Hope Street Project, enabling people to participate in workshops and longer-term training to develop theatre skills. A full-time acting course for the unemployed is planned.

43. The major areas where these concepts have been developed already are in Women's Theatre and gay groups. Only in small, clearly defined groups can the relationship between performer and audience be constructed to allow participation rather than isolation. The political purpose of these groups is worked out through relationships rather than expressed through performances. Some Black Theatre Groups similarly restrict themselves to black audiences, seeing the search for wider audiences as compromising and vitiating their political strength. For theatre and sexual politics see M. Wandor, *Carry On, Understudies*, (London: RKP, 1986). Nothing is available on the Black Theatre position as the groups appear to disdain to publish in white edited journals.

44. Barba's philosophy is clearly laid out in E. Barba, *Beyond the Floating Islands*, (New York: Performing Arts Journal Publication, 1986), from which the quotation comes on p. 208.

3

Personal, Political, Polemical: Feminist Approaches to Politics and Theatre

JILL DOLAN

As by women in other areas of social and political life, a great deal has been accomplished by women in theatre in the United States over the last two decades, and a great deal remains to be gained. The 1970s are remembered, from a 1990s' vantage point, as an era when theatre for women – and more precisely 'feminist' theatre – was born and proliferated. In tandem with the political movement from which it sprang, activist women's theatres with radical techniques and manifestos organised in major urban centres around the country. The groups were innumerable and local, since the theatre they produced spoke directly to its constituents.

The 1980s might be remembered as a decade when, on the one hand, the radical, collective theatre work of the 1970s sputtered and failed, and on the other, women who aspired to careers in professional, mainstream theatre began to gain ground. The visibility of women playwrights, in particular, led to three Pulitzer Prize in Drama awards for women in the 1980s: Beth Henley, for *Crimes of the Heart* (1981), Marsha Norman, for, *Night, Mother* (1983), and Wendy Wasserstein, for *The Heidi Chronicles* (1989). After many years of ignoring women playwrights, the Pulitzer committee – along with the Tony Awards, which honoured Wasserstein's play as the first written by a woman ever to win the Best Play award, in 1989 – seemed finally to take notice of the 'new' talent.[1]

But the apparent success of women playwrights in mainstream theatre obscures several political issues that continue to frame the field of feminism and theatre. The plays most honoured by the prize committees and subsequently most published and produced

44

tend to be the most conservative in content and form. Henley's *Crimes of the Heart*, for example, is a Southern domestic comedy in which three sisters overcome their individual quirks to bond together as family. Few references are made to a larger political setting or to women outside their comfortable white, middle-class, heterosexual situation. Norman's *'Night, Mother* generated much controversy in the feminist press over its protagonist's *a priori* choice to commit suicide and the hopeless, isolated quality of her life. The most recent winner, Wasserstein's *The Heidi Chronicles*, is a critique of the feminist movement launched by a character whose individual liberal humanism is comfortably promoted by the realist dramatic frame she inhabits. The play's rendition of feminism in the 1970s implies that the movement is over and its achievements bittersweet.

While Wasserstein's popular play tolls the death knell of feminism from its safe position in a costly Broadway theatre, something very different is happening on the streets outside. Although alternative feminist theatre remains dormant except for several long-established companies, the liberal and radical feminist movements in the US are regaining an activist stance, prompted primarily by attacks on women's reproductive rights and the reactionary back-sliding of the Reagan and Bush administrations. At the onset of the 1990s, the political climate in the United States and especially abroad, in Eastern Europe, seems potentially reminiscent of the ferment of the 1960s. With abortion and now AIDS activists taking once again to the streets in the US and jarring the complacency of their upwardly mobile generation, one wonders if feminist theatre, too, will once again become a site for political activism.[2]

HISTORICISING FEMINISM AND THEATRE

The potential for renewed theatrical radicalism in the 1990s is best viewed through the historical context of the late 1960s and early 1970s, when the second wave of US feminism followed on the heels of the civil rights movement and the formation of a vocal, active New Left. From within the political upheaval of the late 1960s, activists tried to revise interpersonal relationships and cultural value systems according to more egalitarian ideology.[3]

But within the left's rhetoric of racial and economic liberation, and a re-thinking of cultural values, gender politics remained conservative. The contemporary women's movement in the US re-kindled itself partly out of profound disaffection with the misogyny of the male left. Through a network of *ad hoc* consciousness-raising groups, white middle-class women with some background in radical politics spoke to each other for what seemed like the first time, without mediation. These consciousness-raising groups allowed women to exchange previously unheard details of their personal lives. The apparent commonality of their shared experience provoked a political analysis based on the private sphere their lives inhabited, and the slogan 'the personal is the political' gained currency.[4]

What began in the late 1960s as a grassroots political movement became, through the 1970s, a political and ideological movement with organised impact and increasingly divergent strains. Networks such as the National Organisation for Women, for example, developed strategies for influencing existing social and political systems around women's issues. The liberal feminist movement generated by women within these organisations works to reform US systems toward women's equality.[5]

Radical feminism, in contrast to the reformism of liberal feminism, theorised women's oppression as systemic and began to analyse how patriarchal domination relegated women to the private sphere and alienated them from the power men wielded in public life. Radical feminism in the late 1960s and early 1970s proposed that gender roles were socially constructed and could be changed only after a revolutionary re-structuring of cultural power.[6]

Early women's and feminist theatre began as a voice of radical feminism and the first manifestations of what eventually came to be celebrated as women's culture.[7] The It's Alright to Be a Woman Theatre in New York, for example, one of the earliest groups, transposed the political movement's consciousness-raising format to performance and used the new public forum to help validate women's personal lives. The troupe used agit-prop techniques with a long tradition in political theatre, as well as street theatre and guerilla tactics that they borrowed from the left-oriented experimental theatres that had multiplied in the US in the late 1960s and early 1970s.[8]

The Living Theatre, the Open Theatre, and the Performance Group, for example, broke with the psychological realism that dominated professional US stages. These experimental theatre groups formed collectives that disrupted the politically constricting hierarchy of the playwright/actor/director triumvirate and the separation of spectators and performers formalised by the proscenium arch.[9] The importation from Europe of Grotowski's Poor Theatre, Brecht's alienation-effect, and Artaud's Theatre of Cruelty also radicalised experimental theatre aesthetics in the US. The text was no longer sacred; happenings and rituals became the primary base of theatre work; and social issues and politics explicitly informed every performance choice.

Although the experimental theatre work of the period addressed in vital ways civil rights issues and the protests against the Vietnam war, it did no more for women than the left in general. Women such as Megan Terry and Roberta Sklar, who had both worked in the shadow of Joseph Chaikin's fame at the Open Theatre, left to form specifically women's theatre groups. At the Omaha Magic Theatre and the Women's Experimental Theatre, respectively, they brought along many of the experimental theatres' innovations with theatre form – including ritual-based theory and borrowings from Brecht, Artaud, and Grotowski – but set them in a political arena in which the spectators and performers moved along a revised gender axis.[10]

While such examples of separatist-inclined women's culture thrived through the 1970s, in the 1980s liberal feminism continued to gain viability. The movement's achievements saw Geraldine Ferraro placed on the Democratic presidential ticket in 1984. Although dogged attempts to pass the Equal Rights Amendment failed, marches on Washington and consistent lobbying around women's issues instituted a focus on the 'gender gap' in US politics. The situation of urban black women and other ethnic minorities received little attention on the liberal feminist agenda, but the movement's focus on political and economic equity for white middle-class women became a force with which the dominant culture had to contend.

Mainstream theatre in the 1980s – no doubt as a result of liberal feminism – began to dole out its major awards to women like Henley, Norman, and Wasserstein, while Lily Tomlin and Jane Wagner's *Search for Signs of Intelligent Life in the Universe* (1985) proved a major Broadway success.[11] Women's caucuses in professional theatre organisations and the vitality of Julia Miles' Women's Project at the American Place Theatre helped women playwrights, directors, producers, designers, and actors seem suddenly to appear where they'd never been before in the ranks of Broadway and regional US theatres.[12]

Because of increasing economic burdens and the fractionalisation within radical feminism, however, the tradition of alternative feminist theatres that had flourished in the 1970s failed to sustain itself into the 1980s. Of the numerous radical feminist theatre groups that began in the 1970s, only Spiderwoman Theatre, a collective of American Indian women operating in New York, and At the Foot of the Mountain Theatre in Minneapolis continued to produce and tour by the end of the 1980s.[13] The founding of Split Britches, a popular feminist and lesbian troupe that began in the 1980s in the East Village lesbian community in New York City, was an anomaly in an otherwise stagnant scene.[14] But while alternative feminist theatre practice declined in the 1980s, the decade witnessed the beginning of committed feminist criticism and theory that has become a vital site for activist and intellectual work in the theatre profession and in the academy.

MATERIALIST FEMINISM AND THE NEW CRITICAL THEORY

Feminist theatre criticism in the 1980s began commenting on feminist and women's theatre in an effort to distinguish ideological viewpoints within work by women. Borrowing from such distinctions in other fields, theatre critics and theorists began to sort out the differences in form, content, and context among liberal, radical, and materialist feminists. In feminist criticism and theory, materialist feminists influenced by the Marxist equation of form and content, and by materialism's emphasis on ideology, have been at the forefront of the movement to examine not simply images of women in theatre, but the whole meaning-producing apparatus under which theatre operates.

Materialist feminist theory is concerned with more than just the artefact of representation – the play, film, painting, or dance. It considers the entire apparatus that frames and creates these images and their connection not just to social roles but to the structure of culture and its divisions of power. The theatre apparatus, then, includes the stage, lights, sets, casting, blocking, gestures, the location of the auditorium and the cost of the tickets, the advertising, the length of the run – all the material and ideological forces that shape what a theatre event means. Such theories of representation also consider the spectator an active producer of theatre's meanings.[15]

According to materialist feminist performance theory, placing a woman in representation – the site for the production of meaning in theatre – is always a political act. Female bodies inscribed in the representational frame offered by the proscenium arch, and the frame created simply by the act of gazing through gender and ideology, bear meanings with political implications. Rather than promoting positive or negative images of women – as sociological, liberal feminist criticism first proposed – the materialist feminist approach suggests a new poetics of performance embracing radical revisions of content and form, which might more fully express women's various subjectivities across race, class, ethnicity, and sexual preference.[16]

This 'new poetics' insists on the inseparability of content and form. This stance has provoked a critique of mimesis in feminist theatre work that suggests long-held assumptions that theatre mirrors reality – or, following Aristotle, is an imitation of life – mask the dominant ideology that shapes the image in its mirror. Mimesis is not so much reflective, the theory suggests, as didactic.[17] Materialist feminism's critique of realism proposes that similarly, the form's attempt to re-create reality through psychological identification processes which objectify women, renders it unable to frame subject positions that differ from representation's white, middle-class, heterosexual, male ideal spectator.[18]

These suggestions, needless to say, are unpopular with liberal feminists in the profession still determined to write popular realist plays for mainstream theatre and who believe politics can be separated from aesthetics and 'art'.[19] Materialist feminist theatre and performance theory and criticism developed in the academy, rather than in the profession, at a time when universities in the US were reeling with the influences of European theories that stressed the importance of politics and ideology in shaping a culture's representations.[20] The performance theory described by materialist feminists draws on various French feminist positions espoused by psychoanalytic critics Luce Irigaray, Helene Cixous, and Julia Kristeva; the deconstructive strategies of Jacques Derrida; Michel Foucault's analysis of power and sexuality; revisions of the structuralist psychoanalysis of Jacques Lacan; and post-structuralism's claims for an incoherent, shifting subjectivity that has corollaries in American post-modernism's pop and pastiche style.

Borrowing from so many of critical theory's most popular thinkers has lent feminism in the academy a peculiar respectability. This acceptance has prompted the curious incidence of 'men in feminism', a phrase that ominously predicts the detachment of feminism from the experience – the personal, after all – from which it developed. Similarly, liberal feminism seems to have been so widely accepted – or perhaps, more accurately, co-opted – in US culture and its political systems that the dangerous phrase 'post-feminism' has also gained ascendancy. The uneasy alliances which radical – or 'essentialist' or 'cultural' – feminism has made with the New Right in the anti-pornography debate and with the New Age movement's retreat into spirituality and psychic recovery, has made it vulnerable to critique by other branches of feminism and also to satire in popular culture, both of which neutralise its efficacy.[21]

The trend of recuperating these various ideological strains of feminism into more conservative institutions or cultural contexts can be seen in the use of feminism as content in mainstream realist plays. But the potential for resistance to dominant cultural hegemony remains in the alternative forms of feminist theatre and theory, in which an activist sense of rage at exclusion from power and culture remains potent.

Two exceedingly different theatre texts will serve as examples of US feminism's place in this historical moment. Wendy Wasserstein's *The Heidi Chronicles* is a 'post-feminist' mainstream play that distorts the political history of US feminism from the mid-1960s to the late 1980s. The play trivialises radical feminist gains, suppresses feminist rage, and acquiesces to the dominant culture's reading of the end of feminism. The play's traditional realist form helps to promote its essentially conservative ideology.

Winnetou's Snake-oil Show from Wigwam City, a piece written and performed collectively by Spiderwoman Theatre, uses Brechtian and ritual technique to break from the ideological and formal constraints of realism. *Winnetou* eloquently expresses racial rage over the appropriation of American Indian culture and, through its use of alternative form, expresses the potential for feminist subjectivities. *The Heidi Chronicles* authorises the dominant culture's view of the end of feminism, while *Winnetou* offers evidence that those marginalised by the dominant culture are still filled with a rage that might productively be channelled into re-invigorated activism in the 1990s.

THE HEIDI CHRONICLES: CHOKING ON THE RAGE OF POST-FEMINISM

Wendy Wasserstein's *The Heidi Chronicles* narrates the uncomplimentary view of the feminist movement promoted by the dominant culture. This recent play serves as an ironic bookend to Wasserstein's *Uncommon Women and Others* (1979) which, for all its problems as an upper-middle-class white women's play, still manages to launch some pungent observations about a group of college women's dawning awareness of the necessity of their own liberation through a gender analysis. *Heidi Chronicles* is *Uncommon Women*'s older sister, bitter and chagrined by the unfulfilled promises of the social movement. Heidi is a cipher, who never gives voice to an incisive or adequate political or artistic analysis. While Wasserstein's story is told against the backdrop of feminism, Heidi distances herself from the movement by calling herself a humanist – she reiterates that all people deserve to fulfil their potential. The feminist movement appears to end with the narrative closure of Wasserstein's realist text.

The Heidi Chronicles is told in flashbacks, as art historian Heidi Holland uses the occasion of a course of lectures at Columbia University to reflect on the shape of her life. Heidi's lectures, which open each act, represent a facile liberal feminist art criticism that focuses on images and analogies. For example, Heidi describes Lily Martin Spencer's painting of a solitary young woman, 'We Both Must Fade' (1869), in her opening lecture. She reminds her students (that is, the audience, to whom she speaks obliquely) of high school dances, at which 'you sort of don't know what you want' and 'you're waiting to see what might happen.'[22] The analogy reduces art to the reflection of a universally assumed experience and describes Heidi's reactive, passive position within the history Wasserstein narrates.

The play's series of scenes bounds through twenty years of US history, covering many of the era's most vital, turbulent moments. But history recedes into the background of the relationships on which the play focuses. The first scene returns Heidi to a high school dance in a Chicago suburb in 1965, at which Heidi's friend Susan inculcates her into heterosexual mores. The scene's music is period-appropriate and inspires a jolt of recognition that conjures up a sentimental nostalgia, rather than a more thoughtful consideration of the history the music recalls.

Wasserstein's a-historical approach continues into the next scene, a rally for McCarthy's presidential bid in 1967, at which Heidi meets Scoop, the arrogant editor of *Liberated Earth News*. Wasserstein positions Scoop as the social prophet who knows more about Heidi and her future than she knows herself. When Heidi tentatively explains her nascent feminist politics, Scoop remarks sardonically, 'You'll be one of those true believers who didn't understand it was just a phase.'[17]

Scoop's prophecy, of course, is borne out by the remainder of the play, in which Heidi witnesses the progress of the feminist movement – according to Wasserstein – from a radical separatism to an upwardly mobile, liberal re-integration into the country's economic and political systems. Wasserstein's position on the shift in American – and feminist – values over the last twenty years is provided by Scoop and Susan, while Heidi, bemused and never changing, watches passively.

In an early scene, Susan brings Heidi to a consciousness-raising meeting at the University of Michigan in 1970. The women present are white and middle-class, some are housewives, some are students, and all appear superficial and foolish as they 'encounter' each other's lives. They speak the rhetoric of 1970s pop psychology more than the language of early consciousness-raising, self-righteously explaining they're 'trying to work through' things, and ending the session with a pep rally cry backed by Aretha Franklin's song, 'Respect' (30). Missing in this trivialising scene are the painful exchanges of the stories women had never before told. In their place are glib jokes at the characters' expense and a facile emotionalism. The characters hug continually and repeat that they love each other, as if consciousness-raising was simply about unconditional love between women.

Wasserstein shies away from exploring female sexuality, one of the more important topics consciousness-raising essayed. The presumption of heterosexuality is maintained, as Fran, the scene's only lesbian character, is treated with blatant homophobia. Fran's army fatigues and 'macho' behaviour mark her as lesbian, since Wasserstein trades in dominant cultural stereotypes to create an easy mark for the scene's humour. When Fran confronts Heidi over her choice to sleep with women, Heidi scrapes her chair back an extra foot from the visitor's position outside the circle of women she already inhabits. Heidi's uncomfortable response to Fran indicates Wasserstein's need to distance herself from any display of radicalism, sexual or political. When asked by the other women if her work in art history is feminist, Heidi qualifies, 'Humanist' (26), once again opting for the middle ground.

Even liberal feminist struggles for women's equality appear radical and extremist in this play. For example, a demonstration Heidi joins at the Chicago Art Institute in 1974 is ridiculed in Wasserstein's treatment. Heidi's friend Peter is present on the picket line, but his well-meaning support throws the scene's focus to men's responses to feminist activism, and belittles the feminist analysis of women's exclusion from art history the scene might have launched. The feminist organiser of the demonstration is costumed in black and played as an arch man-hater, which encourages Heidi to opt again for humanism: she remains outside the museum with Peter when he is barred from the women-only demonstration inside.

Peter comes out as gay in the Art Institute scene, announcing his sexual preference by way of insisting his struggle for equality is as valid as women's. In an invidious manner, Wasserstein pits two marginalised positions against each other in competition for audience sympathies. Ultimately, the struggle of male homosexuals is valued more than feminism's struggle for gender equality. Near the end of the play, for instance, as Wasserstein sweeps into the 1980s with a nod to AIDS, Peter dismisses Heidi's individual angst as a luxury, compared to the emotional demands of his difficult, dedicated life among people with AIDS.

The male characters in the play continually predict the women's futures. Susan, for example, represents the separatism of early radical feminism, choosing to live and work on an all-female dude ranch in the west. But at his wedding, the ever-prescient Scoop insists Susan will soon be working on Wall Street. Dancing one last song with Heidi before he honeymoons with someone else, Scoop brings down the Act One curtain predicting, 'You quality-time girls are going to be one generation of disappointed women. Interesting, exemplary, even sexy, but basically unhappy' (52). And, of course, he proves correct.

Act Two's dip into the upwardly mobile consumerism of the 1980s is not a critique of the materialism of 'baby boomer' values so much as a pointed discounting of political idealism in the concerted rush toward 'having it all'. The text safely ensconces feminism in the academy, where the next generation of women reads all about the women who fought for their opportunities. Women's studies replaces the experience of women's lives and bourgeois feminism dissipates into an aggressive movement toward success, acquisition and money.

Susan, the once-'radical shepherdess', becomes a vice-president for a television production company that wants a feminist with a business background, a combination which in the previous decade would have been an oxymoron. But in the 1980s, Susan happily becomes a power broker, parlaying friendships into business contacts. Scoop, too, although less surprisingly, disposes of his once radical politics, leaving *Liberated Earth News* to start *Boomer*, a power magazine for the 1980s. When he sells the magazine for a large sum of money at the end of the play, Scoop intends to run for Congress, neatly completing the re-integration into political and economic systems that characterises the US 'baby-boom' generation. He also expects Heidi's and Peter's votes, assuming that women and gay men will be complicit once again in the white heterosexual male's bid for power.

Heidi, however, remains alone at the play's end. She wonders what the social movements of the 1960s and 1970s were all for and wonders still what she and other women want. Her long mono-. logue in the second act employs self-pity as a political strategy, as she complains that feminism left her isolated. Just as Scoop predicted, she continued to believe, when the others came to regard feminism – and maybe even humanism – as just a fad. Even Susan, in one of the harshest reversals the text constructs, says, 'I'm not political anymore. I mean, equal rights is one thing; equal pay is one thing; but blaming everything on being a woman is just *passé*' (79). Heidi, though, feels stranded and sad, because she 'thought the point was we were all in this together' (84). The woman who pushed her chair back from community finally notices that she is alone.

In the best 1980s fashion, Heidi buys herself the family she has been unable to acquire otherwise. She adopts a Panamanian baby and predicts that things will be better for her daughter. The text eternally defers feminist achievements to more and more distant generations. Heidi sits rocking her baby in a huge, empty loft somewhere in New York, for which – in the 'real life' Wasserstein emulates – the maintenance fees would be enormous. Wasserstein's play and its Broadway context glorifies consumption just as promiscuously as Scoop's magazine.

According to Wasserstein, this is the sadness of liberal feminism – that it isn't possible to have it all, and that to have any of it, for women, requires great personal compromise. Heidi rocks alone with her adopted daughter, but there is no man in her life. Under the system of values the play constructs, life without a man is a supreme sacrifice. By the end of the play, Heidi feels silenced and sad, without the agency promised by the movement to which she supposedly subscribed.

Missing from Wasserstein's play and from the feminist history her realist narrative distorts is the motivating fuel of women's rage at their marginalisation and oppression by dominant discourse. Rather than acknowledging the political power of rage and mourning its repression in the 'New Age', Wasserstein's political project explicitly trivialises women's anger. In the art history lecture that opens the second act, Heidi intends to be showing slides of paintings by Lila Cabot Perry, but accidentally inserts an image of Artemisia Gentileschi's 'Judith Beheading Holofernes', which is an important site of early feminist discourse in art history.[23] Heidi jokes snidely that Perry went through a little-known period of hostility – the painting depicts a woman and her maid viciously cutting off a man's head.

The text scores a laugh with this image – the joke is that the upper-class pretentions of Perry's work have nothing in common with Gentileschi's violence. But the joke underscores the repression of Heidi's hostility and rage, which is never described in the text as part of her feminist development. That the Gentileschi slide is shown accidentally and removed from the scene is typical of Wasserstein's treatment of the history of feminism. Key moments are trivialised and the legitimacy of women's rage is neatly elided. Women aren't supposed to be angry any more.

The Heidi Chronicles is an example of misdirected rage, in which white feminist anger is suppressed by the realist text and erupts inappropriately to trash the history of the movement. *The Heidi Chronicles* uses feminism as content – the movement becomes an historical backdrop against which the same domestic stories traditionally recounted by American realism play out. The play also suppresses race and class difference in its white-washed, consumer-oriented portrait of late-80s America. Wasserstein fails to see that the roots of gender oppression are systemic, not a result of feminism's failure to help white women succeed in 'having it all'.

ALTERNATIVE THEATRE AND THE POTENTIAL FOR RENEWED RADICALISM

The rage that *The Heidi Chronicles* represses finds a more productive expression in Spiderwoman Theatre's *Winnetou's Snake-oil Show from Wigwam City*. The piece's non-linear, non-realist style accommodates the troupe's guiding ideology of gender and racial marginalisation and allows the performers to address their political statements directly to their spectators. Spiderwoman is one of the longest-running, still-producing feminist theatre groups in the country. The backbone of the troupe are three Cuna/Rappahannock American Indian sisters, Lisa Mayo, and Gloria and Muriel Miguel, who borrow the troupe's name from a Hopi goddess:

> We take our name from Spiderwoman, goddess of creation, the first to create designs and teach her people to weave. She always wove a flaw into her designs to allow her spirit to find its way out and be free. We call on her inspiration in the development of our working technique, 'storyweaving', creating designs and weaving stories with words and movement.[24]

Spiderwoman's storyweaving technique results in pieces that are loosely compiled around various themes, all of which relate to the women's gender and ethnicity. They have also injected their own subjectivities into various parts of the dramatic canon, mounting, for example, versions of *Lysistrata* (*The Lysistrata Numbah*, 1977) and *The Three Sisters* (*Three Sisters From Here to There*, 1982), in which the sisters' unrealised dream is to move to Manhattan from Brooklyn. The male characters in this piece were represented by life-sized dolls and the sisters' home movies were interjected into the narrative. The mix of media and an interweaving of various narrative threads characterises Spiderwoman's productions, which are often incoherent and diffuse. The non-linear, improvisatory style, however, is intentional, and allows Spiderwoman to explore and celebrate their gender and ethnic heritage in an alternative theatrical form.

In *Winnetou's Snake-oil Show from Wigwam City*, Spiderwoman satirise the nineteenth-century conventions of popular culture's medicine shows and 'Wild West' shows and the more recent phenomenon of New Age spirituality to formulate a sharp critique of the dominant culture's appropriation of American Indian sym-

bols and shamanism.[25] The piece's structure is loose and uncon-
fining – a cheat-sheet of sorts with the production's essential
structural elements is pinned to the back curtain and frequently
referred to by the cast. The eclectic setting is strictly 'poor theatre' –
a patched quilt of multi-cultural images confronts the spectators as
scenery and a large plastic garbage pail and several cardboard
crates provide set pieces to be transformed as necessary.

The piece opens with a film clip of an American Indian Pow-
Wow, accompanied by theme music from the quintessentially
'American' Marlboro cigarette commercials. This juxtaposition of
cultural elements is both humorous and pointed, as it refers to the
infiltration of American Indian culture by the imperialist mythology of the United States' western expansion. Film clips recur
through the production, projected on a white sheet hanging from
the theatre's three-sided balcony. The clips are often cued visually
or vocally by the actors, breaking the realist convention of masking
production elements. Such Brechtian pointing to the means of
production continues throughout the piece.

In the first episode, a German-accented trapper appears, accompanied by a scout who intends to tell him 'how we hunt in the
West'. Their exchange employs cultural stereotypes of cowboys
and Indians, but the roles are cast across gender and deliberately
overacted to hold such images up for critique. The trapper's German
accent waxes and wanes, mutating frequently into the performer's
native Brooklynese. But the character comes and goes equally
fluidly, as scenes move through various sites in Indian and western lore. The two 'men' appear to be captured or confronted by a
local tribe: Chief Winnetou enters wrapped in an American Indian
blanket and a head-band adorned with symbols of snakes. Under
his outfit, the colourful lamé jumpsuit that the four women performers wear as their basic costume can be seen shimmering.[26]

Spiderwoman appropriate freely and promiscuously from both
high and low culture, often at the same time, to lend texture to
their cultural juxtapositions. The characters begin a ritual ceremony that mixes slapstick physical comedy with allusions to the
witches' scene in *Macbeth*. The garbage pail becomes a cauldron for
a witches' brew, parodying the notion of American Indian rituals
as superstitious. The mops that jut from the pail are soon transformed into horses that the characters ride – accompanied by
fabricated clopping sounds – to the site of Spiderwoman's next
parody.

The subsequent construction of a Wild West extravaganza recalls those which helped to promote the mythology of the American West as an untamed wilderness in which brave white men conquered fearsome, savage Indian tribes. The cultural imperialism of this history is explicitly satirised in this section of *Winnetou's Snake-oil Show*, since the entertainments are provided by American Indian women with names like Minnie Ho-Runner, Mother Moonface, Princess Pussywillow from the Mish Mash Tribe of Brooklyn, and Ethel Christian Christianson.

The women perform a variety of tricks, all of which are intentionally de-mystified for the spectators. Whip tricks are performed in which hats are knocked off the heads of assistants by the assistants themselves. Horse tricks are accomplished by using the mops as capable steeds. A sharpshooter aims at balloons held over an assistant's head, after the assistant is not-so-surreptitiously instructed to burst them with a sharp ring he or she is given to wear. A trick roper performs tricks 'so fine they can't be discerned by the naked eye', for which, of course, the rope is mimed. The de-mystification of these tricks points explicitly to the mystifications of the American West mythology.

The Spiderwoman troupe ad libs enthusiastically and is not at all concerned about presenting a slick illusion of professionalism or reality. Throughout this free-form, circus-style segment, for example, the performers clearly improvise much of the dialogue, and often mistake each other's stage names. They laugh at their own mistakes and, like stand-up comics before a live audience, invite spectators to share their jokes.

These moments of energetic, erratic slapstick parody are interspersed with more expressionistic or ritualistic moments of American Indian storytelling in *Winnetou*. Often, one of the women will narrate a story, while the others act it out behind her or provide atmospheric sound effects. The first of these stories refers to the 'bones of our ancestors', evoking a mystical history of connection to earth that has been trampled by white people's invasion.

The final section of *Winnetou* is a sharp critique of the appropriation of American Indian spirituality by the dominant culture's New Age movement – and, one might interpolate, by the spiritualists of radical or 'metaphysical' feminism. The performers turn a medicine show parody into a 'Plastic Pow-Wow Workshop', at which, for $3000 per weekend, people can be transformed into American Indians. A spectator is chosen to participate and is run through the process. After performing an improvisatory ceremonial dance, he is ushered into a sweatlodge, where he is first given a choice of tribes, then a choice of Indian names.[27]

The names Spiderwoman concoct emphasise the stereotypes American culture has generated for American Indians – the tribes are Rappahamburg, Mish Mash, and Wishee Washee, and the Indian names are Two Dogs Fucking, Old Dead Eyed Dick, Two Sheets in the Wind, and Punctured Eardrum, among others. The participant's choices are presented to him on cardboard placards, which are held up for all the spectators to see. When the spectator has made all his choices and completed the ceremony, he is given a photocopied picture of a 'traditional' Indian – with long hair and head-band – which he must wear in front of his face for the rest of his life. The two-dimensionality of the image he receives refers to the equally flat stereotype promoted of Indian culture, even by liberal New Age types eager to participate in – and implicitly, to appropriate – its spirituality.

The comic tone set by the proceedings is carefully reversed at the end of the piece, when another story is related of a 'face without borders' that refers to the disintegration of American Indian culture and identity. The storyteller directs her remarks to the audience, saying with bitter irony, 'Thank you for discovering me', and 'Don't take your spirituality out on me.' The audience becomes the target of *Winnetou*'s pointed humour and is forced to ponder its complicity in the imperialism the piece describes.

The piece's last moment is also tinged with irony. 'The death of Winnetou' is announced epic-theatre style and enacted in a presentational way. All the seams show and the scene's performance conventions are pointed to emphatically. A kind of eulogy is chanted for Winnetou. 'He sat down and he died' is repeated three times and the purported moral of the story is delivered sardonically: 'Winnetou, lose a two.' But the comic death scene transforms gradually into the final opportunity for Spiderwoman to deliver its more serious political statement.

'There lies Winnetou,' the performers intone. 'There lies the Indian, a sick and dying race.' The digging metaphor, used through many of the stories, is used to suggest that the American Indian must return home to the land underneath white culture. The performers remove even the tenuous, haphazardly constructed mask of character they have worn throughout the piece, to insist that the spectators look at them. 'See me,' they chant in syncopated rhythm. 'I'm talking, loving, hating, drinking too much, performing *my* songs, stories, dances, and now I tell *you*, discover your own spirituality.' Rather than being objectified and appropriated by the spectator's gaze, Spiderwoman insist their ethnic identities be respected as differently constructed.

The charge to white spectators is unavoidable, a moment in which Spiderwoman's rage at their culture's marginalisation and commodification is directly expressed. The comedy used to satirise dominant cultural conventions turns sharply poignant, as Spiderwoman issues a challenge to white spectators to think about their responsibility for the history the piece presents.

Spiderwoman have always used their bodies – which are large and brown and middle-aged – and their lives to fashion political theatre statements. *Winnetou's Snake-oil Show* retains the best of Spiderwoman's eclectic non-linearity while offering its thematic content with such a clear political and emotional investment that its various meanings become difficult to miss or dismiss. The risk Spiderwoman take in crafting what could possibly be an unpopular message among the liberal audiences to whom they play, gives *Winnetou* a vitality that alternative feminist theatre desperately needs to resuscitate and to sustain itself through the 1990s.

In their advance press material, Spiderwoman write:

> Challenging the 'one-size-fits-all view of feminism', this seven woman company uses their diverse experiences as women, as American Indian women, as lesbians, as scorpios, woman [sic] over fifty and women under twenty-five, as sisters and mothers and grandmothers to defy such old generalisations as: 'All blondes have more fun,' and 'All women's theatre is the same.'[28]

Spiderwoman refuses to be subsumed under a heading which might align it with Wendy Wasserstein, whose 'women's theatre', if it fits that rubric at all, speaks from a very different position within dominant cultural privilege from any Spiderwoman will ever have the leisure to inhabit. *Winnetou*, in the best Brechtian style, forces political contemplation from its spectators. *The Heidi Chronicles'* realism panders to its spectators' assumed self-congratulatory a-politicism and, despite its foray into feminism, authorises the dominant culture's conservative ideology.

By exploding the constraints of the realist form, as well as those of a hegemonic notion of feminism or 'post-feminism', groups like

Spiderwoman have the potential to transform feminist theatre once again into a site of radical political action for the 1990s.

Notes

1. See, for example, Mel Gussow, 'Women playwrights: new voices in the theatre', *New York Times Sunday Magazine*, 1 May 1983, in which he highlights Marsha Norman as foremost in a wave of new women playwrights changing the American theatre scene. Gussow's article was sharply criticised for completely overlooking the long history of women working in American theatre, both mainstream and alternative. This kind of a-historicism, however, continues to mark popular media accounts of women's accomplishments in theatre.
2. The theatricalism of social activism that so characterised American anti-war and other demonstrations in the late 1960s seems to be returning to the streets of the United States. Operation Rescue, a rightist anti-abortion activist group, has co-opted leftist guerilla and street theatre tactics to launch its attack on abortion clinics. Perhaps more in the spirit of leftist political theatricality is ACT-UP, an AIDS activist group that lobbies for a legislative and financial commitment to people with AIDS. See, for example, Alisa Solomon, 'AIDS crusaders act up a storm', *American Theatre* 6, 7 (October 1989).
3. Although there are many political and social histories written on this period of American history, see for example Todd Gitlin, *The Sixties* (New York: Bantam, 1987).
4. See Hester Eisenstein, *Contemporary Feminist Thought* (Boston: G. K. Hall, 1983) for an insightful and informative description of feminist thought and political strategies in the early 1970s. Her chapter on consciousness-raising, pp. 35–41, is particularly useful here.
5. For an insightful analysis of liberal feminism in the United States, see Zillah Eisenstein, *The Radical Future of Liberal Feminism* (New York: Longman, 1981). Feminist theorists across disciplines, especially in the 1980s, have taken to drawing distinctions between various strands of feminist ideology. Liberal feminism is generally characterised as a reformist branch of the movement, since its efforts are concentrated on gaining equality for women without radically changing existing social or political systems. The movement is sometimes called 'bourgeois feminism', and continues to be one of the more visible strains of American feminism.
6. See Zillah Eisenstein, pp. 3–41, on this period in the history of radical feminism.
7. Radical feminism's initial focus on gender difference emphasised the constructedness of polarised social roles and sought to change them. Many feminist historians and theorists since have charted radical feminism's subsequent move into a celebration of entrenched gender differences (see Eisenstein, pp. 45–136). See Alice Echols, *Daring to be Bad: Radical Feminism in America 1967–75* (Minneapolis: University of

Minnesota Press, 1989) for a comprehensive history of the ideological changes in the movement. In an earlier article, Echols termed the new version of radical feminism 'cultural feminism', since it explicitly fosters the creation of a separate women's culture (see 'The New Feminism of Yin and Yang', in *Powers of Desire*, Ann Snitow, Christine Stansell, and Sharon Thompson (eds), (New York: Monthly Review Press, 1983). Other theorists call the subsequent ideological position 'essentialist feminism', since it considers women's nurturing roles to be innate and desirable (see, for such a discussion, Diana Fuss, 'Reading Like a Feminist', *Differences*, 1, 2, Spring 1989). Still others characterise variants of this position as 'metaphysical feminism', since it theorises women's spirituality – as opposed to social activism – as the site of their liberation (see Eisenstein, pp. 125–145).

8. See Dinah Leavitt, *Feminist Theatre Groups* (Jefferson, NC: MacFarland, 1980) pp. 18–19, for a brief description of It's Alright to be a Woman Theatre. For information on other early feminist theatre groups in the US, see Helen Krich Chinoy and Linda Walsh Jenkins, (eds) *Women in American Theatre* (New York: Theatre Communications Group, rev. ed., 1987).

9. See Richard Schechner, 'Six Axioms for Environmental Theatre', reprinted in Brooks McNamara and Jill Dolan, (eds) *The Drama Review: Thirty Years of Commentary on the Avant-garde* (Ann Arbor, MI: UMI Research Press, 1986). Schechner's tract, written in 1968, proposed among other things breaking the proscenium arch by mingling the performers with spectators. The totally re-arranged spatial relationship offered the potential for interaction that disallowed the separations of mimesis that realism demanded.

10. See Megan Terry's interviews in Kathleen Betsko and Rachel Koenig, (eds) *Interviews with Contemporary Women Playwrights* (New York: Beechtree Books, 1987) and David Savran, *In Their Own Words: Contemporary American Playwrights* (New York: Theatre Communications Group, 1988). Writings on the Women's Experimental Theatre and Roberta Sklar's involvement can be found in Chinoy and Jenkins, as well as in Karen Malpede, *Women in Theatre: Compassion and Hope* (New York: Drama Book Publishers, 1983). See also Jill Dolan, 'Feminists, lesbians, and other women in theatre: thoughts on the politics of performance', in James Redmond (ed.), *Women in Theatre: Themes in Drama*, 11, (London: Cambridge University Press, 1989) for an analysis of the Women's Experimental Theatre's work in relation to radical feminism.

11. See Jane Wagner, *The Search for Signs of Intelligent Life in the Universe* (New York: Harper and Row, 1986). *Search for Signs*, although quite a mainstream success, is much more radical in form and content than plays by Henley, Norman, or Wasserstein. Its one-woman show format allows Tomlin to use the transformation technique pioneered in feminist theatre by women like Megan Terry and to break with the expectations of dramatic realism. As a result, the play's content is a much more sympathetic, politically invested discussion of American feminism from the early 1970s to the middle 1980s than Wasserstein's

play, discussed below. *Search for Signs'* popularity, however, remains an anomaly on a Broadway scene that generally disallows the presentation of overtly political work.

12. The Women's Project has since left the American Place Theatre and incorporated on its own. The Women and Theatre Program of the Association for Theatre in Higher Education (formerly the American Theatre Association) is a good example of a professional organisation that straddles mainstream and alternative theatre, and advocates for professional and academic women in theatre. In the last several years, the WTP's orientation has become more theoretical and scholarly. But as a result, its annual conferences have produced some of the most interesting alternative performance work by women in the United States. See the special issue of *Women and Performance Journal*, 'Celebrating the Women and Theatre Program', 4, 2 (1989) for critical and historical information on the organisation and its recent work.

13. While the Women's Experimental Theatre produced a series of performances in the early 1980s, it stopped actively creating new performance work by 1986. For information on At the Foot of the Mountain, see Chinoy and Jenkins, pp. 44–50 and 321–325, and Leavitt, pp. 66–78. For a theoretical analysis of their recent work, see Jill Dolan, *The Feminist Spectator as Critic* (Ann Arbor, MI: UMI Research Press, 1988) pp. 92–95.

14. Split Britches – a collective comprised of Lois Weaver, Peggy Shaw, and Deborah Margolin – presented its signature production, *Split Britches*, in 1981, and has consistently produced works in repertory since. *Beauty and the Beast* (1982), *Upwardly Mobile Home* (1984), and *Little Women* (1988) are original, intricately constructed pastiches that re-write popular and high culture from the perspectives of those marginalised by gender, ethnicity, and sexuality. Although Margolin tends to write their scripts and Weaver to direct them, the three women generate their material collectively by improvising around the often eccentric characters they create. Their non-linear scripts work by a kind of accumulation of detail, so that atmospheres and quirky, incoherent personalities are created instead of unifying themes or action-based plots. Their pieces are episodic and repetitious and often simply end, rather than arriving at the point of full disclosure and apparent understanding that realism usually promotes.

Split Britches, and its affiliated producing space, the WOW Cafe, relies on community rather than government funding to produce its work, and frequently tours London, Amsterdam, and other European cities to earn its livelihood. The attention materialist feminists in the academy – discussed below – have focused on the group has also provided them with sustaining residencies at various college campuses throughout the United States. Peggy Shaw and Lois Weaver met while working with Spiderwoman, a group discussed extensively below. For more information on this feminist theatre troupe, see also Dolan, *The Feminist Spectator as Critic*, Chapter 4; Sue-Ellen Case, 'From Split Subject to Split Britches', in Enoch Brater (ed.), *Feminine Focus* (New York, Oxford: Oxford University Press, 1989); and Vivian M.

Patraka, 'Split Britches in *Split Britches*: Performing History, Vaudeville, and the everyday', *Women and Performance Journal* 4, 2 (1989).

15. For a description and application of materialist feminist performance theory, see Dolan, *The Feminist Spectator as Critic*, and Sue-Ellen Case, *Feminism and Theatre* (New York: Methuen, 1988).

16. See Case's chapter, 'Towards a new poetics', pp. 112–132.

17. See also Jill Dolan, 'Gender impersonation onstage: destroying or maintaining the mirror of gender roles', *Women and Performance Journal* 2, 2 (1985) for a discussion of the gender implications of mimesis. Much work has been generated around the topic of realism and mimesis since this early article. For a theoretical extension of the question of mimesis, see Elin Diamond, 'Mimesis, mimicry, and the "true-real"', *Modern Drama* 32, 1 (March 1989). This issue of *Modern Drama* is a special issue on 'Women in theatre', and contains several articles useful to illuminate this discussion. See also the work in Sue-Ellen Case (ed.), *Performing Feminisms: Feminist Critical Theory and Theatre* (Baltimore: Johns Hopkins University Press, 1990).

18. See Dolan, *The Feminist Spectator as Critic*, for an explication of the ideal spectator of representation.

19. See Jill Dolan, 'In defense of the discourse: materialist feminism, post-modernism, post-structuralism . . . and theory', *The Drama Review*, 33, 3 (Fall 1989) for a discussion of the parameters of this debate within the field of feminism and theatre.

20. For an explication of the ramifications of feminist theory in the academy and its influence on theatre research, see Case's introduction to *Performing Feminisms*.

21. For example, *The Kathy and Mo Show*, a popular comedy revue with a long, off-Broadway run through 1989 and into 1990, satirises radical feminism in a scene in which two elderly women enrolled in a women's studies course attend a performance at a feminist coffeehouse. The construction of the scene indicates its authors' familiarity with radical feminist tenets, but its subsequent ridicule of women's culture also indicates they believe radical feminism is archaic in the context of 1980s values.

22. Wendy Wasserstein, *The Heidi Chronicles*, unpublished manuscript, p. 2. All subsequent page references will appear in the text. A published version of the play will be available in 1990 from Dramatists Play Service. See also Phyllis Jane Rose, 'Dear Heidi', *American Theatre* 6, 7 (October 1989) for additional feminist commentary. My observations are drawn from my reading of the unpublished text, as well as the Broadway performance with Joan Allen in the title role, which I attended on 29 July 1989.

23. See Rozsika Parker and Griselda Pollock, *Old Mistresses: Women, Art, and Ideology* (New York: Routledge, 1981) pp. 20–26, for a materialist feminist critical discussion of the Gentileschi painting. I am indebted to Vicki Patraka for helping me make these connections.

24. From Spiderwoman's promotional material. See also Chinoy and Jenkins, pp. 303–305 for more historical information on the troupe.

25. The *Winnetou* manuscript is unpublished. My observations are based on the performance I attended, which was presented at At the Foot of the Mountain in Minneapolis on 8 October 1989.
26. Lisa Mayo and Gloria and Muriel Miguel were joined in this performance by Hortenisa Colorado.
27. At the performance I attended, the participating spectator was a man. I have since heard that other volunteers have been women, so the participant's gender here can be switched.
28. From Spiderwoman's advance press material.

4

The Politics of Theatre and Political Theatre in Australia

RICHARD FOTHERINGHAM

THE POLITICS OF THEATRE

. . . the mode of expression characteristic of a cultural production always depends on the laws of the market in which it is offered. (Pierre Bourdieu, *Distinction*)[1]

The major industries which make and disseminate dramatic texts through Australian society – film, television, and stage – [2] can to some extent be matched to three types of target audience: international (film), national (television), and regional (theatre). The increasing reliance of the Australian film industry on overseas sales received controversial confirmation in 1988–89 when the Federal Government's Film Finance Corporation commenced sending major film production proposals to Los Angeles to assess their saleability in the United States.[3] The influence of Hollywood genres on Australian film narratives as producers attempted to break into the lucrative US market has been noted several times;[4] and to an increasing extent television mini-series have also been specifically directed at known American and British consumers. Dramas for the commercial channels, such as *Bodyline* (1984, on the controversial 1932–33 cricket tour) and for the government-sponsored Australian Broadcasting Corporation, such as *Darlings of the Gods* (1989, about the Laurence Olivier–Vivien Leigh tour of Australia in 1948) were designed to be broadcast in Australia and England. Both these examples adopted narrative perspectives noted by Australian commentators as being alien to national prejudices, with *Bodyline* being told from the English captain Jardine's (and his girlfriend's) point of view,[5] and *Darlings of the Gods* re-invoking the English myth of Australia as a cultural desert. American pressures have become more insistent since financial co-production deals were allowed in government-assisted films in 1985;[6] this has led to a situation where 'national' themes and discourses have been explicitly denied in material marketed, in Australia at least, as 'Australian'.[7] A recent industrial protest involving the Writers' Guild followed the discovery that scripts for the local soap *E Street* were being faxed in from Los Angeles.

Nevertheless, if there is a sense of addressing a national audience in Australian drama, it occurs in the television industry. On the simple level of local drama content, the disastrous failure of governments to impose limits on overseas programme purchases in the 1950s meant that Australian television drama struggled over the next twenty years for a place in the market. Currently television stations are required to broadcast a minimum of two hours of local drama per week; a quota under attack as the television industry finds itself in financial crisis at the end of the 1980s.[8] As well as rules governing the generation of narratives from within the country, there are rules to cover television's target audience(s), particularly by limiting media ownership and networking between different stations. Originally this was designed to limit television's strength as an instrument of national propaganda by insisting on regional control and identity, but most current affairs programmes, game shows, and the major television dramas (*Neighbours*, *A Country Practice*) are viewed nationwide and, unlike *E Street*, are not primarily designed for overseas sale. However, their construction of the national has a constricting influence on Australian cultural diversity, since the major audience for the commercial dramas is in the vast suburbs of Sydney and Melbourne. A programme with even number one ratings in Brisbane or Adelaide (let alone the other major cities or rural Australia) is likely to be cut if it does not rate in the two biggest cities where the most money can be extracted from advertisers wishing to target their products.[9] The serial *Sons and Daughters* set out to maximise its chances in the market by adopting a series premise in which twins separated at birth grew up unaware of the other's existence – one in Sydney, one in Melbourne – met by chance, and fell in love. Most other Australian serials, while aware of the necessity of appealing to the same market, offer fictional locales constructed around the family, using stock binaries: work and leisure, city and country, female and male, old and young. This focus on general myths and problems of Western industrial society, representations of pleasant weather and a moderately affluent lifestyle, using a light and sometimes slightly parodic discourse, combined with low costs-per-unit (approximately two hours are produced each week), have made these programmes highly attractive to overseas buyers, with some thirteen serials currently being broadcast in over thirty countries.[10] Consequently there are both national and international reasons to foreground generalised Western industrial character types and situations; but serials and mini-series have also dealt extensively with Australian history, politics, and even the specifics of geographical localities.

As well as being the major site of anti-colonial struggle in the drama industries, it is in the television dramas that the limitations, sensitivities, and possibilities of a number of constructions of Australia as a nation are most clearly worked out. The major example is in the representation of aboriginal Australians, who since the film and theatre revival in the 1970s have featured strongly as both performers and writers. However, until recently such appearances have been located either in the exotic (in film; for example the roles offered to David Gulpilil in the *Crocodile Dundee* films and elsewhere) or marginalised (in 'alternative' theatrical and film productions). Even Australia's internationally acclaimed aboriginal dramatist, Jack Davis, has had very few performances by groups other than his own small Perth-based Marli Byol Company. Davis's award-winning *No Sugar* (1985) has been seen in Ottawa, Vancouver and London, but in Australia only in Perth and Melbourne. It has not, to date, been performed in Brisbane, Sydney, Adelaide, Hobart or in rural Australia where most aborigines live and where the simple appearance of a professional aboriginal theatre company, together with the play's subject matter – the appalling consequences of government interference in aboriginal family life in the 1930s – would have a major impact.[11]

By contrast the appearance of the black activist Gary Foley in the high-rating commercial television serial *A Country Practice* early in 1989 resulted in a major increase in national awareness of Foley, his career, aboriginal Australians in general, and the issues he used the programme to promulgate. (He was able to exercise influence over research and scripting.) Foley has had a long and distinguished career in aboriginal welfare and arts administration, and as an actor in alternative theatre and films since 1972, but has himself commented:

It seemed to me that what we needed to do as aboriginal people was to reach out and touch that audience we never get to – mainstream middle white Australians. . . I was secretary of the National Aboriginal Health Organisation for about 10 years, and in all that time of political agitating I don't think I was anywhere near as effective as I was in two episodes of *A Country Practice*. I think we really got an important message across.[12]

Representation of class, race, and gender types in popular television in Australia has long been one of the most significant sites of struggle in Australian culture. Little more than a decade ago, a nervous management vetoed the idea of introducing an aboriginal family as tenants into the block of flats which comprised the stock setting for the then long-running soap *Number 96*,[13] and the issue is still a sensitive one today. Actors from European migrant backgrounds have slowly found roles in mainstream television drama, although Asian–Australian performers have yet to achieve similar levels of representation.

If we turn our attention to live theatre in Australia, then it can be argued that there is virtually no national debate or agenda, although the assertion that one exists is a common rhetorical strategy adopted in speeches and newspaper articles. Rather the production and consumption of theatre exists in an economic flux dominated by several interacting factors. The first is the increasing development of the subsidised arts generally as a state rather than federal responsibility, with the Performing Arts Board of the Australia Council (the national arts-funding body) now explicitly defining its central role as being to provide additional special project money to new and existing organisations which are principally funded at the state level. This tendency dates back to the 1960s when it was decided *not* to establish a National Theatre Company (unlike, for example, the Australian Opera and Ballet Companies), but to encourage each of the six Australian states to set up one relatively well-funded company in its capital city. Up to that time the two companies with pretensions to 'national' status, the Melbourne Theatre Company and the Old Tote (predecessor to the Sydney Theatre Company), made several interstate tours with a season of three or four plays; even earlier, theatregoers in all states had the opportunity to see productions of seminal Australian plays such as *Rusty Bugles* (1948), *The Summer of the Seventeenth Doll* (1955), and *The One Day of the Year*, (1960). Since about 1970 however (paradoxically, just as Australian playwriting experienced a major renaissance) this idea that plays of national significance should be given national exposure was abandoned. Touring also became a high-cost activity, and while today a single production is occasionally presented in a second city, this is usually an exchange between two companies presented under the umbrella of the host company, with the play in question chosen for commercial reasons or to promote a wider awareness of the performing company. Promoting a wider interest in the play itself is rarely an issue. Neither critics, academics, nor public in Australia regularly experience theatre other than at the level of the local community. Occasionally newspapers and magazines have employed a 'national' theatre critic (Katharine Brisbane for *The Australian* in the 1970s and Barry Oakley for the now-defunct *National Times* in the mid-1980s were the two outstanding examples), but such experiments have been infrequent. It is extremely difficult therefore to see subsidised theatre in Australia as being more than of regional significance; as the example above of Davis's *No Sugar* suggests, the national impact of texts in performance is consequently significantly weakened. The same is true of even the plays of Australia's most successful dramatist, David Williamson, which may take a decade to be performed (if ever) in all the major cities. The plays of Stephen Sewell and Louis Nowra, two of the most significant dramatists of the 1980s, have been even more arbitrarily selected; until recently Nowra was almost unknown to the Melbourne stage, while conversely Melbourne has several successful writers such as Barry Dickens and Ron Elisha whose work is rarely seen outside that city. Neither Sewell nor Nowra has had a professional production in Brisbane. Sydney sometimes asserts a national London-like centrality in Australian cultural life; a claim opposed particularly by Melbourne and irrelevant to Perth, Townsville or Darwin several thousand miles away.

However, Australians in major cities do share some performance experiences, since a significant if precarious commercial theatre industry does exist. Australian plays are rarely, however, taken up by such managements. For the commercial entrepreneurs Australia is constructed like the British provinces or the American midwest: passive recipients of West End or Broadway hits. Some of the big shows in Australia in 1988–89 were *Cats*, *Les Misérables*, *Big River*, *Anything Goes*, and *42nd Street*, most of which attempted to attract a nation-wide audience by advertising airfare, ticket and weekend accommodation packages in newspapers in other states. Lesser managements tour small-cast comedies around the country; 1989's offerings included A. R. Gurney's *The Cocktail Hour* and three Willy Russell comedies, *Educating Rita, Shirley Valentine*, and *One for the Road*. Few Australian plays have had this kind of Australia-wide exposure; nor, given the lack of a theatre company charged with 'national' goals, is there any sense of canonical texts requiring regular re-consideration and representation. The task of asserting an Australian dramatic tradition is left to school and university text-book lists.

The third factor at play originates in the cultural positioning of theatre, though it has obvious economic consequences. Theatre with a capital 'T' in Australia has always been written, like the arts generally, under the sign of the international, but principally under the sign of London. 'Taste' in theatre, as a determinant of social position and an acquisition offering social mobility, is centred upon Broadway and the West End (for commercial theatre) and on the major London companies, both mainstream and alternative, for subsidised theatre. A major London success like *Les Liaisons Dangereuses* will be staged by most if not all the subsidised state companies in Australia within three years, who will also monitor London activity to help decide which revivals to offer from the classic repertoire. It is no coincidence that recent Australian productions of Aphra Behn's *The Rover* have followed the London staging of the same text. Some at least of the artistic directors of major theatre companies are willing to actively promote Australian product, and their part-reliance on Australia Council funds (where local writing is given more than lip-service in grant allocations), gives them support in their dealings with conservative boards of management and business and subscription managers; but the box office ultimately talks, as increasingly do private sponsors.

The Australian theatre scene exists therefore as a tolerated – even warmly encouraged – 'B' grade industry: smaller plays with smaller casts performed in smaller venues. A major example was the 'World Expo on Stage' season (May–October 1988) held at the Queensland Cultural Centre in Brisbane. Three theatres, the Concert Hall and the Lyric (both 2000 seats) and the Cremorne (300 seats) were used. All international plays were booked into the larger venues, even when they were experimental, non-commercial works like Robert Wilson's *The Knee Plays*; all Australian plays appeared in the Cremorne, even when, as in the case of

Louis Nowra's remarkable and very successful adaptation of the Xavier Herbert novel *Capricornia*, the large set and mixed aboriginal and European cast could barely fit on the small stage. The programme for the Sydney Theatre Company's forthcoming 1990 season also shows this division, with *A Midsummer Night's Dream*, *The Three Sisters*, *The Importance of Being Earnest*, Kaufman's and Hart's *Once in A Lifetime*, and David Hare's *The Secret Rapture* being announced to appear in the Sydney Opera House Drama Theatre (540 seats), and with three Australian plays amongst those offered at the 309-seat Wharf Theatre.

The laws of the market place also work *within* dramatic texts to foreground and background themes and issues, shift generic expectations through staging and advertising, and pressure authors in their approaches to subjects for dramatic treatment. At times, this inevitable play of pressures can degenerate into outright subversion of an author's original intent. A useful example is the Sydney writer Linda Aronson's *Dinkum Assorted*, a play set during the Second World War in a biscuit factory in an Australian country town. According to the author the play started as an overt feminist statement, examining 'the power structures operating within a large group of women', and 'freedom and its price'.[14] This period of history has been of particular interest to Australian feminist artists and historians, since (as happened earlier in Britain during the First World War) it saw the breakthrough in the introduction of very large numbers of women into the workforce. A number of recent books and television programmes have chronicled the subject in both narrative and documentary form, inspired in part by the American documentary film *Rosie the Riveter*.

Dinkum Assorted was written and workshopped over a number of years, and given two professional productions (Sydney Theatre Company 1988, and Queensland Theatre Company 1989). It achieved rare large-theatre exposure in both cities and provided work for an unusually large (between thirteen and fifteen) and uniquely all-woman cast; two major achievements for an Australian play, given the conditions I have analysed above. In Sydney it played to a disappointing 58 per cent capacity audience, but the Brisbane season was more successful and overall perhaps the author's declared intention of taking 'women's issues to a wide general audience' was achieved.[15] Nevertheless its success was bought at a price; certainly by the time of the Brisbane production the script's original intentions had been abandoned in favour of an attempt at commercial success through the use of 1940s' nostalgia and an attempt to market the play as a musical.

From the beginning it seems the all-woman cast caused scripting problems, with narrative threads such as a romance between one of the women and an American airman, a visit by a male documentary film crew, and the stealing of an American Armed Forces' mascot goat, left unresolved and/or simply forgotten in the second act. More subversive to the feminist theme was the introduction of sequences suggestive of *Dad's Army* which, rather than showing women coping without men, showed them being unable to drill, putting gas masks on upside down, failing to resuscitate a victim, being unable to read a first-aid manual, and making elementary mistakes in trying to get a disused oven to work. The Brisbane production further undermined the women's capacity for collective action by casting as the 'militant' leader – the one character shown as resourceful and capable of initiating action – the only actor with a distinctive English accent, reinforcing the common myth that trade union activism is 'the British disease'.

Although the play had only a few songs, its staging attempted to locate it generically as musical comedy, since one strand in the plotting involved rehearsing and performing a Christmas concert. Two other major storylines in the second act were the closing-down of the biscuit factory – a decision greeted with 'we'll muddle through' stoicism – and the inexplicable decision of a single mother, earlier shown fighting tooth and nail to keep her daughter, to abandon her and go off with a lover. Both potentially significant conflicts raising important feminist issues were truncated and forgotten; instead the play ended with the concert, in which the entire cast, dressed as biscuits, lamingtons and jars of Vegemite, sang and danced before offering a final tableau in which they posed attractively as the decorations on a Christmas cake. While some scenes managed both to be entertaining and to maintain a thematic validity (one, where the women danced with male dummies before abandoning them limp on the floor like drunks the morning after, was particularly effective), *Dinkum Assorted* would seem to confirm the belief of those working in alternative, community and consciously political theatre that at present the attempt to reconcile integrity of purpose with mainstream values and expectations is extremely difficult.

POLITICAL THEATRE

If fears of appropriation and subversion dominate in the attitudes of Australian dramatic authors to popular and mainstream narrative forms and institutions, then the corresponding concerns in alternative theatre have been marginalisation and ineffectiveness. Sharing Gary Foley's belief quoted earlier about the relative value of black activism as against using channels of mass communication, many of the writers for political theatre in earlier decades now look back on their work at that time as naïve or futile. Betty Roland, whose work for the Sydney New Theatre in the 1930s ranged from overt agit-prop performed in factories and at demonstrations to the significant prize-winning *Are You Ready Comrade* (1938), remembers that group as offering writers chances to see their work performed and politically committed actors opportunities to express their opinions, 'but I don't think they had much effect on public opinion, or on history.'[16] What later came to be called the New Theatres, based on the Workers' Art Clubs in Germany and Russia, London's Unity Theatre, and the American New Theatre League, were established in most capital cities from 1932 onwards, and did indeed provide a stage for many of the most important dramatic writers from the 1930s to the 1950s. Some New Theatres are still in existence, though press censorship in the 1940s and 1950s and the splits in the Communist Party in 1940 and 1956 minimised their social impact, and the rejection of the old left by younger radicals after 1968 marginalised the groups from even politically-sympathetic audiences.[17] The Melbourne New produced a classic in the folk-musical *Reedy River* (1953), set in the aftermath of the unsuccessful 1891 shearers' strike which gave rise to the Australian Labor Party. It and Odets' *Waiting for Lefty* were amongst the most enduring of the plays in the New Theatres' repertoires, but *Reedy River*, produced first at a time when several newspapers banned reviews of New Theatre productions, is still largely ignored by Australian theatre history. Although it has been performed by at least one amateur group throughout the country every year since its premiere, *Reedy River* to date has never had a professional production.[18]

The Cold War paranoia of the Menzies government, with its security files on supposedly left-wing artists, may help to explain why there seems to have been little other overtly political theatre in Australia throughout the 1950s and early 1960s. However the post-1968 wave of alternative theatre, significant then as a breaking free from this repressive era, is also now remembered by participants such as Alison Richards as a time when actors, writers, and directors were 'young, raucous, and terribly sure of themselves. . . Wonderful how sure you can be of changing the world trudging from coffee shop to coffee shop in Carlton [near Melbourne University], with an occasional foray out to a factory for contact with the working classes.'[19] Australia's involvement in the Vietnam war gave a direct-action urgency to much political theatre, performed mostly by and for university students. This strident and predominantly anti-American agit-prop dissipated after the election of the Whitlam Labor government in December 1972 and the immediate withdrawal of Australian forces from Vietnam, and did not revive in any organised way after the sacking of that government by the Governor-General just under three years later.

However, the experience was not without its useful lessons, with many of the non-mainstream theatre artists from that period moving to *institutionalise* alternative, and sometimes overtly political, theatre practices, and evolving a technique of *narrowcasting* (to borrow a mass-media concept) to assist the effective communication of their ideas and to cut across the supposedly a-political but nevertheless selective appeal of mainstream theatre. Amongst Australian authors a key figure in this shift has been John Romeril, whose early work *Chicago Chicago* (1969) was one of the few directly political texts of its time to be published, and who has provided numerous scripts for both mainstream and alternative companies in the ensuing thirty years. Reconsidering the dilemma of what Graeme Blundell, in the Introduction to *Chicago Chicago*, called 'the ambiguities of motive' in working for professional, box-office dependent theatre,[20] Romeril has noted, thirty years later:

> It's almost the case [now] that a theatre without money, a theatre without box office, is a theatre that doesn't exist in Australia. I think too that, finally, you have to be intent on reaching an audience and maximising that audience, even if it is a specialised audience, like the show I did about single parents. Obviously you take as your audience all possible single parents in Australia and try if you can to get them to come.[21]

Targeting specific audiences has become the major strategy for alternative theatre in Australia in the 1980s, with companies directing their work towards geographical, ethnic, gender, class, lifestyle and special interest groups. This has tended to blur the identification of 'political' theatre *per se*, since many groups would argue that their choice of *audience* is the major political statement by which they challenge the present construction of the Australian *polis*, particularly in its continuing adherence to a middle-class and middle-aged male Anglo-Celtic hierarchy, and the present appeal of mainstream theatre to middle-class, middle-aged female Anglo-Celtic audiences. Thus the decision of companies such as Sidetrack in Sydney's Marrickville, West in Melbourne's Footscray, Street Arts in Brisbane's West End, Junction in Adelaide's Mile End, and Deck Chair in Fremantle in Western Australia to base themselves in industrial suburbs, often with significant though no longer first-generation migrant populations, links together a wide variety of performance styles and subjects. Deck Chair's *Fleets of Fortune* (1987, revised 1988) offered a history of the Italian fishing community in Fremantle but, though it contained direct political comment on migrant policies and problems, essentially celebrated the experiences of a community whose voice was previously heard only in its own sub-culture. The foregrounding of other traditions of Australian life is the major political statement of such plays; a matter to which we will return later.

The most enduring product of the institutionalisation of alternative theatre and the targeting of particular audiences has been the 'Art and Working Life' Project, established by the Australia Council in 1982 in response to 'a resurgence of interest by the Trade Union movement in arts activities'.[22] The major group in the 1970s which triggered this 'resurgence' was the Popular Theatre Troupe, a small professional company with a repertoire of short documentary plays on contentious subjects such as racism, multinational companies, women in the workforce, and uranium mining. A season of factory performances in 1976 at the Adelaide Festival of Arts and elsewhere led the next year to a tour of Sydney job sites sponsored by the Amalgamated Metal Workers' Union – the first significant financial commitment of this kind made by a trade union. At about the same time Trades and Labor Councils in several states appointed arts officers, and a number of alternative theatre workers moved into positions of authority within federal and state arts-funding bodies, initiating policies which challenged the hegemony of the state theatre companies over the arts-subsidy dollar.

From 1982 it became possible under the Art and Working Life Scheme for a union and a theatre company to jointly devise a proposal for a performance project partly funded by the union, and to receive significant government financial assistance for that project. Although at the end of the 1980s the increasing conservatism of Australian politics caused the Theatre Board (now the Performing Arts Board) to suggest that other community organisations as well as unions could apply for support from this programme, union-backed projects continue to dominate the field. The possibility of financial reward for what many actors had assumed to be 'radical' and unpaid performing caused a sudden and significant increase in 'political' theatre, with a consequent degree of cynicism from older artists whose work preceded such unexpected government beneficence. In a short 1984 article provocatively entitled 'Art and Working Life – Bourgeois Theatre in Overalls?', the playwright and actor Allen Lyne demanded:

> Where do the artists come from who wish to work in this kind of theatre? What is their reason for working? Few have any political framework of analysis: our theatre training institutions do not teach politics. Working with political theatre companies in Australia and on Art and Working Life projects, I have been dismayed by the almost complete lack of knowledge of working-class history. Most people working in the field know nothing about their own union [Actors' Equity], let alone anyone else's; or about the trade union movement generally – its history, its direction, its strengths and weaknesses. In two supposedly political theatre companies I've had to insist that the staff become unionised.[23]

In a more considered article written five years later (1989) the academic David Watt noted that Art and Working Life projects have oscillated between this essentially opportunistic desire by a-political performers 'to "colonise" a new market area', and an overcompensatory 'revolutionary zeal' on the part of young Marxists which he regards as more dangerously inappropriate to the political situation of unionism itself as Australia, following Thatcher's Britain, moves towards the de-regulation of the labour market.[24]

Watt privileges in his analysis one company – Melbourne Workers' Theatre – which has concentrated its work exclusively within the Art and Working Life area, and which he argues has therefore 'developed a closer collaboration than most of the community theatre groups which have worked with unions as part of a larger pattern of activity.' This is debatable; although a major writer, Andrew Bovell, and one possibly enduring play, Bovell's *The Ballad of Lois Ryan* (1988), have emerged from this organisation since its inception in 1986, it is perhaps more accurate to see as central to the Art and Working Life scheme a number of companies (including Sidetrack, West, Junction and others mentioned above) co-operating with individual unions in their geographical vicinity, and performing short plays on industrial issues like Sidetrack's *The Number One Thing* (1984, on worker participation, produced in conjunction with the NSW Trade Union Training Authority) and Junction's *What's New* (1987, on industry re-structuring, supported by the South Australian Trades and Labor Council). Bovell's *The Ballad of Lois Ryan* is in subject matter unremarkable; it concerns industrial safety (the most common 'soft' subject in Art and Working Life projects since like motherhood it can't be questioned). It achieves moving strength not as a direct comment on that issue but as a study of the complexities of modern living which would lead a woman to be alone late at night operating an unsafe machine, while being represented on union committees by male shop stewards like her former husband who see her own leadership qualities and working conditions as being of lesser importance than theirs.[25]

The major difficulty with the narrowcast concept in general has been the tendency of writers and theatre companies to ignore wider issues and other discourses (thereby limiting their work's impact), and a corresponding tendency – ironically similar to the problems in mainstream theatre which have been discussed above – to fudge themes and approaches which might be less 'popular' with the target group. What makes *The Ballad of Lois Ryan* significant, in addition to its complexity, is that it challenges its intended audience rather than expressing their prejudices. It is this issue of women's rights which in particular has focused attempts at dialogue (rather than co-operation) between theatre companies and unions. One remarkable work which succeeded in negotiating a difficult and sensitive topic was Vitalstatistix's *A Touchy Subject*, on sexual harassment in the workplace. Devised initially in Adelaide in 1987 for technical college students but later taken to offices and worksites in at least three states, *A Touchy Subject* depended for its effect on its all-woman cast, whose light comic portrayal of both male and female characters in a wide variety of workplace situations used Brechtian techniques with cathartic results.[26]

While unquestionably there is a loose grouping of companies, writers and performers who share considerable common theatrical and political ground, a wider view of political theatre in Australia in the 1980s, as indicated earlier, has to consider a large number of other groups who have made a primary commitment to providing platforms for new voices and addressing new audiences other than trade unionists. While most alternative professional theatre work in the 1980s has occurred under the umbrella concept of 'the community theatre movement' (a phrase which gained a wider currency after the establishment of a Community Arts Board at the Australia Council in 1977–78), the very vagueness of the term 'community' has tended to conceal some significant disagreements. Because it is a less confrontational term than 'alternative' or 'political', 'community' has proved useful in the search by nearly all small theatre companies for both government grants and corporate sponsorship, and the sense of a larger movement has also been asserted as a lobbying tactic, supported by several National Community Theatre Conferences and at least one professional lobbying agency which in 1989 organised a nation-wide survey of groups asking them to identify what they consider essential community theatre practices. However it is hard to sustain these assertions of either ideological or organisational commonality in the face of the clearly divergent and at times opposed attitudes and practices of different companies.

It is self-evident that lifestyle celebrations such as the gay Mardi Gras in Sydney each February, and lesbian plays like Zootango's *Hallelujah Lady Jane*, have political importance, beginning with their acceptance without major controversy into public life. The former has become a major annual festival with professional organisers; the latter had successful Hobart and Brisbane seasons in 1988. It speculated on what the wife and sister of the nineteenth-century Governor of Tasmania and explorer Sir John Franklin, and an Australian convict woman they encounter, may have been doing to relieve their boredom and frustration while he was busy failing to discover the North-West Passage. Other important new voices include the aboriginal performers mentioned earlier and a number of disabled-actor theatre companies, with the NSW Theatre of the Deaf completing its first decade of fully-professional work in November 1989 with a major success *Wolfmoon*, performed at Sydney's Wharf Theatre. While these groups have by and large worked independently of the community theatre movement (partly because their funding has been from other sources), they would presumably have small quarrel with it.

The same cannot be said of many of the groups formed from the Euro–Australian community who have created works dealing with continental European migrant experiences. While a number of companies within the community theatre movement, including Sidetrack, Street Arts, West, and Deck Chair, have consciously set out to achieve a multi-cultural identity, comprised partly of non-to Anglo actors and, include ethnic issues within their plays, there is also a number of successful European migrant groups whose plays see Australia much as new English migrants did in the nineteenth century: as a socially and culturally barren land with second-rate artists (themselves excluded), and who construct a colonial/neo-colonial memory of Europe as the centre of intellect, culture, and community. Others see the migrant experience primarily as an opportunity to exploit a more affluent economy without engaging in the life of that country. A published example is Theodore Patrikareas' *The Uncle from Australia*, a popular success with Greek–Australians and in Greece. Its central character is a migrant who has succeeded financially in Australia but who has taken his money back to his childhood home, where he exhorts the villagers:

> Life as a migrant is full of struggle – hard pitiless struggle. You've got to fight battles every day not just for your bread but even more for your soul. . . . stay in your own country. That's the advice I'd give to every young man.[27]

The Uncle from Australia is an earlier (1964) play written towards the end of the period of mass European migration to Australia, but its popularity with a later generation of Greek–Australians, in a 1987 revival, shows some continuing colonial tendencies of migrant communities. This construction of 'the (distant) homeland' as against 'the (present) other' continues to appear in many plays emerging from ethnic spaces, but no scripts are presently available for a more detailed examination of an aspect of ethnic theatre which has little appeal to other cultural groupings.

One interesting aspect of Phil Thomson's and Ken Kelso's script for Deck Chair's *Fleets of Fortune*, mentioned earlier, was that it tried to objectify such attitudes by analysing the attraction of Mussolini's regime for Italo–Australian migrants during the 1930s.

It offered a story segment in which, during the early days of the Second World War, a fisherman was pressured by his fascist workmates into forwarding money to the Italian Embassy to assist Mussolini's war effort, and was consequently interned. However, this potentially complex situation was resolved by a simple-minded attack on the inhumanity of the Australian government in taking the father from his family – even though he was later shown to have been allowed to return home.[28] The subject, it seems, is still too sensitive for the Italo–Australian community to allow a more rigorous exegesis of conflicting loyalties and rights, and is another example of the limitations to the freedom which writers and performers have sought in alternative theatre.

If such work has caused barriers to be erected on both sides of the discourse of the national in Australian theatre, so too has much of European ethnic theatre's attitude to questions of gender and race. A remarkable popular success (though predominantly with Euro–Australian audiences) has been the revue *Wogs Out of Work*, a joyous celebration of their life experiences by actors from Greek, Italian and Spanish backgrounds, which began at a Melbourne Comedy Festival in 1987, was picked up by a commercial management and played almost continuously for the next two years throughout Eastern Australia, with a second company also being formed in September 1988. No text is available (and there were significant differences between the scripts for the two productions), but in performance many of the sketches in both versions of *Wogs Out of Work* seemed to be constructed on assumptions about gender differences which did little to disperse the bigotries about Italian men which circulate in Australia, as elsewhere. Both versions also included gratuitous racist references to aboriginal people and to Anglo–Australians; while the latter might well be endured as the justice of revenge, the former suggested the insularity of much of the Euro–Australian community from those questions of discourse and representation in Australian theatre which are, if anything can be so called, truly national concerns. Several plays (the 1984 *Nuovo Paese* project with Sydney's Italian community in Leichhardt was one)[29] have attempted to counter this insularity by including a scene in which the old first-generation migrant parents return to their country of origin for a holiday, only to find it is now also a modern industrial state, and that the changes (feminism, cultural diversity and tolerance) which they had seen as problems to be resisted by ghettoism are in fact changes in Western rather than Australian society. However, such plays have not to date achieved popular or widespread exposure.

It seems then that, while the 1980s have seen a remarkable expansion of professional theatre of both a consciously political and a socially diverse nature, many of those who initially supported the emergence of new voices on Australian stages rather too naïvely assumed that such utterances would confirm 'progressive' 'Australian' attitudes. As in any field of debate there is a struggle for popular and influential utterance, with new areas of assertion and challenge opening up, though hampered by the continuing regional and narrow audience base for most productions. Professionalisation has meant that, however diverse the sources of non-box-office income for individual companies, most stage work is now produced in an increasingly similar cultural and financial matrix (certainly in comparison with the very different conditions which obtain in the film and television industries). The divisions asserted between commercial and state-subsidised versus community and political theatre (with the accompanying connotations of conservative and radical, compromised and free) may increasingly fail as adequate or useful categories in which to locate political theatre in Australia, in both the narrow and the wider sense of the phrase, in the 1990s.

Notes

1. Pierre Bourdieu, *Distinction: A Social Critique of the Judgement of Taste*, trans. Richard Nice (Cambridge, Mass: Harvard University Press, 1984) p. xiii.
2. Radio drama cannot be discounted, although it is increasingly limited to the Australian Broadcasting Corporation's FM stations and is both 'national' and 'narrowcast' in the same way as is the ethnic television channel SBS, as discussed later in the article.
3. See e.g. *The Australian*, 22 May 1989, p. 4.
4. E.g. Ruth Abbey and Jo Crawford, 'Crocodile Dundee or Davy Crockett?', *Meanjin* 46, 2 (1987) pp. 145–152; Peter Hamilton and Sue Matthews, *American Dreams, Australian Movies* (Sydney: Currency, 1986).
5. For a comment on *Bodyline* see Stuart Cunningham, 'Kennedy–Miller: "House Style" in Australian television', in *The Imaginary Industry: Australian Film in the late '80s*, ed. Susan Dermody and Elizabeth Jacka (North Ryde: Australian Film, Television, and Radio School, 1989) pp. 177–199.

6. Elizabeth Jacka, 'The Industry: Chapter 4: Overseas Links', *The Imaginary Industry*, p. 58.
7. Jacka, p. 50.
8. *The Australian*, 19 October 1989, p. 2.
9. E.g. the fate of the programme rating number 1 in Brisbane, 'Australia's most wanted', in September 1989.
10. 'Invasion of the Aussie Soaps', *Sydney Morning Herald*, undated clipping from 1989, 'Good Weekend', pp. 24–28.
11. Pamela Payne, 'A season of magic', *Sydney Morning Herald*, 21 October 1989, p. 87.
12. Jo Litson, 'The angry young heart-throb', *The Weekend Australian*, 8–9 April 1989, Weekend 11.
13. Interview by the author with Robert Caswell (former scriptwriter for *Number 96*), 6 October 1983.
14. Programme notes for the Queensland Theatre Company production, March 1989.
15. Linda Aronson, *Dinkum Assorted* (Sydney: Currency, 1989) p. ix.
16. 'Interview: Betty Roland Talks to Drusilla Modjeska', *Australasian Drama Studies* 8 (April 1986) p. 68.
17. Paul Herlinger, 'A New Direction for "the New"?' *Australasian Drama Studies* 8 (April 1986) pp. 97–112.
18. However, the script was eventually published in 1970 and recently republished. Dick Diamond, *Reedy River* (Sydney: Currency, 1989).
19. Alison Richards, 'And Here We Are Again', in R. Fotheringham (ed.), *Community Theatre in Australia* (North Ryde: Methuen Australia, 1987) p. 33.
20. Graeme Blundell, 'Introduction' to Buzo, Hibberd, Romeril, *Plays* (Ringwood: Penguin, 1970) p. 12.
21. '"A Hybrid Talent": An Interview with John Romeril by Leah Mercer', *Australasian Drama Studies* 17 (October 1990), forthcoming.
22. 'Unions and Art', *Art and Working Life Festival Programme*, 1985, p. 4.
23. Allen Lyne, 'Art and Working Life – Bourgeois Theatre in Overalls?', in R. Fotheringham (ed.), *Community Theatre in Australia*, pp. 46–47.
24. David Watt, 'The Trade Union Movement, Art and Working Life and Melbourne Workers' Theatre', *Australasian Drama Studies* 14 (April 1989) p. 5.
25. Andrew Bovell, 'The Ballad of Lois Ryan', unpublished script for the 1988 Melbourne Workers' Theatre Production.
26. Darrelyn Gunzburg, Ollie Black, Margaret Fischer, *A Touchy Subject* in *Australasian Drama Studies* 14 (April 1989) pp. 65–86.
27. Theodore Patrikareas, *The Uncle from Australia*, trans. Con Castan, *Australasian Drama Studies* 15/16 (October 1989/April 1990) pp. 145–46.
28. These comments are based on the revised version performed at Brisbane's World Expo on Stage, 27 September – 1 October 1988. A script was not available.
29. See Robin Laurie, 'Twelve Weeks in a *Nuovo Paese*' in *Community Theatre in Australia*, pp. 89–94.

5

Community Theatre:
Carnival or Camp?

PETER REYNOLDS

The tradition created among the European bourgeoisie by Ibsen, Strindberg, Chekhov, Shaw, Galsworthy, Anouilh, Cocteau, Giraudoux, Pirandello became a strong self-confident tradition. It declared, without too much bother, that the best theatre is about the problems and the achievements of articulate middle-class men and sometimes women, is performed in comfortable theatres, in large cities, at a time that will suit the eating habits of the middle-class at a price that only the most determined of the lower orders could afford, and will generally have an air of intellectuality about it – something to exercise the vestiges of one's education on and to scare off the Great Unwashed. There will be critics to make it more important by reviewing it in the important newspapers, and learned books written about it to prove that it really *is* 'art'.   (John McGrath)[1]

. . . I was dissatisfied with theatre: it's hard to say why except that perhaps it seemed totally unimportant in most people's lives.   (Ann Jellicoe)[2]

As we approach the end of the twentieth century it would appear obvious to all but the most blinkered observer of social trends that the vast majority of the population in Britain care nothing at all about the theatre. If they do pause to consider it they probably only experience a sense of alienation and mild irritation. For, despite the international reputation some of its directors and actors enjoy in the trans-cultural marketplace, and the wholly dispro-portionate attention given to the theatre in the 'quality' press, and in radio and television arts coverage, potential audiences resol-utely stay away in droves. Who can blame them? For those few who do regularly frequent professional theatre in Britain, their role is clear: they are creatively impotent, seldom consulted, and always expected to remain passive (and appreciative) consumers of the production of others.

Most conventional British theatre companies, like the now defunct Stalinist regimes of Eastern Europe, are monolithic and moribund; they play the same kind of material to the same audience over and over again. They cannot be reformed from within: not only are the vested interests too entrenched, they are also extraordinarily difficult to penetrate. Once inside, all the unwritten rules conspire to protect and preserve the status quo. The British theatrical establishment operates like an exclusive gentleman's (sic) club, with power concentrated in very few hands. Work is inevitably obtained through a network of 'contacts', and actors who wish to continue to work are compelled to acquire and sustain a 'co-operative' (that is, unquestioning) reputation, however uncongenial they may find their work, or however much they may disagree with the play and/or the methods of their director. The directocratic structure, or, if you prefer, the hegemony of the Cambridge-educated Mafia, ensures that most, if not all of the significant decisions regarding the processes of making texts into performances are controlled by that powerful élite. Actors are seldom involved in decision-making; audiences, never.

Professional theatre in Britain is a closed community. Any significant challenge to the status quo existing within it, and to the control of the few over the means of theatrical production, has to come from outside the established theatrical institutions. In the 1960s and 1970s it seemed for a time as if that challenge was going to come from agit-prop and street theatre, and from so-called 'Alternative' theatre groups like Belt and Braces, Red Ladder, and Monstrous Regiment. But, despite mounting what was, for a short time, an effective counter-culture, their impact on mainstream theatre was, at best, marginal. Many promisingly progressive companies, founded on democratic principles, became absorbed into the mainstream, floundered on the careerist aspirations of some of their members, or, more often than not, simply folded up through insufficient funding. But, at the end of the 1980s, it was possible to detect the birth of another challenge to traditional British theatre. Just as the decade ended with the apparent triumph of democracy over autocracy in Eastern Europe, so a more enlightened and democratic theatrical form had been evolving in Britain: Community Theatre. Like its European political counterpart, Community Theatre was a movement for greater democracy and openness: it sought to break the mould of exclusivity and élitism surrounding conventional theatrical activity. And just as the workers, students and intellectuals of Eastern Europe built their revolutions on the streets, Community Theatre began to build its reputation not in large purpose-built metropolitan theatres, but in communities. Above all, both revolutionary movements – and I think Community Theatre is, potentially at least, revolutionary – attempted to break away from the dictatorship of one or two all-powerful individuals and institutions. Both sought to bring about a more open, co-operative and responsive form of organisation alerted to, rather than alienated from, the needs both of individuals and of communities. In this process they gave many more people genuine responsibility for the interpretation of their past, the construction of their present, and the direction of their future.

Anyone even vaguely interested in British theatre could not have failed to notice the tremendous increase in the 1980s of events advertised as Community Plays. Unless, however, you happened to attend a performance of one, you might still be left none the wiser as to what you had seen; and even if you had, you might still be left in the dark about its significance. Indeed, many of those who eagerly seized upon the fashionable label 'community' and attached themselves to it with alacrity, did so only to provide themselves with a new marketing device to sell the tired and familiar products of mainstream theatre companies. If you read their submissions to the Arts Council of Great Britain for funding, you could be forgiven for thinking that almost all theatres in Britain today were totally committed to serving the interests of the communities in which they are located, whether that community is defined in local, regional or national terms. Even progressive theatres like the Glasgow Citizens, and the Theatre Royal Stratford East, operate on the traditional assumption that theatre is essentially a service industry. However, in practice their idea of 'service' is usually restricted to supplying people with a particular theatrical product which they are expected to purchase and consume on the premises. Whatever theatres may say and try to do by way of 'serving' their communities (many now employ a community advisor or 'outreach' team), what they *do* seldom if ever reaches a point of genuine community involvement in the theatrical manufacturing process itself.

However, during the 1980s the work of one organisation in

particular sought a genuine rather than a token involvement of the community in the process of play-making: the Colway Theatre Trust (CTT). By their work they have invited a re-definition and re-thinking of ideas about the community and its relationship to theatre. The form of Community Theatre CTT developed during the 1980s was very different from the activities that have characterised most conventional theatre in Britain since the end of the Second World War. CTT sought to break the conventional relationship of active producer and passive consumer, and to replace it with a more genuinely collaborative and mutually responsive enterprise. CTT sought to blur the distinction between amateur and professional by involving both in a shared and co-operative experience in which the *process* would always be acknowledged as of equal importance to the theatrical product.

Dorset is an unlikely place to begin a theatrical revolution, but the Colway Theatre Trust was founded there by the playwright Ann Jellicoe in 1979, following the presentation in the previous year of her play *The Reckoning* in a school in Lyme Regis. Both the performance and the play were unusual for several reasons. Jellicoe, a professional dramatist whose work has been widely performed on the British stage and is best known for her play *The Knack* (staged in 1962, and later made into a commercially successful film), had chosen to write a new play which drew for its inspiration on the history of the town in which she lived: Lyme Regis. She decided to dramatise some of the events surrounding the Monmouth rebellion which began in Lyme in 1686, and to present them neither in London nor in a theatre (the usual venues for a playwright of her status), but in a school located in the town. The decision to use a public space for the performance rather than a conventional theatre (all bar one of CTT's subsequent productions have avoided theatres) removed at least one potential barrier to the involvement of a wider spectrum of local people. Those who were either unfamiliar with theatregoing as a social habit (the vast majority of the population) or uneasy with the idea of entering a building whose use is associated with the narrow cultural preoccupations of the educated middle class, did not have to negotiate a social ritual with whose conventions they were unfamiliar.

In order to present the play, Jellicoe decided to involve both professional *and* amateur theatre workers. The West Country group Medium Fair, together with Ann Jellicoe herself (as both writer and director) plus the services of Carmel Collins as designer, formed the professional core who worked with a large amateur cast. A total of seventy performers were involved, made up of both adults and school children, all drawn from the local community. Another traditional barrier to a more intimate and immediate experience was removed by the crucial decision to avoid a conventional end-on presentational style and to go instead for a promenade performance. The promenade style suited the amateur cast and made for a much less formal but more spontaneous atmosphere. It also contrasted with the conventional theatre's continual signalling of the literal and metaphorical separation of performer and audience. So successful was the promenade convention that it was adopted for all but one of CTT's subsequent productions in the 1980s.

The Reckoning was not only a *local* success, but, perhaps because of Jellicoe's reputation as a writer and former literary manager of the Royal Court Theatre, it also received some attention from the national press. The *Guardian* spoke of it as ' . . . a splendid piece of theatre. Dramatic, exciting, bloodthirsty, totally absorbing and above all maintaining an air of spontaneity . . .'[3] More significant for the future development of CTT, it was also seen by the playwright Howard Barker, who subsequently agreed to write a community play. His *The Poor Man's Friend* was staged in Dorchester in 1981 and confirmed that the work of CTT was of national interest and importance.

Experience of *The Reckoning* had convinced Ann Jellicoe that using a core of professional performers combined with amateurs did not work in the collective interests of the company as a whole: the amateurs tended to defer to the professionals. Thus the cast of *The Poor Man's Friend* (over 150 individual parts) was entirely amateur. However, as in Lyme, a promenade style performance was used. Performances took place not in a theatre but, as in *The Reckoning*, in a school hall. Barker's play was based on the nineteenth-century local history – carefully researched by a team of local people – of the town of Bridport. Although no professional actors were used, there was again a core of professionals that had now grown to include a writer, director, designer, musical director, and stage-manager. But in order to facilitate a production using 150 performers (*all* given a specific role and not used merely for 'crowd scenes') a huge back-up team was required consisting of costume, set, and property makers, as well as those involved in research, publicity, administration and, not least, fund-raising. All these people came from the Bridport area. Crucially, no one who expressed an interest in becoming involved was denied an opportunity of doing so. The whole project was designed to include as many members of the local community as possible, and, by the time the play had finished, as many as 50 per cent of the total population of this small market town had been involved in its genesis.

The whole scale of the operation, the professional and amateur collaboration, the fact that the play addressed the history of the town, and therefore issues and events of significance to the local community, and above all the commitment demanded and given, clearly distinguished *The Poor Man's Friend* from the identity of either amateur or professional theatre. The play was an enabling device for community activity. Although still mirroring in some respects the conventional (and strictly hierarchical) professional model of theatre production – a producer (CTT) commissions a writer and director, the director in turn commissions a designer, musical director and so on – the actual power of this professional group to produce the product depended entirely on the *voluntary* collaboration of a very large number of people. Howard Barker relied heavily on the material gathered for him by local people, Ann Jellicoe (the director) had no choice other than to rely on the commitment of people who, unlike their professional counterparts, did not have to depend for their future livelihood on the goodwill and patronage of a director. Apart from the obvious strengths of the text itself, the play provided a focus and a reason for a sustained community initiative which was both uniting and celebratory. It was the nature of the *process* of making *The Poor Man's Friend*, as much as the *product* itself, that was really significant in the long term.

The Poor Man's Friend was a tremendous theatrical and social success. Like its predecessors it also attracted the attention of the national media who universally praised Barker's play, Jellicoe's direction, and the infectious energy of the many Bridport people who had made it possible. A BBC documentary was made ('A Play for Bridport' – BBC-2 *Arena*) which told the story of the play's genesis. Thus, in less than four years, Community Theatre as defined and practised by the CTT had begun to be a movement with influence beyond the confines of the West Country.

Soon the attention of the theatrical establishment was drawn to what was happening in Dorset. David Edgar's play *Entertaining*

Strangers, written for the CTT as a community play for Dorchester in 1985, was re-presented in a revised and scaled-down version at the National Theatre's Cottesloe theatre with a professional cast directed by Sir Peter Hall and led by Dame Judi Dench. Nick Darke's community play, *The Earth Turned Inside Out*, (directed by Jon Oram, a co-director on *Entertaining Strangers*, and successor to Ann Jellicoe as director of the CTT), was also transferred to the National under the new title *Ting Tang Mine*, directed by David Rudman. Although this was a kind of recognition of and tribute to the power of the drama created in those towns, and a very welcome source of finance for the writers concerned, what was transferred to the National had nothing to do with Community Theatre. Removed from the context that created it, *Entertaining Strangers* or *Ting Tang Mine* were no longer community plays. The National Theatre had been able to buy the product; they could not reproduce the process that had given rise to it and that had made it what it was. Of course it was in their interests *not* to reproduce that process. *Amateurs* could hardly be allowed to act in Britain's Royal National Theatre! Ann Jellicoe (not an amateur, but not known and recognised by 'the profession' as a director either) was passed over as director in favour of Sir Peter Hall.

It is possible to see the National Theatre's decision to remove these plays from the context that produced them as a cynical attempt to expropriate and therefore regulate this new form of theatrical activity by attempting to absorb it; and, in doing so, to take away its radical potential. This has certainly happened elsewhere. For example, in the summer of 1989 the Chichester Festival Theatre performed a version of Thomas Hardy's play *Victory*. It was advertised as a performance that would involve the local community. What actually happened was that all the speaking roles were performed by professional actors, and a group of some two or three dozen unpaid extras were used to create atmosphere in crowd scenes. For most of the time the play was performed entirely onstage in the Festival Theatre. However, on certain nights performances began in the Cathedral and concluded in the theatre, the audience being conducted from one location in the town to another by the enthusiastic group of amateurs dressed to resemble the good folk of Chichester c. 1815. Such, and no more, was the extent of community involvement!

The advent of what is obviously a challenging new form of theatre in Britain has not come about by accident. It is in part a response to the failings of the British theatre establishment, to which the Community Theatre movement of the 1980s may, in the future, be recognised as having created a viable radical alternative. But CTT's brand of Community Theatre not only seeks to create a new openness, to physically involve people in taking responsibility for their own entertainment: it also seeks to challenge some of the dominant theatrical conventions which are responsible for the separation of producer and consumer in more traditional theatrical activity, including that of more so-called 'radical' theatre companies.

Community Theatre offers an alternative to the passive consumption of illusionist fictions. Illusionism is the dominant theatrical convention of late twentieth-century British theatre. It requires audiences to suspend disbelief, to identify not with the performer, but with the character s/he is representing. Indeed, the illusionist performer does not draw attention to him/herself but pretends to *be* the character; those who do this most successfully are the most highly rewarded. On the whole, audiences are schooled not to enjoy watching the spectacle of an actor 'acting', but instead are encouraged to watch the scrupulously imitated experience of a character. Thus a performer's skill and craft in the creation of the character remains mysterious. Further, although the spectacle presented to audiences is highly conventionalised, those conventions are hidden. The actor's preparations for performance are very private; most rehearsals, if not actually secret, forbid the presence of any outsiders. The training of actors too is shrouded in mystery, and the general public knows little or nothing about how they obtain work and the true nature of their occupation. Seldom in history can there have been so public a trade as that of the actor, yet consumers/audiences, despite their intimate familiarity with what the actor produces, remain in almost total ignorance of the processes and conventions involved in manufacturing it. The objective of CTT's work is to make known to as many people as possible within a community how the theatre works. Community Theatre counters the negative passivity of illusionist conventions by opening up the process that constructs them. Part of CTT's policy is that anyone who wants to play a role *can*, anyone who wants to learn how a play is produced *can*. The promenade convention also helps to counter the physical and intellectual passivity engendered by illusionism by requiring performers and audience to share the same space.

The social rituals of theatregoing which are still unfamiliar (and uncongenial) to the vast majority of people, although countered by the use of a non-traditional performance space, have still to be negotiated if the audience for community plays is to be broadened beyond a narrow section of the middle class. Anyone who has ever attended a Community Play mounted by CTT will immediately be struck by the informal and relaxed atmosphere that contrasts so strongly with that encountered in most conventional theatres. This is helped by the fact that most of CTT's productions are preceded by a Fair held in an adjoining space. Local organisations – the Women's Institute, the Samaritans, the Red Cross and so on – have the opportunity to set up stalls.[4] All participants in the Fair are encouraged to dress up in an appropriate period costume, and those who have a skill can demonstrate it to others – juggling, singing or dancing for example. Stalls sell craft work, food and drink. The Fair acts as rite of passage to the performance. Audience and performers mix not as characters and spectators, but as recognisable members of the same community. As in amateur productions, there is the shared warmth that comes from mutual recognition of a neighbour, friend or passing acquaintance, and the experience of the event is made a familiar rather than a strange one. The liveliness and bustle of the Fair are not dispelled by the subsequent performance, but taken up by it and carried forward by the classic elements of popular theatre: audience participation, music, song, dance and, in all Colway's productions, a driving narrative. This is nothing like conventional theatre where performances are invariably received by a hushed, reverential, and highly self-conscious audience, more often than not resembling those taking part in a penitential religious ritual rather than a shared celebratory event.

Despite the anti-democratic and élitist nature of professional theatre in Britain, it nonetheless has, from time to time since the end of the Second World War, thrown up a product that offers a radical critique of contemporary society. From the late 1950s an attempt was made to produce plays that critically addressed social issues. But for the most part, however, and despite an honourable tradition of radical drama mostly but not exclusively centred on London's Royal Court Theatre, theatrical activity as a whole in Britain has never been taken very seriously by many of those on the radical left. Important issues have undoubtedly been dramatised, and debates initiated, but by and large the preachers who occupied the stage of the Royal Court and elsewhere were preaching to the converted, and despite their insight, energy, and commitment, their drama never seriously constituted an instrument with which it was possible to advance *real* social change. Indeed, it is questionable whether the professional theatre industry in Britain can *ever* be a radical and significant force for change, given the way it is currently organised, and when entry into it is so strictly regulated.

But although the monolithic nature of existing theatrical institutions seems impenetrable, the problem of encouraging a new theatrical process, product, and participant, is not insoluble. Community Theatre is potentially a radical and energising force for effecting, if not a transformation of society, then at least a model for the transformation of the theatre back into a more genuinely popular and democratic art form. This new theatrical movement offers a possible model for the development of a new form of theatre for a new century; one that challenges traditional expectations of what theatre is, and what it can do. It dispels mystique, and allows ordinary women and men to work together in a less strictly hierarchical and more genuinely collective way.

How then should the work of the Colway Theatre Trust be evaluated? Should it be dismissed, like Morris dancing, as a picturesque but arcane irrelevance? Are both the products *and* the process of Community Theatre reactionary in political terms, merely reinforcing the values of the national culture and the dominant conventions of its theatrical expression; or is it, as is sometimes claimed, 'a unique formula' that not only challenges traditional views of the theatre but also succeeds in bringing people together in a genuinely celebratory community event? It is certainly possible to take a negative view of CTT's work if too much attention is paid to the artistic philosophy of its founder. Ann Jellicoe's book, published in 1985, *Community Plays and How to Put Them On*, was, in almost equal measure, both helpful and unhelpful to the subsequent development of Community Theatre. It not only revealed, in detail and with practical application, how CTT set up the organisation necessary to bring about a community play; but it also contained, in addition to such useful practical guidance, its author's personal statement about the significance of the process. What she said has alienated some people, especially those on the left, and diverted attention away from the actual day-to-day working practices of CTT. For Jellicoe's ultimate justification for what she was doing and attempting to do appears to lie in the Arnoldian notion of art as a civilising force in society. In his book *Culture and Anarchy* (published in 1869) Matthew Arnold advocated the centrality of classical culture. Such a cultural tradition would serve to counter and correct what Arnold saw as the barbarism of actual nineteenth-century communities, and what he regarded as the crudities of provincial culture. It is arguable that on Ann Jellicoe's own journey into provincial life (from London to Lyme Regis) she took with her a luggage of classicising discourse:

> Art can be a rehearsal for life. It can educate us in social and moral behaviour. Art refines and strengthens and enriches: through enjoying and understanding art our eyes and ears can learn to distinguish the true from the meretricious, the strong from the inflated, the sensual from the lifeless.[5]

Although she does not give a great deal of space to it in the book, Jellicoe's creed appears to be that the process of being involved in an *artistic* event is potentially an experience of spiritual transformation. What she says also seems to contradict the focus in the work of CTT on community involvement and shared responsibility for constructing a performance, because Jellicoe elevates the individual artist to God-like status, and thus potentially reinforces the passivity of the mass of less gifted human beings to whom it is not immediately given to distinguish between the 'true and the meretricious'. Ironically, an example of such a cult of personality (and of attempted appropriation of a collectivist achievement by a conventional oligarchy) was given by Anamaria Wills, sometime director of the Towngate Theatre, Basildon, Essex, who commissioned CTT and the dramatist Arnold Wesker to make a Community Play for Basildon in 1988. Her preface to the play's programme makes it very clear just whose play she though it *really* was:

> Arnold Wesker is a formidable man. His reputation goes before him, and you draw breath, quickly and silently, before you say hello. There is something about him that makes your knees shake when you meet him – you are dealing with a giant of twentieth-century drama. He views Basildon through his own perspective – the research, the history, the past and the present all feed in, influence and distort. But eventually it is the perception of one man – the artist.[6]

Another reason for some hostility towards Ann Jellicoe has come through her refusal to attempt to use Community Theatre as a tool in political consciousness-raising. She knows that to alert individuals to the inherent economic and class contradictions and conflicts within their own communities would be to fragment the mythology of social cohesion that keeps such communities as those in the West Country relatively stable. Ann Jellicoe argued fiercely with Howard Barker in order to

> convince him that he must not write a political play, that such a play would divide the town when we were seeking to unite it . . . we agreed he should compromise, not write a political play but one which should celebrate resistance.[7]

Ann Jellicoe is apparently concerned with the spiritual transformation of the isolated and unique individual, rather than with the processes by which a society constructs such conceptions of individual autonomy. In her book she uses particular language with which to speak of the power of art, language which echoes that of the poet T. S. Eliot's *Four Quartets*. As Jellicoe expresses it, the objective of the CTT is to act as a kind of cultural missionary who will 'help communities create a work of art'. And when the anxious natives ask what 'art' is, they presumably are told 'Art is a means to the still centre, the moment of balance, the unchanging truth'[8] and left none the wiser.

In addition to being put off by Ann Jellicoe's philosophy of art, there is also a suspicion that the work of CTT is almost exclusively addressed to, and staffed by, the middle class. But while no one would claim that the working classes are flocking to see performances of community plays, any more than taking a large role in their creation, Colway's army of volunteers is certainly *not* exclusively middle class. Nor is the fact that it is undeniably predominantly middle class any reason to suppose that it will automatically continue to be so. There have been a significant number of blue-collar workers who chose to join projects and, as the movement spreads geographically away from the South-West, that proportion may increase. More significantly, from the beginning, a large number of young people from a wide spectrum of social classes have participated in the production of community drama.

But I would argue that whatever the doubts concerning the true constituency addressed by the work of CTT, and despite the expressed views of its founder regarding the 'civilising' role of art, the *process* she helped to establish remains important whatever ideological framework its principal author chooses to impose upon it. The socialist dramatist David Edgar, author of the tenth community play produced by CTT (*Entertaining Strangers*, Dorchester, 1985), takes a retrospectively positive view of his CTT experience. His play was performed in St Mary's Church, Dorchester High Street. Edgar likened the play to 'a kind of theatrical carnival' in which traditional barriers that divide performers and audience are broken down, and where the community as a whole, and not just a narrow section of it, takes responsibility for making its own means of celebration.

> One of the remarkable things about the proto-carnival theatre as I experienced it in St Mary's Church Dorchester is its amazing flexibility. Somehow, because in the promenade form the audience is able to choose what to look at, to construct its own spatial relationship with the event, it is able to switch not just the direction but the very *mode* of its attention, if not in the twinkling of an eye, then certainly in the turn of a head . . . In *Entertaining Strangers*, the audience evinced a remarkable capacity to switch its attention and its mode of perception from a race-meeting to a church, from a participatory drinking song to the witness of a silent man at prayer.
>
> In this form, then, the theatre does seem to be more capable than we might have thought it to present experience with a variance, a simultaneity, and most of all the *unevenness*, which is metaphorically at least akin to the experience of actual carnival in real streets.[9]

In the same article, Edgar also acknowledges the power of Howard Barker's statement that 'a carnival is not a revolution . . . after the carnival, after the removal of the masks, you are precisely who you were before.'[10] But, whilst that statement contains a literal truth, it nonetheless ignores the *possibility* that, as a result of actually participating in the process, people may have learnt something important: not only how to construct their own theatrical event, but that they are *capable* of doing so. In order to effect social change you have to create the mechanism to effect such change, and Community Theatre can potentially be used as part of that mechanism. By teaching people new skills, by harnessing those they already have, and always by encouraging self-confidence, Community Theatre can hand back to ordinary people the means through which issues of relevance to them and to their communities may be articulated and explored.

Since 1985, when Ann Jellicoe resigned as director of the CTT in protest at South-West Arts' failure to continue to fund their activity adequately, the work has developed independently of its founder. By the end of the 1980s Arts Council incentive funding had facilitated the appointment of a triumvirate to run CTT, which included a full-time Community Development Officer. The latter's role is to establish regular contact with the community concerned at least eighteen months before the proposed date for the production. A request for CTT to begin work in a community must come from that community initially, and the community is required to demonstrate that there is the necessary basis of popular support before CTT will agree to take up the contract. CTT also employs a full-time play officer for each production. S/he is responsible for coordinating the enterprise and lives in the community for at least six months prior to the opening night. The director is also required as a condition of his/her contract to live in the community in the three months leading up to the performance, but, in addition, s/he is also required to hold regular workshops for performers in the previous three months or so during which the casting is finalised. The designer, musical director and stage manager will also live in the community for the production period. All the professionals involved on the production side will offer regular workshops.

What CTT have also achieved, and it is a very significant achievement indeed in the context of British theatre in the 1990s, is the promotion of new writing. CTT's policy is always to commission a new play and, at a meeting at the Arts Council late in 1989 where thirty-six applications for contract writer's awards were being discussed, 50 per cent of them were for community plays! CTT has also succeeded in widening its geographical base to include areas outside the West Country. Basildon's play was the first in a new town, and there are plans for further work in London (Southwark and Southall) as well as traditional industrial areas further north (Warrington and Bassetlaw). Colway's work has encouraged others to make community plays in areas far removed from the well-established and generally well-heeled residents of Dorset, such as Birmingham (1989), and Glasgow (1990).

Whatever happens to conventional professional theatre in

Britain in the future, the energy released by Community Theatre ought to be harnessed by those on the left who claim to be interested in alternative theatre. Despite the romantic philosophical aesthetics of one of its founders, the achievements of CTT are real. The successful co-operation seen in the 1980s between amateur and professional theatre workers in manufacturing carnivalesque community events has left behind a good deal more than a hangover for the 1990s. Whatever its faults, Colway Theatre Trust has shown by example that there *is* a real alternative to established British theatrical institutions, one that is always potentially capable of being both radical and innovative.

Notes

1. J. McGrath, *A Good Night Out: Popular Theatre, Audience, Class and Form* (London: Eyre Methuen, 1981) p. 15.
2. A. Jellicoe, *Community Plays: How to Put Them On* (London: Methuen, 1987) pp. 2–3.
3. The *Guardian*, 16 December 1978.
4. During the preparations for the Colyford village play (*Colyford Matters*, 1983), a row blew up when a group wanted to include a CND stall in the Fair. CND were refused permission to participate. (see Jellicoe, *Community Plays*, pp. 26–27.
5. See Jellicoe, *Community Plays*, p. 47.
6. From the 'Theatre Director's Letter', printed as part of the programme sold to audiences attending performances of *Beorhtel's Hill*, Towngate Theatre, Basildon, Essex, June 1989.
7. See Jellicoe, *Community Plays*, p. 17.
8. D. Edgar, *The Second Time as Farce*, (London: Lawrence and Wishart, 1988) pp. 241–2.
9. See Edgar, *The Second Time as Farce*, p. 243.

6

Shaustück and Lehrstück: Erwin Piscator and the Politics of Theatre

GRAHAM HOLDERNESS

It is logical to include in a book of this kind an essay on Erwin Piscator, and not merely because he was the author of a book with a similar title – *The Political Theatre* (1929) – which staked out for the first time the territory of 'political drama' as it has been understood and practised throughout the twentieth century. It is with the dramaturgical, directorial and technical work of Piscator in Germany, and with that of Meyerhold in Russia, that the specifically 'modern' forms of political drama first emerged. Here drama developed in close relation to social and political factors generally considered indispensable to the theory and practice of political theatre: a Marxist philosophy and a revolutionary Marxist movement; the immersion of theatre workers in materialist theory and proletarian cultural practice; the feasibility of a politicised working-class audience which such a theatre could hope to entertain, engage and urge towards further political consciousness.

Both Meyerhold and Piscator worked respectively in characteristically modern political contexts. Each saw a great nineteenth-century empire overthrown or reformed by revolutionary or social–democratic political struggle; each lived to see his society – the revolutionary Soviet state, and the social–democratic Weimar Republic – subordinated to a ruthless dictatorship. Each met a fate typical of twentieth-century European politics: Meyerhold dying (probably shot) in one of Stalin's prisons, Piscator forced into exile from the power of Hitler's tyranny. In the life and work of each man can be traced the characteristic contours of the modern political world.

Yet it is also the case that the political world through the birth-pangs of which they lived, and which gave shape to their respective theatrical careers, appears now to be coming to its close. In this respect the fate of Meyerhold, repudiated as a 'formalist', and then rehabilitated in 1956 when Stalin himself was posthumously ac-. cused (in Krushchev's 'secret speech' at the twentieth Congress of the CPSU) of political 'crimes', is in many ways more 'contemporary' than that of Piscator. Piscator's work seems by contrast welded indissolubly to the political structure of a vanishing age. His theatrical practice was deeply committed to the basic tenets of a Marxist philosophy which has been thoroughly revised, and is now repudiated even by many who would ten years ago have called themselves Marxists.[1] In terms of party loyalties Piscator was a hard-line Communist rather than a non-aligned socialist or revolutionary Marxist: a member and supporter of that party grouping which has astonishingly, during the period in which this book has been composed, submitted to free elections and surrendered its monopoly of power throughout the socialist states of Europe.

Piscator's concept of revolution in the theatre, like Lenin's concept of revolution in the economy, was predominantly technological: centred in practical terms on exploiting the mechanical instruments of theatre technology, and wedded in theoretical terms to a characteristically modernist vision of society transformed by the uninhibited development of mechanical and technological means of production, man forging his future in the white-hot furnaces of revolutionary industrial change.[2] In a post-Chernobyl age of nuclear contamination, global warming, depleting natural resources, knowledge of the possibility of irreversible pollution and the 'death of the planet', that rhetoric of unstoppable industrial progress (fundamental to traditional Marxist economics) rings particularly hollow and discordant.

It is only when a significant historical period begins to draw to its close that its overall shape and constitutive structure begin to become clearly visible. The political world in which Piscator lived, worked and fought can be viewed only now with a certain objective clarity. It is precisely because our conception of the politics of theatre, and indeed of the politics of culture in general, is likely to be so far removed from Piscator's, that a theoretical review of his theatrical practice is both timely and feasible.

DAS POLITISCHES THEATER

Piscator's book *The Political Theatre* (1929)[3] describes the author's work in the German theatre up to the end of the 1920s. Here Piscator's theatrical experiments are formally located in the history to which they obviously belong. The book begins with the First World War, with the author a serving soldier on the Western front; traces his career in the theatre through the German revolution and into the Weimar Republic; and ends with a deepening economic crisis and the rise of the Nazi Party. By 1931 Piscator had left Germany for the Soviet Union, and did not return to his native country until after the war.

As a written text, *The Political Theatre* is constructed in a style reminiscent of Piscator's theatrical work: a montage of narrative, extracts from journals and diaries, newspaper clippings and reviews, passages of comment from the people discussed. As a narrative it is lively, comprehensive and diversified, conveying accurately the flavour of Piscator's personality, the character of his theatrical experiments and the nature of the period he lived and worked through – the history which formed him and which he in turn helped to form.[4] Piscator's opening chapter ('From Art to Politics') begins:

> My calendar begins on August 4, 1914.
> From that day the barometer rose:
> 13 million dead.
> 11 million maimed.
> 50 million soldiers on the march.
> 6 billion guns.
> 50 billion cubic meters of gas.
> What room does that leave for 'personal development'? Nobody can develop 'personally' under these conditions. Something else develops him. The twenty-year-old was confronted by War. Destiny. It made every other teacher superfluous.
>
> *(The Political Theatre*, p. 7)

An autobiographical narrative thus begins with an interrogation of the very premise of autobiography. Is a biography the description of an individual's 'personal development', a narrative construction taking its shape from the integrity and coherence of an individual life? Or does such a narrative rather describe, through the account of an individual's work and political engagement, the historical context which ultimately provided the structure and shape of that development? Who is the subject of this narrative, 'Piscator' (here disparagingly referred to as a mere 'twenty-year-old') or the historical forces (especially 'War') that confronted him with a shocking and determinant 'Destiny'?

Paradoxically, to begin a description of his 'personal development', Piscator has to characterise his whole age, the world of his time. His personal development as an individual begins from that point at which the 'person' abruptly realises that his life is determined by an immense, apparently uncontrollable process of inhuman destructiveness. Who is the subject of an autobiography constructed in such conditions: the individual or history? What is the significant trajectory of an individual life: the person's relation to himself, or his engagement with the world of politics?

Piscator entered the war thinking of himself as an artist. He emerged from it convinced that art is inseparable from politics. Ordered to dig himself in under an artillery bombardment on the Ypres salient, Piscator found that he couldn't. 'What do you do for a living?' asked the NCO.

'Actor'.

The moment I uttered the word 'actor' among the exploding shells, the whole profession for which I had struggled so hard and which I held so dear in common with all art, seemed so comical, so stupid, so grotesquely false, in short so ill-suited to the situation, so irrelevant to my life, our life, to life in this day and age, that I was less afraid of the flying shells than I was ashamed of my profession.

Art – true, absolute art – must measure up to every situation and prove itself anew in every situation. I have since gone through worse things than the shellfire in the trenches of Ypres, but at that time my 'personal profession' was levelled like the trenches we occupied, lifeless like the corpses around us.

(*The Political Theatre*, p. 14)

Piscator was of course historically correct: the war had an enormous and irreversible effect on European culture. It accelerated and confirmed developments which had certainly been operating beforehand (after all, the war itself did not appear from nowhere): the later nineteenth century was a period of enormous cultural change, to which belong Naturalism and Expressionism in the theatre, the fictional experiments of Conrad and Henry James, the early poetry of the Modernists, the beginnings of modern science fiction, and radical innovations in music and the visual and plastic arts. Nonetheless the culture of the 1920s would have remained inconceivable without the preceding enormity and incredible violence of the First World War. *The Waste Land, Ulysses, Women in Love*, the German political theatre of the 1920s, all bear the traces of a new and previously undreamt-of historical crisis.

One of the ways in which art sought to engage with that crisis (and it was only one among many) was by seeking a new and closer relationship with politics. The theatre artist, dramatist or director, felt a new sense of responsibility: the need to intervene in history, to use art and ideas to shape the world anew. 'We now ask you actors . . .' Brecht wrote 'To change yourselves and show us the world of man/ As it is: made by man and subject to change.'[5] Piscator wrote in 1928: 'Our art was created from a knowledge of reality and inspired by the will to replace this reality. We founded political theatre' (letter to *Die Weltbuhne*, 1928).

The other important influence – so important as to constitute, like the war, a fundamental premise of Piscator's work – was the Bolshevik revolution of 1917. The German revolution, which according to the dominant Marxist programme of the time should logically have followed the same pattern as the Russian, ended in defeat, with the left crushed and fragmented by an alliance between the surviving military hierarchy and the revisionist Social Democratic Party. There was no transfer of power to the people, and the SDP was left in charge of an essentially bourgeois republic. The left, of which Piscator was a member, remained wounded and bitter in defeat. They looked to the victory of the Bolsheviks in Russia as a great red hope, as a demonstration that the Communist revolution could be successful.

The precise extent of specifically theatrical influence from Russia to Germany in this period is difficult to measure. Piscator's experiments have been connected with Meyerhold's,. though Piscator himself denied this, suggesting that little was known, at the time, of those comparable developments. His own view was that parallel historical developments and a shared common philosophy independently produced similar theatrical experiments (see *The Political Theatre*, p. 93). The society formed by the October Revolution – the USSR – is today, together with the political philosophy on which it was founded, in the process of radical transformation and huge structural change. Piscator and Meyerhold belong to the revolutionary inception of a historical epoch now drawing to its startling and unforeseen close. Where does that leave the concept of political theatre developed and formulated in those increasingly distant historical conditions?

PROLETARISCHES THEATER (1920)

Entering the world of the Berlin theatre in 1920, Piscator could find no space appropriate for the kind of political theatre he wanted to create. The only theatre in existence which stood in any sense outside the establishment of municipal and commercial theatres was the *Volksbühne*, which had in the view of the left become corrupted, commercialised and conservative. In 1889, Berlin had seen the founding of the *Freie Bühne* (modelled on Antoine's *Théâtre Libre* in Paris) which offered to a select public a platform for European naturalist plays by Ibsen, Tolstoy and Strindberg. A separate organisation, the *Freie Volksbühne*, followed it in 1890, aiming to take the same sort of repertoire to a broader, more genuinely popular audience. Eventually this organisation sought to pursue its aim of taking art to the people by becoming a large block-booking agency within the commercial theatre. In 1910 it established a permanent company, the *Neues Volkstheater*, which from 1914 had its own house in the *Volksbühne*. In this way by the outbreak of the war the chief institutions of Berlin theatre had moved from a position in the radical avant-garde, through a democratic populism, to a wholly commercial policy, drained of all social commitment and dominated by the sophisticated and opulent theatrical style of Max Reinhardt. (*The Political Theatre*, pp. 35–6).

Piscator's response to a situation deemed by the left to be one of theatrical decadence, in which the mainstream theatre had become hopelessly out of touch with the revolution of the times, was to found a theatre outside the established cultural apparatus, to create a space within which he could create the kind of drama he felt was necessary. This was the 'Proletarian Theatre' (*Proletarisches Theater*), founded in Berlin in 1920. It was an agit-prop group, concerned as much with propaganda as with drama. Turning his back on the fashionable theatre, Piscator took his actors into the slums, performing simple sketches with typified characters and direct appeals to the audience for solidarity with the Communist movement. Performances took place in halls and meeting rooms, with theatrical resources pared down to a minimum. 'A few props, some black drapes and a couple of spotlights would be transported in a handcart' (*The Political Theatre*, p. 39). The audience was entirely working class: men kept their hats on, mothers brought their babies, the audience commented vociferously on the staged events, and critics from the bourgeois press were refused entry.

The Proletarian Theatre was an economic failure, since Piscator kept admission charges to a minimum, and charged nothing to the unemployed. Even with this minimalist, shoe-string theatrical economy, and even when the houses were packed (as they often were) the company made losses. The enterprise ended abruptly when the police refused to extend the company's six-month licence. Piscator later returned to the agit-prop form with a production called the Red Review, (*Revue Roter Rummel*) which was played at some fourteen locations around Berlin in 1924. This used the revue or cabaret form, with music, songs, acrobatics, statistics, sketches, combining entertainment with propaganda. It began with what appeared to be a fight in the audience: two men pushed and argued their way onto the stage. Identified as a wholesale butcher and a piece-worker, they were met by a bourgeois figure in a top hat, who invited them to spend the evening with him. They all remained onstage throughout the performance, enabling a running commentary on the action from both bourgeois and proletarian standpoints. Slide-projections were used: in one scene, as a judge sentenced a Communist to prison, the interiors of real prisons were displayed on the screens. A sketch called 'The Revenge of the Bourgeoisie' was accompanied by back-projected pictures of the 1919 revolution being suppressed by the army. Here there was no attempt at naturalism, either in acting or in stage technology. A typical sketch was the 'Electoral Boxing Match', in which representatives of the various political parties sparred gently with each other, until the Communist candidate climbed into the ring to knock them all out. Actors impersonating Lenin, Karl Liebknecht and Rosa Luxemburg delivered speeches to the audience as if the occasion were a public meeting. The show ended with performers and audience singing the *Internationale* together.

Piscator jokingly told a story symptomatic of theatre practice in these cultural conditions, in which he claimed that his designer

John Heartfield (who rejected his German name Helmut Herzefelde as a protest against Teutonic imperial chauvinism) was the real inventor of 'epic theatre':

> John Heartfield, who had agreed to produce a backdrop for *The Cripple*, was as usual late with his work and appeared at the back of the hall with his backdrop rolled under his arm when we had reached the middle of the first act . . . Heartfield: 'Stop, Erwin, stop! I'm here!' . . . I stood up, abandoned my role as the cripple for the moment, and called down to him: 'Where have you been all this time? We waited almost half an hour for you [*murmur of agreement from the audience*] and then we had to start without your backdrop' . . . Since he refused to calm down I turned to the audience and asked them what was to be done, should we continue to play, or should we hang up the backdrop? There was an overwhelming majority for the backdrop. So we dropped the curtain, hung up the backdrop and to everybody's satisfaction started the play anew. (Nowadays I refer to John Heartfield as the founder of the 'Epic Theatre').
>
> (*The Political Theatre*, pp. 39–40)

The anecdote is rather more than a joke because it was, significantly, in that kind of situation – a theatre without technical resources, but with a living, engaged, participating, even *intervening* audience; a situation in which dramatic illusion could be temporarily suspended, and in which performers could relate directly to an audience – that 'epic theatre' of the Brechtian kind could happen, if only by accident.[6] Piscator's own conception of 'epic theatre' was as we shall see quite different from Brecht's; but he always aimed for this kind of audience involvement, because his primary objective was to politicise the audience through art, or to give the audience the opportunity of politicising itself. The attractiveness of the revue form to him was that it 'coincided with the disintegration of bourgeois drama. In a revue there is no unity of action, effects are lifted from any areas which can be made to connect with the theatre; the revue is untrammelled in its structure and at the same time quite naïve in its appeal . . . the revue offered a chance of "direct action" in the theatre.' (*The Political Theatre*, pp. 81–2). One reviewer offered an illuminating description of the spectator's experience:

What is basically new about this theatre is the curious way in which reality and the play merge into one another. You often don't know whether you are in a theatre or in a public meeting, you feel you ought to intervene and help, or say something. The dividing line between the play and reality gets blurred . . . the spectator is involved in the play, everything that is going on on stage concerns him.

(The Political Theatre, p. 54)

The element of *confusion* experienced by this spectator, that sense of boundaries shifting and distinctions becoming blurred, recalls Brecht's 'estrangement-effect' (discussed in more detail in the next chapter by Christopher McCullough), and testifies to the theatrical power of these techniques. Such a response would hardly however have pleased Piscator himself, who always emphasised the need for clarity in exposition, for unmistakable certainty in the communication of meaning. Speaking of his production of Hauptmann's *The Weavers* at the Grosses Schauspielhaus in 1925, he defined the nature of audience involvement rather differently:

The masses took over the direction. The people who filled the house had for the most part been actively involved in the period, and what we were showing them was in a true sense their own fate, their own tragedy being acted out before their eyes. Theatre had become reality, and soon it was not a case of the stage confronting the audience, but one big assembly, one big battlefield, one massive demonstration.

(The Political Theatre, pp. 96–7)

The highest tribute Piscator can pay a performance is to claim that the stage abolished itself and replaced itself with 'reality'. The spectator's experience ceases to be a specifically theatrical one, and becomes indistinguishable from the experience of various 'real-life' collective situations. The gap between theatre and reality is closed, and the masses 'direct' the action with a unified certainty. In Brecht's phrase: 'Not politics trying to take over the theatre, but the theatre politics'.[7]

There is clearly a fundamental difference in the nature of the spectator's experience, visible even in Piscator's own description, between the proletarian agit-prop work, and Piscator's subsequent attempts to create a revolutionary Communist drama within the framework of the professional commercial theatre of Berlin. We will consider the constitution of the spectator in the latter context presently: it is fairly clear however that rarely in Piscator's professional work in commercial theatre buildings could the kind of opportunity for actor–audience dialogue to actively shape the nature of the production, have happened as it happened when Heartfield arrived with his belated backdrop. Walter Benjamin defined the basic principle of 'epic theatre' as a theatre in which the audience is shown that 'it can happen this way; but it can also happen quite a different way.'[8] The audience which was consulted for its opinion on the installation of a backdrop was being shown exactly that.

THE VOLKSBÜHNE

Piscator's theatrical ambitions did not, however, stop with shoe-string agit-prop: he was determined to build what he later called a 'revolutionary professional theatre' alongside the 'proletarian amateur theatre' advocated by many in the Communist movement. In 1923 he took over the Berlin Central-Theatre, associated previously with operetta and farce, and put on three naturalistic productions of plays by Gorky, Tolstoy and Romain Rolland. He saw this as a retreat from the position he had reached by 1921: the Central-Theatre was participating from the fringes in a mainstream commercial theatre, rather than playing experimental works from a position of political commitment to a proletarian audience.

It may however have been the relative tameness of his work at the Central-Theatre that led to his next job – as a director in the *Volksbühne*, where he was to work from 1923 to 1928. Piscator's own verdict on the *Volksbühne* at this period was severe: 'The *Volksbühne* had abandoned every last vestige of aggressiveness, it had been absorbed and digested by the bourgeois theatre system. The war failed to open a new era for the *Volksbühne*, unless it was the era of its final and irrevocable capitulation to the ruling powers.' (*The Political Theatre*, p. 62). It was not, however, until after his tenth production at the *Volksbühne*, *Gewitter über Gottland* (*Storm over Gotland*, 1927) that Piscator and that theatre finally parted company. He went on to form his own theatre companies in his own theatres, the first and second '*Piscator-Bühnen*'.

Piscator's first *Volksbühne* production was a play *Flags* by Alfons

Paquet. Based on the struggles of immigrant workers in Chicago in 1886, it is a Brechtian parable of class injustice, showing labour leaders framed and convicted by an alliance of corrupt politicians, lawyers and police. The play shows a peaceful workers' demonstration bombed into violence by *agents provocateurs*, hired by the capitalist boss Cyrus McShure. The workers' leaders are arrested and tried: one commits suicide in jail, the other four are hanged.[9] The play was sub-titled 'An Epic Drama', the description deriving initially from its twenty loosely-based, episodic scenes with a morality-play subject in which the outcome is clearly predictable, and the message unmistakable.

But Piscator also employed what he called an 'epic' mode of production, using 'techniques from areas which had never been seen in the theatre before'. By those 'techniques' Piscator meant particularly the use of film (or in this case, as there were technical difficulties with film, slide-projection) as an integral part of the production. The play opened with slides of the historical figures on which the characters were based projected onto a screen behind the proscenium arch, while a ballad singer with a pointer introduced them to the audience. It was thus established at the outset that the 'characters' on the stage merely 'stood for' real figures whose significance extended beyond the physical boundaries of the theatre. Two other projection screens outside the proscenium arch were used throughout the production to record captions (like the inter-shot titlings on silent movies) or comments on the action from outside it. Newspaper cuttings and telegrams were flashed up to make points or to relate the action to exterior reality.

Piscator was able to develop these experiments much further when, after resigning from the *Volksbühne* in 1927, he established his own theatres, calling them '*Piscator-Bühnen*'. Here he had a much freer hand to develop the technical infrastructure and elaborate sets he wanted, and on that basis was able to mount his three major productions, *Hoppla, wir leben!*, *Rasputin*, and *The Good Soldier Schweyk* (1927–8). *Hoppla, wir leben!* and *Rasputin* both used extremely elaborate sets: one a kind of high-rise scaffolding construction providing eight separate acting areas with complex spatial relationships, moving parts, facilities for back-projection, and so on; the other an enormous tinfoil globe. The actors could only rehearse by occupying these contraptions: so during the run of *Hoppla*, after each night's performance, sixteen men had to work for three hours dismantling the scaffolding. A similar shift of workers had to erect the *Rasputin* set for rehearsals the next morning. At 4 p.m. rehearsals ended, and twenty-four men had to prepare the stage for the evening performance of *Hoppla*.[10]

Although the characteristic technical innovations appear right across the spectrum of Piscator's work, we can see his theatrical practice dividing into two linked but separable strands of activity. In the performances of the Proletarian Theatre, and in the Red Revue, a diversified mixture of conventions and styles within the general agit-prop framework bestowed a different significance on the technical experiments themselves. Where *Flags* used the drama as an allegory of the real world, the Red Revue invited the audience to become involved in a cabaret-style performance in which events took their own appropriately theatrical shape – a boxing match, a juggling turn, a comedy sketch – and by a radically creative montage *produced* a vision of the world. Where the intensified realism of *Flags* merely mimed a real world which could only be grasped by other means than the theatrical, the Red Revue constructed a satirical vision of the world, accompanied by utopian fantasies of a new world the audience themselves could help to bring into being.

These experiments in agit-prop theatre contrast with the kind of theatre, represented by *Flags* at the *Volksbühne*, or *Hoppla, Wir Leben!* at the *Piscator-Bühne*, with which Piscator is now preeminently associated. In the Proletarian Theatre and in the Red Revue, we have the example of a theatrical practice conducted outside purpose-built theatres, and outside the economic and political structure of the mainstream theatre altogether. Here was a theatre which sought a new audience, and was prepared to dispense with many of the conditions traditionally associated with theatrical convention. Here was a theatre that sought flexible and impromptu methods of staging and performance, and a new interrelationship between drama, entertainment, education and political agitation. Here was a theatre which pointed clearly towards the more democratic side of Brecht's work and influence (discussed below by Christopher McCullough), and towards what Peter Reynolds calls the 'revolutionary' innovations of modern 'community theatre'. Piscator's subsequent theatrical practice points in quite a different direction, towards the spectacular and high-technology spaces of our modern subsidised and commercial theatre.

It is possible even from these brief descriptions of Piscator's productions to recognise that his interest in stage technique could work in different directions. In one sense the montage principle is the opposite of naturalism, since by juxtaposing discrete images it breaks or suspends the realist illusion. At the same time Piscator's practice was to make the dramatic spectacle, incomplete and fragmentary in itself, figure forth a totality which actually lay beyond it – the 'real world', the dimension of history and politics, of which the dramatic action formed a component element. The spectator was discouraged from identifying directly with the events on stage, or believing them to be 'real'; but at the same time encouraged to grasp a conception of totality, the complex and comprehensive structure of the real events which the play could only signify. It is on the one hand ironic, on the other predictable, that one of Piscator's characteristic innovations, the use of back-projected film to supply historical context, came to function in the cinema as a naturalistic means of simulating location in the studio.

Obviously there is more than one meaning of the word 'epic' in play at this point. Piscator's conception of 'epic theatre' was consistently simpler than that of Brecht. It consisted largely of the idea that, in political drama, the events on the stage should never be perceived in isolation from the social and historical reality which they imitate or symbolise. Piscator's technical innovations in staging were to a large degree directed towards achieving a continual system of cross-referencing between the microcosm of the stage and the macrocosm of political events in the circumambient world of history. The use of projected slides and film, cartoons and newspaper headlines, were all designed to force the audience to link, by parallelism or contrast, what they saw and heard on stage with what was going on in the world at large.

It was about the extension of the action and the clarification of the background to the action, that is to say it involved a continuation of the play beyond the dramatic framework. A didactic play was developed from the spectacle-play. This automatically led to the use of stage techniques from areas which had never been seen in the theatre before.

(*The Political Theatre*, p. 74)

That passage (interpolated in the revised 1963 edition of *The Politi-*

cal Theatre) appears as Piscator's comment on a review of *Flags* by
Leo Lania, where the same notion of epic is formulated with even
greater simplicity:

> The author consciously avoids any kind of artistic treatment and
> lets the naked facts speak for themselves. The play has no
> 'heroes' and no 'problems', it is one long epic of the struggle of
> the proletariat for freedom.
>
> *(The Political Theatre*, p. 72)

Flags was, according to Lania, 'the first Marxist drama', and Piscator's production 'the first attempt to make the forces of materialism
tangible and comprehensible' (p. 74).

Both Lania and Piscator were working here with theoretical
distinctions obviously derived from the 'base/superstructure'
model of contemporary Marxism, which presupposed that cultural
production took place in a secondary realm of ideas and spiritual
impulses, symptomatically related to a determining economic
'base'. Piscator's distinction between 'spectacle' and 'didactic'
plays, Lania's between 'art' and 'naked facts', both construct a
hierarchy of discourses in which 'culture' is assumed to be demon-
strably secondary or inferior. Within this ideological problematic
(which Piscator only partly accepted) events in the theatre could
never be more than an imitative representation of real events; and
the only way of actualising the theatre, making it a medium for the
communication of reality, would be to formally articulate it with
the primary realm of economic competition and 'real' political
struggle. While working with the Proletarian Theatre, Piscator
complained about the inadequacy for his purposes of the plays
being written:

> Time and again what we received were 'plays', fragments of our
> times, sections of a world-picture, but never the whole, the
> totality, from the roots to the ultimate ramifications, never the
> red-hot, up-to-the-minute present, which leaped to overpower
> you from every line of the newspapers. The theatre still lagged
> behind the newspapers, it was never quite up to date, it never
> intervened actively enough in the events around it, it was still
> too much of a rigid art-form predetermined and with a limited
> effect.
>
> *(The Political Theatre*, p. 48)

The conception of 'totality' here is one of the most theoretically contentious issues in modern Marxist debate, it is one of the points at issue in the famous quarrel between Brecht and Georg Lukács, and it is an issue over which Piscator felt he and Brecht took radically different views: '. . . our views of totality differ: Brecht unveils significant details of human life while I attempt to give a conspectus of political matters as a whole.'[11] The 'totality' alluded to here stands initially for the comprehensive structure of a social organisation developing as a historical process. At another level, however, it represents the kind of synthesising philosophy which claimed to comprehend that historical totality, historical materialism or Marxism. Here any statement of 'fact', even a newspaper headline, invokes the totality more authentically than a fictional theatrical representation, and is therefore regarded as more 'real'.

The crucial theoretical problem with this philosophical model, as Brecht appreciated and as most Marxist cultural theoreticians have subsequently confirmed, is simply that it denies the 'material' nature of art and culture. In this, theoretical problematic art can never be regarded as 'real', can never be more than a shadow of reality. Brecht attacked the great Marxist critic Georg Lukács for treating literature as a finished model of reality, capable of a comprehensive depiction of a historical totality, but complete in itself and impervious to change.[12] However much literature is valued in Lukács's theory, it is always perceived as a second-order imitation of the real. Brecht was more interested in the *analogies* between art and reality, in culture as a sphere of social activity; and as a theatre worker rather than a literary critic, he was much more inclined to see art as a process of cultural production, always experimental and provisional, never finalised and complete. So too, in practice, did Piscator: but Brecht's position was much closer to what we now call 'cultural materialism', a Marxist theory which recognises art as social production; as distinct from the 'economistic' Marxism accepted by Piscator, where art could realise itself only by converting itself into social reality. The term 'epic' meant to Piscator much what it had meant to Aristotle: a narrative form whose contents were not confined by the dramatic 'unities' of time and place. Just as the classical epic could narrate a story extended in time and widespread over space, so the modern epic drama could burst out of the confines of the theatre and take the world as its stage. If the stage itself resisted this totalising function, it must be revolutionised. If theatre writers declined to produce appropriately comprehensive visions of historical change, the director/producer must compensate for their shortcomings: 'My technical devices had been developed to cover up the deficiencies of the dramatists' products.' (*The Political Theatre*, p. 188)

TOTAL THEATRE

Piscator's great dream was to be able to direct in what he called a 'total theatre', a theatre building equipped with all the mechanical equipment necessary to realise the full potentialities of modern stage technology. He wanted not just a revolving stage, but a theatre with several stages which could be mechanically altered, even during a performance: a conventional proscenium arch stage could become an apron or thrust stage, the seating could revolve to form an amphitheatre or theatre-in-the-round. The 'total theatre' would be fully equipped with film cameras to project visual material literally everywhere in the auditorium. It would be the perfectly mechanised and automated space for drama – a 'theatre machine'. This theatre was never built, but Piscator succeeded in getting it designed, by no less an architectural expert than Walter Gropius of the Bauhaus.[13] The design, which involved flexible stages, a reconstruction of the auditorium, and the provision of elaborate stage machinery, was conceived by the architect as 'a great space machine' to be exploited by the director, but also as a 'theatrical instrument' for the re-positioning of the spectator: '. . . to make him a part of the space in which the events are taking place and prevent him from escaping from them under cover of the curtain.' (*The Political Theatre*, pp. 182–3)

It is abundantly clear that to identify the quality of the spectator's experience in such a 'total theatre' it is necessary to invoke our earlier distinction between the kind of 'alienation-effect' felt at a performance of the Proletarian Theatre, and the kind of 'participation' available to the audience in this precision-made 'theatre-machine'. In the one case, the spectator, as in Brecht's 'epic theatre', is drawn towards an understanding of the social totality by a dramatic form that is precisely, in itself, not a totalising structure, and is therefore able to adumbrate the character of society in terms of its contradictions, incomplete achievements, unfinished processes of development. In the 'total theatre' the

spectator is obliged to encounter an image of the social totality
which is in itself a totalising structure, so that the spectator is
internalised within its experiential medium. Here there can be no
distance, no opportunity for reflection, no exercise of the sceptical
intelligence, no fostering of difficulty and contradiction, no 'estrangement' of the Brechtian kind. Piscator expressed the difference clearly:[14]

> B[recht]'s starting point is episodic succession.
> P[iscator]'s is political fatality.
> B. demonstrates it in miniature.
> P. on the big scale. I wanted to comprehend fate as a *whole*,
> showing how it is made by men and then spreads beyond them.

The political strategy of the 'total theatre' was to constitute the
spectator as the co-producer of a powerful *Gesamkunstwerk*, an
organically unified theatre event symbolising an organically-
unified social totality, encountered in one form as existing bourgeois society, projected into the future as the achieved one-party
Communist state.

A further contrast between the respective theoretical positions of
Brecht and Piscator can be advanced by considering the position of
the actor in Piscator's 'total theatre' and in Brecht's 'epic theatre'.
Unlike Brecht, Piscator made no contribution to the development
of new styles or theories of acting: there was no 'epic' style of
acting to accompany the epic structure of the dramatic narratives
he employed. Meyerhold thought Piscator was on 'the wrong
track', since he 'concentrated entirely on developing the *material*
aspects of theatre technique'. In Meyerhold's view 'the stage and
theatre are a framework, to which the actor's voice and gestures
have to be accommodated.'[15] Piscator's comments on acting are
interestingly ambivalent, swinging from a democratic acknowledgement of the actor's need to find a style appropriate to the
artistic and political tasks of the production, to a bureaucratic
insistence on the actor accepting a purely instrumental role: 'I see
the actor in the first instance simply as fulfilling a function, just as
do light, colour, music, scenery, script.' (*The Political Theatre*, p. 121)

The authoritarianism of this directorial attitude towards acting, the
demand that the spectator participate in theatre as a function of a

disciplined technological operation, the dream of a 'total theatre', all seem to justify George Grosz's perceptive identification of Piscator as something of a 'Wagnerian':

> . . . vestiges of the old Wagnerian longing still cling to him, and he is often to be found on the thorny path which leads to 'the total work of art'. What a dream, what a thought, what a possibility, what tremendous scope for modern stage magic!
>
> (*The Political Theatre*, p. 266)

Of course such 'stage magic' is nowadays readily available at the flick of a switch to a theatre as well-resourced and fully-equipped as Piscator could have wished: though its ideological functions are scarcely commensurate with his politico–theatrical programme. The kind of 'magic' produced by stage technology is effectively the opposite of the spectator's 'astonishment' at the recognition of humanity aimed at by Brecht:

> That man can be changed by his surroundings and can himself change the surrounding world . . . all this produces feelings of pleasure. Not of course if man is viewed as something mechanical, something that can be put into a slot, something lacking resistance, as happens today under the weight of certain social conditions. Astonishment, which must here be inserted into the Aristotelian formula for the effects of tragedy, should be considered entirely as a capacity. It can be learned.[16]

'PROLETARIAN AMATEUR' VERSUS 'REVOLUTIONARY PROFESSIONAL' THEATRES

The distinction I have been making throughout this chapter – between, on the one hand, a political theatre developed in the spaces and on the infrastructure of the bourgeois commercial theatre, and on the other an unlocalised, low-budget drama developed as an extension to political or 'community' oganisation – is not something that never occurred to the theatre workers of the 1920s. Piscator frequently found himself at the centre of sharp controversies within the Communist movement, vigorous and sometimes acrid debates about the necessary relationship between artistic and cultural production, and the revolutionary movement itself. If the October Revolution was a proletarian revolution, should not the art of the new Soviet state, and of the other revolutionary movements struggling to build such states, be proletarian art? The basic idea of the Soviet *Proletcult*, propagated by the Russian Association of Proletarian Writers – that revolutionary art should develop out of the working class, and take the working class as its sole audience – had deep roots in Russian society (it owed a great deal to Tolstoy's teaching, particularly in his essay *What is Art?*, 1898), and was challenged by, for example, Trotsky in *Literature and Revolution* (1924). Piscator's work was attacked on *Proletcult* grounds, and his reply appears as a chapter on 'The Proletarian Amateur Play' in *The Political Theatre*. Piscator grants the importance of proletarian theatre, and claims his own seminal achievement within its medium: 'The forms which I devised for the first Red Revue have proved to be right for what the proletarian amateur groups are trying to do.' (p. 101). Piscator also claims an equivalent status for the 'revolutionary professional theatre':

> . . . the development which this theatre has followed in my enterprises to date shows that it developed out of the proletarian amateur propaganda play. Secondly, the two types of theatre are fighting on different sectors of the cultural front and they consequently face different tasks.
>
> (*The Political Theatre*, p. 100)

Each type of theatre had its characteristic strengths and limitations; both would have a significant role to play in the new socialist society: 'Both the revolutionary professional theatre and the revolutionary amateur theatre are moving towards a proletarian cultural theatre, and this will be the form the theatre will take in the cultural life of a socialist community once the economic and political foundations have been laid.' (p. 101). The historical issue is of course the fate of such a theatrical movement in conditions not anticipated by these observations: the temporary victory of fascism in the 1930s, the post-war stabilisation of Western European and American capital, the consolidation of the Cold War, the ultimate collapse of centralised Communist regimes, the re-emergence of separate European nationalisms. From the perspective of those conditions, it is possible to identify Piscator's work in professional theatre as a distinct form of 'revolutionary modernism',[16] ideologically opposed to the reactionary nature of the modernist movement in general, but inextricably involved with corresponding currents of cultural authoritarianism. And just as Piscator's work assimilates readily to the modernism of the early twentieth-century avant-garde, so the work of Brecht interestingly parts company with that of his comrade and compatriot, and begins to disclose – as Christopher McCullough goes on to argue in the following chapter – distinct features of a 'post-modern' cultural and theatrical practice.

Notes

1. The Italian Communist Party (PCI) is about to re-launch itself with a new name. The theoretical and discussion journal of the British Communist Party (CPGB) is likely to renounce its title *Marxism Today*, and the party itself is considering its future as a separate organisation.
2. On Lenin's definition of Communism as 'Soviets plus electrification', see H. Marcuse, *Soviet Marxism* (1958, Harmondsworth: Pelican, 1971).
3. E. Piscator, *The Political Theatre* (1929), ed. and trans. H. Rorrison (London: Eyre Methuen, 1980).
4. The original edition of 1929 used occasional double columns and insets in various typefaces, as well as photographs and illustrations, to intensify the 'montage' effect of the narrative. These were stripped out when the book was revised and published in 1963 by the Rowohlt Verlag, Reinbek/Hamburg. The translation already cited restores some of this narrative diversity in the original, by using illustrations of documents, theatre programmes, etc.
5. B. Brecht, *Poems*, ed. and trans. J. Willett and R. Manheim (London: Eyre Methuen, 1975) p. 234.
6. On the other hand scarcity of resources could on occasion contribute to an intensified realism. When Piscator directed Tolstoy's *The Power of Darkness*, an appropriate dramatic atmosphere was created by an icy draught blowing from stage to auditorium. Piscator had stripped out the central heating pipes and sold them to a scrap-merchant to defray some of the company's debts.
7. Brecht quoted in J. Willett, *The Theatre of Erwin Piscator* (London: Eyre Methuen, 1978) p. 191.
8. W. Benjamin, *Understanding Brecht* (1966), ed. and trans. S. Mitchell (London: New Left Books, 1977).
9. Interestingly the same incident, with a completely opposite interpretation in which the bombs are thrown by revolutionary anarchists, was employed as the apotheosis of an anarchist saint in Frank Harris's novel *The Bomb* (1908). See G. Holderness, 'Anarchism and Fiction', in *The Rise of Socialist Fiction, 1880–1914*, ed. H. Gustav Klaus (Brighton: Harvester, 1987) pp. 144–7.
10. The technical difficulties are described by Piscator's stage manager

Otto Richter, quoted in *The Political Theatre*, pp. 190–3. Martin Kane provides a detailed description of the production of *Hoppla*, taking Piscator's theories at face value and recognising no theoretical difficulties, in M. Kane, 'Erwin Piscator's 1927 production of *Hoppla, We're Alive'*, in D. Bradby, L. James and B. Sharratt (eds) *Performance and Politics in Popular Theatre* (Cambridge: Cambridge University Press, 1980). See also M. Patterson, *The Revolution in German Theatre, 1900–33* (London: Routledge and Kegan Paul, 1981) pp. 134–46, and C. W. Davies, *Theatre for the People: the story of the Volksbühne* (Manchester: Manchester University Press, 1977).

11. Piscator quoted in Willett, *The Theatre of Erwin Piscator*, p. 188.
12. For an account of the Brecht–Lukács controversy, see T. Eagleton, *Walter Benjamin: Towards a Revolutionary Criticism* (London: Verso, 1981) pp. 84–90.
13. See W. Gropius, *The Theatre of the Bauhaus*, trans. S. Wensinger (1961, London: Eyre Methuen, 1979). J. Styan relates the Bauhaus to other contemporary developments in the arts, in his *Modern Drama in Theory and Practice*, 3 (Cambridge: Cambridge University Press, 1981) pp. 136–9.
14. Piscator's diary, quoted in Willett, *The Theatre of Erwin Piscator*, p. 187.
15. Meyerhold quoted in Willett, *The Theatre of Erwin Piscator*, p. 125. Edward Braun by contrast emphasises the parallels between Meyerhold, Brecht and Piscator in E. Braun, *the Director and the Stage* (London: Methuen, 1982) pp. 153–4.
16. W. Benjamin, *Understanding Brecht*, p. 89. But for an eloquent defence of the 'revolutionary professional theatre' see D. Edgar, *The Second Time as Farce: Reflections on the Drama of Mean Times* (London: Lawrence and Wishart, 1989) pp. 24–47.

7

From Brecht to Brechtian: Estrangement and Appropriation

CHRISTOPHER J. MCCULLOUGH

In November 1984, Howard Davies directed a new translation of *Mother Courage and Her Children* for the Royal Shakespeare Company at the Barbican Theatre. The theatrical script employed was developed, at Howard Davies' invitation, by Hanif Kureishi from a literal translation made by Sue Davies. Together Kureishi's version and Davies' staging represent an intriguing case of cultural appropriation. In an interview Kureishi dismissed Brecht's concept of 'estrangement' (*Verfremdungseffekt*, usually translated 'alienation-effect', and abbreviated to 'A-effect') as irrelevant to *Mother Courage*, in both its new manifestations, textual and theatrical.[1] The aim of both translator and director was to 'make it warm and funny', instead of 'a long, tedious, stodgy anti-war play'.[2] A basic strategy in this operation was the aim of focusing the audience's attention upon the individuality of Mother Courage, bringing out her warmth and 'randyness'. Here clearly Brecht's aspiration to reveal character as a social construct was subordinated to a notion of character as an absolute and trans-historical essence. In Brecht's Marxist aesthetic, epic drama is constructed to re-direct the focus of theatrical attention from a psychological empathy with the unique trans-historical human essence, to a revelation of the process by means of which individual lives are shaped by ideas and events. The Kureishi–Davies collaboration explicitly set out to reverse this relationship, re-establishing what Brecht had over-turned. This operation was not offered to the public as a suppression of Brecht, but as a liberation of the true spirit of the artist from the thraldom of a political ideology.

'Brechtian' is a term often used quite separately from any sig-nificant ideological association with the work of the German playwright. Yet the term has found its way into common parlance, among groups of theatre workers who use it to mean any theatrical construction in which the actors admit to being actors on a stage. Those same actors would probably, if they were fully cognisant of the underlying political ideology, almost certainly reject it in one sense or another. The formal and overt disavowal of Brecht's Marxist theoretical base has, in many theatrical and literary institutions, occurred in the most subtle of ways.[3] Rather than suppressing or ignoring the plays and theoretical writings, it has proved more opportune to effect a strategy of liberal, humanistic appropriation, which has the effect of marginalising the political ideology. Underneath the cold Marxist exterior beats a heart of pure poetic tragedy. An interesting process of logic forms the basis of this argument. The later plays (*Mother Courage, Galileo, The Good Woman of Setzuan, The Caucasian Chalk Circle*) can plausibly be regarded as the product of an artist possessed of great humanistic sensibility. Yet the ideology Brecht espoused is known as a cruel and authoritarian political system that seeks to destroy individuality. It must therefore follow that no artist who produced such plays could truly espouse such an oppressive ideology. Through the mediation of such persuasive argument, Brecht's writings and theatrical practice have ironically been moved from a marginalised to a central position within many British theatre institutions. Liberal–humanist culture can simultaneously absorb and control the works, naturalise them into the scheme of bourgeois hegemony, and confirm its own power by claiming to rescue 'art' from 'politics'.

The common understanding has been that apart from a small minority of theatre scholars and practitioners, the works of Bertolt Brecht were largely unknown in this country before the Second World War. This is more or less the case if we are talking about full-scale productions in mainstream theatres; the only major production being one of *The Seven Deadly Sins* at the Savoy Theatre in 1933.[4] However, it is possible to distinguish two types of 'Brechtian' theatrical production in this period: the performance and critical reception of his later and most widely accepted plays, and the work accomplished with much earlier plays in the explicitly political, often amateur theatre groups before and since the war. If these two levels of reception may be identified in the performance of Brecht, the influence of what we term 'Brechtian' may likewise be described on two levels. There is on the one hand an appropriation of the outward appurtenances of Brechtian style – half-curtains, placards, unnaturalistic bright lighting and a cool style of acting, all of which can be deployed without any commensurate ideological purpose. On the other hand there is the measurable influence of Brecht's theory and practice on left-wing radical theatre from the pre-war Unity Theatre through to contemporary companies such as 7:84.

In the subsidised national theatres Brecht flourished between 1933 and the late 1970s, with *Mother Courage* and *The Caucasian Chalk Circle* by far the most popular choices (with around twenty different professional productions of each play). Outside the two national subsidised theatres, there are only two recorded productions of a Brecht play in what may be described as the commercial London theatre: *The Threepenny Opera* (Prince of Wales Theatre, 1972 and Sadler's Wells, 1976). For the rest, some 141 productions of a variety of plays (including seven of *The Exception and the Rule*) have been produced in the regional subsidised theatre, or in fringe and community theatre companies. The conclusions that may be drawn from these rough statistics point to an almost universal indifference on the part of commercial theatre, which, ideologically speaking, should be entirely logical, leaving the contemporary subsidised theatre (as a product of post-war welfare capitalism)[5] and the 'fringe' to make their various appropriations of the playwright and his works.

It was not until 1956 that the London stage was exposed in any significant way to Brecht's work. Then the critical reception was largely antagonistic: not only on isolated aesthetic grounds, but inevitably, in the international tensions of the Cold War, when anti-Communist hysteria was running strong both here and in the USA, on political grounds. This prejudice seems to have consisted of an insular distrust of the foreigner, but also a revulsion against what were referred to in our own xenophobic Thatcherite decade as 'alien political philosophies'. Both were exemplified in a review of *The Caucasian Chalk Circle* pre-dating by two months the visit of the Berliner Ensemble.

But, oh dear, what a terrible old Germanic bore this Brecht can be and what aeons of fatigue we shall have to suffer in the future owing to the Communist deification of this stuck-in-the-Twenties playwright! For isn't Brecht, as the master theatrical mind of our age, just another Communist ramp – another talent plumped up into genius by incessant and skilful propaganda?[6]

Despite the aggressive tone, this reviewer was engaged, albeit grudgingly, in an attempt to disentangle Brecht the artist from a political ideology that is judged to be an antiquated doctrinaire philosophy: 'like many another good talent Brecht is being ruined by an old-fashioned ideology. He is obviously much better than his creed allows him to be.' Brecht emerges from this process of ritual condemnation and forgiveness as a good man fallen among Marxists: a liberal–humanist artist who committed the tragic error of identifying a compassion for the oppressed with the dogma of Communism.

This sundering of Brecht the artist from Brecht the political theorist is a continuing process of attempted appropriation which seems consolidated rather than questioned by recent new translations and productions, such as the RSC *Mother Courage* of 1984. The work and example of the historical materialist theorist and playwright is accommodated into a humanist concept of unchanging human nature. The result is a return of what Brecht himself struggled to suppress: naturalism. The hegemony of naturalism in the Western theatre is one of the means by which liberal capitalism continually reinforces its power base by 'naturalising' a particular view of human behaviour. Brecht expressed this essential dichotomy as 'Theatre for Pleasure or Theatre for Instruction':

> The dramatic theatre's spectator says: Yes, I have felt like that too – Just like me – It's only natural – it'll never change – The sufferings of this man appal me, because they are inescapable – That's great art; it all seems the most obvious thing in the world – I weep when they weep, I laugh when they laugh.
> The epic theatre's spectator says: I'd never have thought it – That's not the way – That's extraordinary, hardly believable – it's got to stop – The sufferings of this man appal me, because they are unnecessary – That's great art: nothing obvious in it – I laugh when they weep, I weep when they laugh.[7]

A radical leftist development of Brecht, aimed at countering the phenomenon of liberal–humanist appropriation, would have to begin with this fundamental distinction. Only by adapting Brecht's epic strategy of 'estrangement', making the familiar unfamiliar, challenging our perceptions of a fixed world of unchanging and universal values, can we harness the 'Brechtian' for the purposes of a progressive cultural politics.

When the Berliner Ensemble performed in this country in September 1956 at the Palace Theatre, the company not surprisingly attracted a fair amount of journalistic attention, most notably from Harold Hobson and Kenneth Tynan. The disparity of response between Hobson and Tynan is curiously marked by their respective descriptions of the Ensemble's rendering of the British national anthem, still the expected etiquette in British theatres of the period. Hobson in *The Sunday Times* observed: 'Their playing of *God Save the Queen*, hauntingly arranged by Elizabeth Lutyens, on Monday evening came as a revelation, with its high tense, silver trumpet note.' However, Tynan's perception of the event struck an entirely different note: 'But the clearest illustration of the "A-effect" comes in the national anthem, which the Berliner Ensemble have so arranged that it provokes, instead of patriotic ardour, laughter. The melody is backed by a trumpet obligato so feeble and pompous that it suggests a boy bugler on a rapidly-sinking ship.'[8]

Both critics praise the theatrical effect achieved here: but for diametrically opposite reasons. It would be a mistake, however, to read the responses of these two influential critics, on the basis of assumptions about their ideological predispositions, as crude polarities; the one progressively supportive of the Berliner Ensemble, the other expressing conservative hostility and reactionary opposition. True, Kenneth Tynan's response is the more enthusiastic, but Harold Hobson's is by no means lacking in understanding of the Ensemble's methods; nor is Tynan's response as perfectly in tune with the theatrical ideology of the company as he himself might have believed.

Hobson managed to articulate a perceptive but ambiguous response to the company's work. He recognised that the company's intention was to *estrange* the British national anthem by an act of re-contextualisation: but for him the effect was not one of ideological subversion, but rather an intensification of patriotic feeling, as the familiar song appeared surprisingly framed by that 'tense' and 'haunting' musical setting. Commenting on the casual dress adopted by the musicians, he at once draws the distinction between the accepted formalities of West End conventions (of which, it is implied, he approves), and the quite deliberate flouting of those conventions by the visiting company. This action, he makes quite clear, is not a result of carelessness. 'When this company ignores a convention to which we are accustomed, it is evident that it does so because it considers that convention either irrelevant or positively injurious to its purposes.' Hobson's own disorientation when confronted with a subversion of conventions did not prevent him from perceiving the subtle structures of the Berliner Ensemble's leftist radicalism.

Articulating with great lucidity the received notion of Brecht's 'epic theatre' – 'The Berliner Ensemble does not seek emotion: it seeks understanding' – he identifies Brecht's work, not in direct opposition to his own ideological position, but as one option in the ideological complexity of European Marxism. He recognises quite clearly that Brecht was distanced from the British theatrical hegemony of naturalism, but equally distanced from the vanguard of Soviet theatre in the 1950s. 'These purposes are quite different from those of the Western stage which Miss [Helen] Hayes adorns. More curiously, they are quite different also from those of the Moscow Art Theatre, with whose political ideas this East Berlin company might be supposed to be in sympathy.' Though sharply dissociated from his own theatrical culture, the Berliner Ensemble could offer Harold Hobson an alternative common ground. However bleak their ideological perspective ('The Berliner Ensemble's view of life is therefore an austere one'), on occasion Brecht couldn't help but allow beauty to break through, '. . . as in the charming episode of the swan and the young lovers on the banks of the Severn in *Trumpets and Drums*'.[9] Hobson simultaneously supports the critical approach that seeks to identify Brecht as a romantic irrationalist, while (for his own purposes) alerting the reader to ideological diversities possible within the Marxist movement. Thus it may be argued that we can perceive a contradiction in the ranks of journalistic reception of Brecht in Britain. Certainly Hobson's comments subvert the earlier critical view of T. C. Worsley that Brecht is, 'just another Communist ramp'.

Kenneth Tynan's review in The *Observer* presents us with a rather different set of perspectives. To most theatregoers and readers of journalistic theatre criticism in the 1950s and 1960s, Tynan was the *enfant terrible* of his profession. The undeniable enthusiasm and expertise with which he fulfilled that role tend to characterise him (even today, some years after his death) as occupying a more radical position than was actually the case. Certainly the first paragraph of his review of the Berliner Ensemble goes beyond mere eulogising of the production towards questions about the role of the audience in Brecht's theatre: 'By contrast with the blinding sincerity of the Berliner Ensemble, we all seemed unreal and stagey.'[10] Tynan celebrates the arrival in Britain of a new and vital approach to theatre; but at the same time he seeks, albeit on a sub-textual level, to rescue Brecht the poet from a theory that will ultimately choke his artistic talent. His review of the Royal Court Theatre's production of *The Good Woman of Setzuan* exemplifies his method of appropriating Brecht as a romantic irrationalist, producer of theatrical emotions so intense as to swamp his own self-imposed theoretical constraints: 'At every turn emotion floods through that celebrated dam, the "alienation-effect". More and more one sees Brecht as a man whose feelings were so violent that he needed a theory to curb them. Human sympathy, time and again, smashes his self-imposed dyke . . .'[11] Tynan saw Brecht's Marxism primarily as a personal therapeutic control, a puritanical check on his raging artistic soul. Despite his commitment to a rationalist ethic ('Brecht wrote morality plays', Tynan said of the Berliner Ensemble's production of *Mother Courage*, 'and directed them as such') Brecht emerges from Tynan's celebration as a romantic individualist railing against corruption and debauchery. Brecht's talent consisted for Tynan in cutting the experience of his stage characters to the bare essentials of raw human *reality*, which mattered far more than any new theatrical structure, any re-definition of the relationship between art and reality, any reconstruction of the relationship between audience and stage. Tynan's Brecht is synonymous, to a large degree, with the romantic figure of Baal in Brecht's early play of that name. Brecht's concern for re-defining landscapes is here reduced to a preoccupation with the characters who inhabit those landscapes; the opportunity to examine how and why those landscapes form those characters is lost.

It is from the foundation created by those early British receptions of Brecht's work that much contemporary interpretation and appropriation of Brecht's plays in production operates. That initial induction of Brechtian theatre practice into British culture formed the basis for a process of institutionalising his plays within the cultural hegemony of our major theatres. The experience of the RSC's 1984 *Mother Courage* is perhaps one of the most salutary. Mention has already been made of the genesis of the playhouse copy: and the production itself confirmed that the play's radical potentiality was being suppressed under the weight of an interpretative reliance on sophisticated theatre technology. The theatrical product was enclosed within the chrome auditorium doors of the London Barbican theatre, where, once the metaphorical curtain had risen, the production worked in a spectacular and musical medium, providing great visual excitement, and well-loved tunes to stir the memory. Mother Courage's wagon, which relied upon an electric motor to power it around the stage, was the reason I saw the play failing to start more often than not, providing perhaps the only – unintentional – alienation-effect. The songs were fully incorporated into the stage fiction, with musicians, unlike those of Harold Hobson's experience, glimpsed as hooded figures, swathed in stage smoke, appearing in gaps of the cyclorama encircling the acting area; thus no disturbing contradictions in relation to the proprieties of theatrical attire were allowed to arise. The audience was constituted as the recipients of a finished cultural product, required to do nothing more than to passively consume a fetishised cultural commodity.

The term Brechtian is also widely used in British theatre to describe productions of plays by authors other than Bertolt Brecht. Perhaps most notably the term has found its way into the vocabulary of post-war Shakespearian production. In this instance we have to recognise the potential complexity of the issue, for on the one hand the use of the term 'Brechtian' may well indicate simply the appropriation of certain stage effects, employed with little reference to the ideological practices that created the need for them. However, it may equally be argued that Brecht's own twentieth-century theatre practice had more than a relationship of similarity with the theatre practice of the Elizabethan–Jacobean public playhouses. He himself described the Elizabethan drama as 'full of alienation-effects'; and Walter Benjamin, in *Understanding Brecht*, proposed that the remarkably dialectical and materialist dynamics of sixteenth-century stage practice, buried at the Restoration, were revived in Brecht's own 'epic theatre'.

Again, however, we find ourselves approaching the territory of appropriation. The transposition of ideas and structures from one century to another is an unsatisfactory business, always likely to produce some confirmation of the timelessness of Shakespeare, 'not for an age', perpetually 'our contemporary'. This problem is further heightened when we consider the outcome of allegedly Brechtian meta-theatrical and self-reflexive techniques applied to the production of Shakespeare's plays. One such example was a production of *Richard II*, directed by John Barton for the Royal

Shakespeare Company in 1973. The production was well received, simultaneously by both liberal–left theatre observers and rather more conservative literary scholars, a consensus which points to the slippery pluralism of these techniques when adopted at a purely formal level, internalised as theatrical devices rather than contextualised as ideological critique. Barton's methods were both visually and orally lucid and articulate challenges to naturalistic acting techniques and pictorial scenography. The setting relied upon a pattern of symbols representing the rituals of hierarchy within the play, and emblematic and metonymic elements employed in particular contexts such as the references to 'England's ground'. The acting further intensified the disturbance of illusion, by making the characters of Richard and Bolingbroke interchangeable between two actors, Richard Pascoe and Ian Richardson, who alternated in the two roles with each performance. The choosing of the roles for the performance was carried out during a prologue, in full view of the audience, by a surrogate Shakespeare figure![13] The final effect of these devices was not one of *Verfremdungseffekt*; despite the challenge to illusionistic staging, the type of theatre produced here does not raise questions about status and hierarchy. Instead the elaborate artifice and ritualistic style of presentation imply an outward world consisting of self-conscious formalised role-playing, which in turn neo-platonically represents a greater fixed truth by which the actions of the protagonists may be judged.

A more genuinely 'Brechtian' approach to Shakespeare can be exemplified by a 1984 Royal Shakespeare Company production of *Henry VIII*, directed by Howard Davies. This production, while by and large poorly received by the critics, seemed to achieve a great deal in politicising a play that is often marginalised by literary critics and, if performed at all, is performed as a rather vacuous pageant. The stage devices, which could certainly be described as 'Brechtian', appeared to be commensurate with this director's interpretation of the dramatic content. The setting was a bare stage, occasionally intruded upon by heavy furniture, notably a large table upon which women folded linen – an acting exercise recommended by Brecht – and by sliding screens appearing like cardboard cut-outs, emblematic rather than pictorial, representing historical locations. The actors frequently performed directly to the audience, including Richard Griffiths as a Henry who successfully engaged the audience with many conspiratorial winks. The ensemble of musicians, sitting downstage right, ostentatiously displaying modern dress and contemporary instruments, playing a jazz-influenced score suggestive of Kurt Weill, would have worried Harold Hobson and Miss Helen Hayes. The most intriguing aspect of the production was to be found in the contradictions created between (on the one hand) its obvious intention to simultaneously open up the machinery of the play's political structure, and the machinery of its own cultural production; and (on the other) the theatrical and social space in which it was presented.

Because *Henry VIII* is generally regarded as a poorly written 'brown-nose job on the Tudors',[14] the overwhelming theatrical tendency has been to dress up the piece as pageantry, re-affirming the mythology of an Elizabethan golden age. Certainly in post-war Stratford Festival productions this approach has been used, and has proved persistently apposite to the social occasion. As that same cultural ethos still predominates at Stratford and the Barbican, Howard Davies' production of *Henry VIII* can be read as an attempt to exploit contradictions between different elements constituting the theatrical space: in this case the socio-architectural environment, and the conventional expectations of a bourgeois audience. This type of cultural intervention into the process of institutional reproduction may be regarded as one of the most exciting possibilities for 'Brechtian' experiment in the mainstream theatre.

I have been speaking of the term 'Brechtian' as indicative of a process of appropriation, by means of which the example of Brecht's theoretical practice can be institutionalised and domesticated within the ideological structures of British theatre. This should not however be taken to imply that the theoretical practice itself is a fixed entity, unchanging and unresponsive to the process of historical development, unaffected by the dialectics of historical change, tied inexorably to the artistic consciousness and intention of its 'author'. Certainly the attitude and behaviour of the Brecht estate, which retains a tight hold over copyright and translation, might point towards such an assumption of private property in cultural production.[15] To think of Brecht's 'work' as a constant quantity, constructed in permanent form by an unmediated aesthetic consciousness – whether that premise is based on the liberal–humanist notion of the art-work as organic whole, or on the rather less idealistic motives of the Brecht estate – is to miss the most salient feature of Bertolt Brecht's contribution to the social and political function of art. Brecht's own historical practice, as director, playwright and theorist, defies any attempt to fix his work as a trans-historical yardstick by which our contemporary theatrical efforts may be measured. In his own adaptations of other play-wrights (Shakespeare's *Coriolanus*, Marlowe's *Edward II*) and direc-torial enterprises (Synge's *Playboy of the Western World*) Brecht did not subscribe to any notion of fidelity to imputed authorial inten-tion. His practice of challenging the concept of art as a fixed entity independent of ideological formations, whether an autotelic for-malist unity, or a fetishised commercial commodity, is one reason why Brecht's work is so apposite to the concerns of contemporary post-structuralist theory. While most theatrical and critical atten-tion is given to the late *great* plays, and to a somewhat ossified conflation of Brechtian epic theory, it is in the early writings, and particularly in the concept of the *Lehrstück* ('teaching play'), that a real potential for radical developments in Brechtian theatre may be explored.

Although post-dating the first British performance of Brecht by three years, the second and third recorded performances (in, respectively, 1936 and 1938) offer us a rather more radical prospect than does the 1933 staging of *The Seven Deadly Sins*. The contact in 1936 was not a formal theatrical occasion, but rather a political link between Brecht's work and the British Labour movement. In the Co-operative Hall, Tooting, and elsewhere in London, the London Labour Choral Union gave amateur performances of the Brecht–Eisler learning oratorio *The Expedient*; and at the same time the Workers' Music Association was publishing the scores of Brecht and Eisler for performance by its singers. This socialist cultural-internationalism was further developed when, in 1938, the left-wing Unity Theatre Club produced a translation of *Señora Carrar's Rifles* by Herbert Marshall (under the title of *Mrs Carrar's Rifles*). These events were in some ways more important as interventions in political theatre than any of the more formal theatrical productions of Brecht's work that have taken place in Britain since the last war. In this more democratic form of political drama, the audiences were constituted as active participants in the drama, rather than as spectators fulfilling their appointed role as passive consumers of an institutionalised 'Brecht'. 'It was, so to speak, art for the pro-ducer, not art for the consumer.'[16] Although these events in Lon-don were not identified specifically as *Lehrstücke*, they shared with that theatrical form a strategy of engaging the audience in the means of cultural production. The term *Lehrstück* is often translated into English, with a fair degree of antagonism, as didactic[17] or propagandist[18] plays. Perhaps a more accurate translation would be 'teaching plays', in the sense that the best teaching involves a learning experience on the part of all concerned.[19] For the essential task of the *Lehrstück* is to enable the participants to observe experientially that the world is capable of change. The emphasis is further placed on what the performers themselves may learn through their involvement in the action of the play. 'These experiments were theatrical performances meant not so much for the spectator as for those who were engaged in the performance.'[20]

Brecht's concept of the *Lehrstück* challenges both the traditional function and the conventional structure of theatre, and forms the ideological base from which his specific idea of the epic grew. Elizabeth Wright in her book *Post-Modern Brecht* distinguishes the *Lehrstück* from epic drama in terms of their respective potentialities for radical cultural intervention. Her argument foregrounds the *Lehrstück*, in which 'art' is conceived as social practice, whereby the actors, usually amateurs (as in the early links with the British Labour movement) perform a dual role of performer and spectator, and exchange their roles according to the development of ideas being worked out in the drama. The later 'epic theatre', on the other hand, while retaining the technique of *Verfremdungseffekt*, and certainly possessed of the power to expose contradictions within a hegemonic theatrical structure, is also perpetuating the very institution (the bourgeois theatre) within the physical and ideological confines of which it is being produced.

It is in the concept of *Lehrstück*, perceived not as a fixed body of theory, but as a continually changing and developing theatrical practice, that we find the possibility of a radical theatre for the future. The signs of a theatrical activity capable of such mobilisation are certainly not to be found in the institutionalised productions of Brecht's plays; nor in the activities of many of the contemporary radical left-wing playwrights. Important and challenging as Bond, Brenton, Churchill, Edgar and Griffiths obviously are, they are still to a degree (in Elizabeth Wright's terms) working within, and by implication perpetuating, the very institutions they are challenging.

The practitioners of the *Lehrstück* are more likely to be found outside the professional theatres. They may be found exploiting the uses of drama and role play in specific communities, as in Augusto Boal's proposals for a guerilla theatre. They may be discovered in dramatic events such as John Arden and Margaretta

D'Arcy's project of an October carnival in the streets of Bradford, celebrating the Russian Revolution. They may appear in the alternative cabaret, in the multi-cultural carnival, in the large-scale devised theatre game.[21] There is no guarantee that such activities, simply by virtue of their democratic and participatory nature, necessarily carry the ideological force necessary for the kind of dialectical revolution in theatrical perception attempted by Brecht in his early experiments. But their very resistance to easy appropriation, their refusal to assimilate readily either to the formalist's artefact or to the bourgeois theatre's commodity, bestow on them a challenging, obstructive power. If there is to be a revolutionary praxis of drama relevant to contemporary and future theatrical discourse, here in the Brechtian *Lehrstück* is one of the locations from which it might begin to grow.

Notes

1. R. Julian, 'Brecht and Britain: Hanif Kureishi in interview with Ria Julian', *Drama*, 155/1 (1985) pp. 5–7.
2. Ibid., p. 6.
3. Examples of this process in critical work can be found in M. Esslin, *Brecht: A Choice of Evils* (London: Eyre Methuen, 1959), R. Gray, *Brecht the Dramatist* (Cambridge: Cambridge University Press, 1976), and J. Hilton, *Performance* (London: Macmillan, 1987).
4. B. Brecht and K. Weill, *The Seven Deadly Sins* (*Anna, Anna*), The Savoy Theatre, July 1933, with Lotte Lenya and Tilly Losch, choreography by Balanchine. There were three performances. London reviews of foreign productions of Brecht appeared in *The Times* ('The Threepenny Opera': a Berlin Burlesque, 25 September 1928), and in The *Observer*, ('The Caucasian Chalk Circle* at the Paris Drama Festival', reviewed by Kenneth Tynan, 26 June 1955).
5. The Local Government Act of 1948 allowed local authorities to levy a rate of sixpence, a practice which laid the foundations for post-war state subsidy of the arts and the setting up of a number of civic and national subsidised theatre companies.
6. T. C. Worsley, *New Statesman*, 14 July 1956, reviewing a production of *The Caucasian Chalk Circle*, performed by students of the Royal Academy of Dramatic Art, London. For more recent interventions along the same lines, see Michael Billington, 'Brecht to the Wall', *Guardian*, 24 April 1990, and Christopher Hampton, 'The Wicked Person of Berlin . . .', *Independent on Sunday*, 29 April 1990.
7. 'Theatre for Pleasure or Theatre for Instruction', in J. Willett, ed. and trans., *Brecht on Theatre* (London: Methuen, 1964) p. 71.

8. H. Hobson, *The Sunday Times* (2 September 1956); K. Tynan, *Observer* (2 September 1956).
9. See. H. Hobson, *The Sunday Times* (1956).
10. See K. Tynan, *Observer* (1956).
11. K. Tynan, 'The Good Woman of Setzuan at The Royal Court', in *A View of the English Stage* (London: Methuen, 1984) p. 184.
12. See K. Tynan, *Observer* (1956).
13. I am indebted to Robert Shaughnessy for the use of material on Barton's production gathered for inclusion in his doctoral thesis on Shakespearian production.
14. S. Grant, *Time Out* (20 September 1984).
15. An example of the problems involved in dealing with the Brecht estate is recorded in J. Hiley, *Theatre at Work – Galileo* (London: Routledge, 1981) pp. 4–7.
16. See B. Brecht 'The German Drama: pre-Hitler', in Willett (ed.), *Brecht on Theatre* (1964) p. 80.
17. See Esslin, *Brecht* (1959).
18. See R. Gray, *Brecht the Dramatist* (1976).
19. See Brecht in Willett, *Brecht on Theatre* (1964) p. 80.
20. E. Wright, *Post-Modern Brecht* (Routledge, 1989) pp. 10–23. See also R. Steinweg, *Das Lehrstück: Brechts Theorie einer ästhetischen Erziehung* (Stuttgart, 1972).
21. A. Boal, *Theatre of the Oppressed* (London: Pluto, 1979); D. Edgar, *The Second Time as Farce: Reflections on the Drama of Mean Times* (London: Lawrence and Wishart, 1988); A. Hunt, *Hopes for Great Happenings* (London: Methuen, 1976).

8

The Political Dramaturgy of John Arden

JAVED MALICK

There is a contemporary tradition of political drama in Europe which goes back from the radical theatre groups and artists of the 1960s and 1970s, through Brecht and Piscator, to the early Soviet theatre. Developed in conscious opposition to the ideologically and socially bourgeois character of the established forms of drama, this tradition is characterised mainly by an endeavour to re-widen the range of artistic, cognitive, and social resources and possibilities of the theatre, both as an art form and as a social institution.[1] In dramaturgic practice, this has meant mainly two integrally related things: one a focusing on the shared life of the community and its tensions; and two, a conscious return to the conventions, techniques and styles of the traditional, historically plebeian, cultural forms. Further, in terms of theatrical feedback, the effort to revitalise the theatre and to bring back to it those larger plebeian sections of society which the bourgeois theatre has systematically banished has involved some radical reconstruction of the naturalist stage, often breaking out of the fixed and enclosed locations of the conventional, middle-class theatres (with their fixed and individually marked seats, polite atmosphere, financially and socially restricted admission, and so on), and performing instead in open-air parks, noisy restaurants, crowded market-places or busy shop-floors, where the theatrical experience acquires a more pointed and, in Bakhtinian sense, truly 'dialogic' character.

John Arden belongs in this tradition of political drama. He shares with it a number of fundamental aesthetic and ideological preferences and orientations. This, however, is not always appreciated by his critics. When his first plays were produced in an atmosphere of revival of the socially committed form of naturalism on the English stage, it was felt that, contrary to the current fashion, Arden's drama revealed no clear bias in favour of one or the other side of a dramatic argument. For an audience accustomed to illusionistic dramaturgy and its moral spoon-feeding – an audience that, for example, had identified readily with Jimmy Porter's historically impotent but emotionally and rhetorically powerful 'anger' against the Establishment – it was bewildering, if not altogether outrageous, that a dramatist should write plays about what seemed to be recognisable problems of contemporary metropolitan life – such as municipal corruption, prostitution, incompatible neighbours – without taking sides. Soon, however, there was a reversal of attitude as Arden's 'moral ambivalence' came to be seen as his peculiar strength, and 'ambiguity' became the main value of his dramaturgy.[2] The result of this liberal valorisation of Arden's supposed 'impartiality' is that his and D'Arcy's recent overtly political and explicitly partisan plays are seen as a corruption or degeneration of his 'true' artistic talents.

In the following pages, my endeavour shall be to demonstrate that, the 'conversion' theory of certain critics notwithstanding, Arden's dramaturgy has evolved following its own inner logic. I shall argue that, although it is true that his early plays evinced no overt declamatory morals and no illusionist empathy with good protagonist as against black villains, and although his political position has changed radically from the early, vaguely left-wing form of liberalism to the recent, openly revolutionist stance, and that this change is significantly reflected in his work, a fundamental feature of his work is that it invariably focuses on the problems and experiences of the group or the community, rather than of the individual. I shall further suggest that it is this critical focus on the shared social life and its tensions, this dramaturgic practice of foregrounding the public and the social, privileging it over the private and the psychological, which makes his drama more deeply political than the 'socially conscious' liberal dramas of the Ibsenian tradition. In other words, while the openly and committedly political character of his later plays stems from his more mature perception of society and politics, it also signifies a culmination of certain artistic and ideological tendencies inherent in his dramaturgy from the very beginning.

REJECTION OF BOURGEOIS TRADITION

Right at the outset, Arden rejected the individualist assumptions and emphases underlying the established forms of modern drama in favour of a more communal or collectivist focus, re-worked from the older traditions. He was aware of the significance of the dramaturgic choice he was making, and also of how radically it deviated from the general neo-naturalist trend of the 'new' post-war British drama. In an early essay, he explained his artistic creed, distinguishing it clearly from the choices made by some of his contemporaries. He wrote:

> To use the material of the contemporary world and present it on the public stage is the commonly accepted purpose of play-wrights, and there are several ways in which this can be done. Autobiography treated in the documentary style (Wesker). Individual strains and collisions seen from a strongly personal stand-point and inflamed like a savage boil (Osborne). The slantindiculor observation of unconsidered speech and casual action used to illuminate loneliness and lack of communication (Pinter). . . . What I am deeply concerned with is the problem of translating the concrete life of today into terms of poetry that shall at the one time both illustrate that life and set it within the historical and legendary tradition of our culture.[3]

Arden believed that social criticism, if 'expressed within the frame-work of the traditional poetic truths, . . . can have a weight and an impact derived from something more than contemporary docu-mentary facility'.[4] In his mind, the adherence to the conventions and techniques of the plebeian cultural forms was clearly and integrally linked to the project of writing socially meaningful drama. He recognised that he belonged 'in the same tradition as Brecht', because, like himself, Brecht too had 'taken all his drama-tic styles and devices' from a rich tradition of popular–plebeian culture which goes back to the Middle Ages, running vitally through the medieval and the Elizabethan dramaturgies and theatres, and which could still be seen until a few decades ago, albeit in a residual and highly de-vitalised form, in the music-hall and the pantomime. In his view Brecht's main contribution was 'to revive this type of theatre as a style of writing and producing and then apply it to modern problems and modern ideologies and modern audiences'.[5]

From *The Waters of Babylon*, his first professionally staged play, to *The Island of the Mighty*, his and D'Arcy's last professionally staged play, and beyond that to their recent work outside the professional theatre circuits, Arden's drama testifies to a persistent and increasingly conscious endeavour on his part to perfect a form which is rooted in the contemporary social experience, but also free from 'contemporary documentary facility', or, to borrow a phrase from Raymond Williams, from 'the false commitment of the inserted political reference'.[6] His work does not simply 'translate' the 'concrete life of today' into terms of traditional poetics, but does so in such a way that that life is seen mainly in its shared, socio-historical aspects, and, what is more, seen critically, from below.

Completely ignoring the ideologically and artistically constricting naturalist preference for the private, familial, and 'psychological' types of action, Arden has from the beginning put on the stage actions of a more social and political kind, involving public and semi-public situations and institutions as well as a rich, socially differentiated range of agents and relationships. A chronological reading of his plays reveals that he has not only sustained without diminution this expressly socio-political emphasis of his dramaturgy, but, in consonance with his own political development, has also further perfected and deepened it. We find, for example, that the locus of action in his drama has developed significantly from the relatively restricted civic neighbourhoods of *The Waters of Babylon* and *Live Like Pigs*, or from an even more strictly localised clinic-cum-old-people's-home in *The Happy Haven*, through the entire, if small and isolated, communities of *Serjeant Musgrave's Dance* and *The Workhouse Donkey*, to the much vaster and more complex national and international politics of *The Royal Pardon*, *Armstrong's Last Goodnight*, *Left Handed Liberty*, *The Hero Rises Up*, *The Island of the Mighty* and *The Non-Stop Connolly Show*. The thematic concerns too have similarly progressed from the micro-level politics (that is, local forms of political corruption in municipal politics, the problems of specific kinds of social outcasts, and so on) to an investigation, in specifically class terms and from an openly committed position, of such problems of pressing global import and magnitude as war and peace, imperialism and socialism, oppression and freedom, the strategies for revolution and radical social change.

However, the socio-political emphasis of Arden's dramaturgy stems not so much from *what* he writes about as from *how* he writes – in other words, from his characteristic method of formulating a dramaturgic action.

EPISODIC CONSTRUCTION

Arden's characteristic style of writing in short, discrete scenes is common to all traditional narratives as well as to the Brechtian 'epic theatre'. It is obviously in sharp contrast to the naturalist dramaturgic practice of formulating the action as a smooth, unilinear, causal flow of mounting intensity – an almost imperceptible process without interruptions, without even any formal signals to mark a play's commencement and conclusion. Just as the unilinear, causal method, which carries with it a sense of continuity and inexorability, reinforces the individualist/subjective standpoint of the naturalist drama, the episodic composition allows the playwright to dramatise a complex, historical view of social reality.

In Arden, a scene is usually defined and delimited in such a way that some socially significant aspect of the dramatised events, relationships, and/or behaviour is foregrounded. This allows it to acquire a *gestic* quality in the Brechtian sense of the term. Almost every play in Arden's opus comprises a variety of such gestic scenes. Therefore, as the action jumps from scene to scene, time and space come across as experientially variegated and eminently alterable – and not merely phenomenologically but with a richness suggesting socially significant texture. For instance, in *The Workhouse Donkey*, the change from I.ii to I.iii signifies a cognitively significant shift from a private space to a public one, from the formal and constrained atmosphere of a dinner party to the casual and free atmosphere of a pub, from a restricted number of formally invited guests from a predominantly upper-class background to a richly variegated and relatively freer community of lower-class drinkers, from a safe situation in which the main activity is polite conversation to a potentially explosive one in which the activities range from boisterous jokes, laughter, songs, betting, borrowing and lending money, through illegal and confidential medical consultation, to a mischievously manipulated committee meeting with its mockery of 'democratic procedure', and finally to a police raid. These are clearly two qualitatively distinct social situations, or, more precisely, class chronotropes, which determine what kind of people might be found in them as well as how they might relate to each other.

Thus, a play composed in this manner becomes capable of encompassing a wide range not only of physical time and physical space but also of human existence and experience. In Arden's case, this dramaturgic practice helps his work to communicate a panoramic and complex view of society and to foreground the fundamental plurality of socio-economic states, interests, and possibilities. This is particularly evident in the supra-individual emphasis of his agents and agential relationships.

SOCIAL DEFINITION OF AGENTS AND RELATIONSHIPS

While a character in the orthodox forms of modern drama as a rule suggests a full-fledged, psychologically complete and complex subjectivity, typical Arden protagonists are individualised only to the minimum, functionally necessary extent. As individual characters, they possess only a few rudimentary details, mainly of a biographical and temperamental kind, subsumed under a proper name. These semantic traits individuate an agent, allow her/him to be distinguished from others, and thus add to that agent's imagined 'reality'. However, they do not suggest an isolated subjectivity or allow individual subjectivity to become the dominant focus of dramaturgic interest. On the contrary, they are usually so conceived as to allow the psychological and the social, the individual and the typical, to be dialectically linked. Musgrave, the protagonist of the play named after his bizarre dance, is an example in point. What really defines him as a character is not only his military background and experience, which he shares with his fellow-soldiers, but also, and especially, his rigid moral code and obsession with discipline and religion. These traits individualise him and allow him to be distinguished from the other characters in the play. However, they also suggest the Puritan, Cromwellian soldier, and, thus, a specific ideological legacy of the bourgeoisie. Furthermore, in Arden's dramaturgic treatment of it, this connection is deliberately foregrounded.[7]

Dialogue, as Peter Szondi says, is 'the common space in which the interiority of the dramatis personae is objectified'.[8] However, a character's ability to communicate itself exhaustively and clearly to others (and to the audience) is inversely related to that character's inward orientation. That is why, in an interesting paradox, the very preoccupation with the inner life of the character in the individualist dramaturgy precludes the possibility of full and clear realisation of that character on the manifest level of the text. His/her intensely introspective feelings and experiences tend to render him/her increasingly inarticulate, creating difficulties in fluent and unambiguous speech. Therefore, spoken words and actions are made to communicate their meanings only obliquely or impressionistically, so that the textually manifest aspects of the character, like the visible tip of an iceberg, become significant not in terms of what they actually say or disclose – and thus render evident and verifiable for the spectators – but mainly for what they merely suggest and cannot fully express.[9] Much of the peculiar richness and intensity of this kind of drama derives precisely from this nagging sense of uncertainty, inarticulateness, and ambiguity of experience which is correlative to the interiorisation of the character and the loss of overt, dialogic action.

Because they are delineated so broadly and selectively, Arden's characters are free from obsessive introspection. And precisely because they are so free, they are able to, as it were, constantly turn themselves inside out by talking freely, readily, and unambiguously to one another as well as, and frequently, to the audience. This generates an abundance of verbal and gestural activity in a play, which dialogises the agents and enhances their theatrical interest. It also makes Arden's characters among the most communicative fictive beings in modern drama, who remain quite communicative even under such extraordinary circumstances as would render naturalist characters introspective and incoherent, if not altogether speechless.

By constantly exteriorising themselves in speech and action, such characters emphasise their own lack of individualist closure and, as it were, direct our attention away from their separate selves towards some larger world of the collective and, therefore, also towards a more complex perception of the dramatic action as a whole. Moreover, Arden's use of various forms of direct address (such as formal commentary, asides, soliloquies and songs) allows him to further de-privatise his agents so as to preclude any individualist or purely subjective perception of their status and roles, and to re-invest them, instead, with an emphatically supra-individual (that is, socio-political, or socially typical) significance.

POLARISED DRAMATURGIC SPACE

The most crucial cognitive consequence of this non-individualistic approach to dramaturgic agents – which makes a web of agential relationships rather than the individual character the pertinent analytical focus of his drama – is that the interest in a play remains focused, not on one or a very few isolated individuals and their private lives and consciousnesses, but on socio-historically significant polarities of collective human existence and experience.[10] The fact that Arden's agents usually function in clusters, forming themselves into distinct groups on the basis of identity of social status, interests and goals, has the effect of polarising the agential space of a play.

Polarisation of dramaturgic agents according to their social and/or ideological positions has existed in his drama from the beginning. The nature and scope of such groupings, however, have undergone significant development over the years. The early plays, where the struggle was usually for mere survival under a hostile system, tended to concentrate on some local and historically marginal segment of the socially underprivileged. The central focus in these plays was on some specific conflict of interests between such a counter-hegemonic (or deviant) group and the dominant social and moral order. The hostile establishment was as a rule represented in these plays by its official representatives or functionaries, who, insofar as they *objectively* represented or defended the interests of the dominant order against the divergent interests of an unassimilated (often inassimilable) group, simultaneously came across as a single group, or at least as representatives of various sub-groups within the unity of an hegemonic order.

For example, in *The Waters of Babylon*, the central conflict is between an alien (largely immigrant and non-English), morally 'deviant' group of crooks, pimps and prostitutes and a hostile social system (represented in the play by a municipal councillor, two MPs, and a policeman). In *Live Like Pigs*, likewise, a freely constituted household of irrepressible gypsies conflicts with the established middle-class environment into which it has been forcibly moved and with which it is socially and morally incompatible. The dominant 'order' is represented in the play not only by its official administrative and political functionaries (the Housing Estate Official, the officially appointed doctor, and the policeman) but also by the Jackson family, whose preoccupations with stability, security, and respectability exemplify the hegemonic power of the dominant ideology. Similarly, in *The Happy Haven*, a group of elderly but mentally active patients in a medical institution find themselves in conflict with the interests of their doctor and, beyond him, with the interests of a larger social group signified in the play by the politically and economically powerful patrons of the doctor's research.

These early plays thus focused upon the antagonisms between some specific, and foregrounded, category of the socially underprivileged and the framing social and moral order. Arden's subsequent plays continued the practice of dividing the agential space (a) horizontally, into the upper and the lower socio-ideological realms, and (b) vertically, into sub-groups within a shared but diversified socio-political space. These plays continued to foreground the lower realm by focusing mainly on groups of ordinary people in a struggle against the hegemonic order. However, they also marked a significant progress in the direction of a fully developed political drama.

EMERGENCE OF A CLASS-BASED PERSPECTIVE

There are two ways in which Arden's progress towards openly political drama can be described: first, there was an expansion of the dramaturgic focus so as to include a whole community (and not just a specific and marginal fragment thereof, as in the previous plays); and, second, in a significant cognitive shift, the main agential divisions came to be perceived increasingly in class terms.

This process began with *Serjeant Musgrave's Dance*, which presented social conflicts arising out of the existence of an unjust order which produces bitter class conflicts at home and conducts brutal colonial wars abroad. The main agential polarisation in the play is between the hegemonic order – represented by the mayor who, significantly, is also a mine-owner (thus signifying the identity of economic and political powers), the parson (who is also a magistrate), the policemen, and the dragoons – and those opposed to that order (namely, the soldiers, the miners and the women).

However, the first full articulation of the class-based perspective is found in *The Workhouse Donkey*. On the surface, this play seems to be a satire on corruption in municipal politics, focused mainly on the conflict of interests between the two organised political factions, their electoral rivalries and intrigues. On closer scrutiny, however, it reveals itself to be more complex in design and import, and comes across as an indictment, from an expressly and cheerfully plebeian standpoint, of the 'legitimate' political alternatives in post-war Britain, as well as an acknowledgement of the necessity – and indeed the possibility – of finding a different, genuinely plebeian and revolutionary alternative.

At this cognitively higher level of the play, the focus shifts from electoral rivalry to the more fundamental conflict between social classes. The conservatives believe that 'today/ Class-struggle is concluded' (II.i), and the narrow political and social perspective of the orthodox section of the Labourites amounts to an agreement with this view. Butterthwaite, alone among the politicians, insists that 'By solid class defence and action of the mass alone can we hew out and line with timbered strength a gallery of self-respect beneath the faulted rock above the subsidence of water!' (III.ii).

This is an entirely new voice in Arden's work. It marks an important stage in his development towards political radicalism. In *Musgrave* he had touched upon the class question, but he could not fully reconcile it with the over-riding pacifist moral stance. Here, in the *Donkey*, he has foregrounded it. For, as we move from the surface to this deeper level of this play, a different kind of polarisation of the agential space comes to the fore. We see the two political factions, the police, and their bourgeois allies, as belonging to the same side of the conflict – the side which supports and perpetuates the existing class-structure.[11] The other side of this class conflict is represented by Butterthwaite and his plebeian supporters. Butterthwaite, who describes himself as a plebeian Messiah (II.vi), brings into a legitimised, 'orderly' power struggle within the bourgeois system an officially unacceptable 'discordance' of class conflict. Conceived as a colourful embodiment of the spirit, interests, and historical experience of the working masses, he, even when actively involved with the Labour party, never loses his class perspective. Outmanoeuvred by the orthodox faction in Labour, he prepares himself (and on May Day, too) for the final conflict by activating the hitherto dormant plebeian sections of the electorate within a horizon fusing politics and ethics, revolutionary hope and carnivalesque licence. For a brief moment in the last scene – when he leads a carnivalesque procession of his followers into the new art gallery, a symbol of the hegemonic culture as also of the renewed Labour–Conservative unity in the play, and disrupts what was officially envisaged as a polite, formal, and restricted ceremony – the existing social order is turned upside down. The play, thus, clearly demonstrates that the real conflict is not between the different power-groups struggling for a greater share within the hegemonic system, but between the dominant power-structure as a whole and the plebeian masses.[12]

POLITICAL FACT AND HISTORICAL FICTION

After *The Workhouse Donkey*, first performed in 1963, Arden turned increasingly towards historico–legendary subjects. Again, his method of dramatising history is radically different from that of the individualist dramatists. For example, in *Luther*, John Osborne took a historical subject and, through a curious mixture of some surface devices from Brecht and psychology from Erik Erikson, turned it into a psychopathological character-drama. The play seems to illustrate Christopher Fry's idea that history in the theatre 'means people rather than events. What they do is less important than what they feel and suffer while doing it. Their success or failure isn't measured in worlds conquered or lost, but *in the private battlefield, in the vale of soul-making as Keats called it.*'[13]

Contrary to this, the emphasis in Arden's historico–legendary plays is firmly oriented to 'doing' rather than 'suffering'. He focused on conflicts, turmoils, and developments which have, at specific and significant junctures of the past, so intervened in the course of European history that everybody's 'soul-making' was deeply affected, making any division between public and private untenable. Agential relationships in these plays are therefore conceived in such a way that they evoke the impression of huge collectivities in conflict, a sharply polarised political order in transition.

These plays are not mere historical spectacles or documentary chronicles. They are written rather as complex investigations into the nature of political power and social change. Plays like *Armstrong's Last Goodnight*, *Left-Handed Liberty* and *The Hero Rises Up* re-examine history from a specifically contemporary, politically subversive standpoint. They centrally involve collusions and contradictions among divergent social and institutional factions, and focus on the complex, dialectical, and not always honourable or noble, processes through which political power is acquired and maintained. Furthermore, they demonstrate how at various junctures in history certain alternative possibilities were set up, missed or deliberately thwarted. *Left-Handed Liberty*, for instance, is concerned not so much with a chronology of events leading to the signing of the Peoples' Charter as with making a critical examination of a myth in English political history, pertaining to law and power.[14] It dramatises a complicated pattern of political conflicts and alliances between several powerful groups and institutions, each motivated by its own class or factional interests rather than by any concern for the general good of the Commonwealth.

VIEW FROM BELOW

These historico–legendary plays as a rule focused on factional conflicts within the ruling class, and, therefore, were primarily concerned with the privileged sections of the dramatised society. However, not content with depicting the situation in terms of its surface politics alone, Arden, since there was no attempt at 'documentary facility', often departed from the text versions of events and also incorporated into his plays some comment from the standpoint of ordinary people. For example, in *Armstrong*, Meg's bitter lament over the dead body of her treacherously murdered lover (I,4), reinforced by Lindsay's comment articulating the political import of her experience (I,5), suggests such a view from below. Even more pointedly, the inclusion of the singing girls of London and the village folk of Gotham in *Liberty* signifies the inclusion of the standpoint of the alienated common people of England in a play which centrally deals with a bitter struggle for hegemony in the upper realms of the established social order. By allowing us a glimpse of that order's underbelly, by showing us the indifference and cynicism with which ordinary men and women view the struggle between the king and the nobility, Arden is making a significant political comment. This comment becomes explicit in the ballad which sums up the popular position in relation to the Charter and mocks the promised 'liberties' (III,5). The Mayor's comments on this satirical song – somewhat like those of Lindsay's on Meg's grief in *Armstrong's Last Goodnight* – reiterates and underscores this popular criticism of the Charter from the standpoint of the nascent mercantile class: 'It's not only that particular ditty, there's others as well, worse: there's a bad feeling in the streets. And I can't say that I blame them: they've heard enough pious pronouncements about liberty over the last twelve months to make the Fleetditch mud larks vomit. . . . But what have we got – in practical terms to show to the people? What bales of cloth, as it were, to lay upon my counter?'

Arden's practice of deliberately incorporating a view from below into events and developments in the upper social realm is not an idiosyncratic departure from the 'authentic' facts of history, but a conscious and profoundly significant dramaturgic gesture of viewing history critically – even subversively or 'left-handedly' – from a plebeian stance. In plays like *Armstrong* and *Liberty*, this stance not only reveals the class-bound nature and significance of the dramatised power-structures but also implies that true human values lie with society's oppressed. A logical extension of such a value-judgement could envisage not only axiological but also pragmatic inversion, that is, in favour of which, social groups might the course of history be radically altered. As already noted, the first open expression of a radical plebeian alternative to existing history dates back to *The Workhouse Donkey*, but its best and most categorical presentation so far is to be found in Arden and D'Arcy's epic trilogy, *The Island of the Mighty*. It is in this play that, for the first time in Arden's professional career, the revolutionary potential of the disinherited multitudes is directly articulated and celebrated.

The play – which comprises a system of three linked historico–political parables, each dramatising a specific aspect of a world which is sharply and explosively polarised between oppressive rulers and the disinherited and oppressed masses – casts the masses as the protagonist, investing them with the driving thematic force, and indeed heroism. This has the effect of making the plebeian perspective axiologically as well as agentially the dominant one.[15]

The dramaturgy of the play is interwoven with critical and celebratory impulses. On the one hand, it offers one of the most sustained and radical critiques of imperialism, militarism, political hegemonism, and class-, ethnic and gender-based oppression in modern drama. On the other, using an approach which is illustrative of what Brecht called 'a fighting conception' of the people, the trilogy celebrates the people's collective strength, their will and ability not only to survive but to survive subversively.[16] Aneurin's song, with which it concludes, and which is simultaneously a threat of revolutionary apocalypse and the promise of a plebeian millennium, celebrates the undying determination of the disinherited people to come back and take possession of 'the whole world'. However, the play also makes it clear that this plebeian millennium is not to be instituted from above (by God's ordinance – as in the Grail legend) but is to be wrenched from history by a powerful and willed collective effort of the many ('Two thousand or three') who have for centuries been 'muffled' and pushed 'under' by the few ('score or two').

BREAK WITH PROFESSIONAL THEATRE

The Island occupies a crucial position on the trajectory of Arden's development as both a *culmination* and a *turning point*. It marks the culmination of his and D'Arcy's preceding artistic and political development, as it also inaugurates the subsequent, more integrally revolutionary phase of their work in the theatre. It was finalised at the end of the radical activist decade of the 1960s, a decade of crucial significance for Arden, as it was for many others in Western Europe and America.

Throughout that decade, Arden and D'Arcy had continued to work in the community and fringe theatres. This work – which includes *The Business of Good Government* and *The Royal Pardon* as well as several events without fixed texts but with distinctly theatrical character, and which is directly linked in form, style and orientation to the openly political work since 1972 (for example, *The Ballygombeen Bequest*, *The Non-Stop Connolly Show*, *Vandaleur's Folly*) – had a deep and lasting influence on the development of Arden's dramaturgy as also on his attitude towards the British professional theatre. By offering them the freedom to experiment and to try out in practice their own ideas and notions, this experience outside the professional, metropolitan theatres necessarily showed up the relatively restrictive and rigid structure of the professional theatre. It is not surprising, therefore, that the period of their increasing dissatisfaction with London's professional theatre, the late 1960s, coincided with the period of Arden and D'Arcy's increasing involvement with amateur and fringe theatres.

This dissatisfaction was further reinforced in 1968 by a quarrel with the Institute of Contemporary Arts over the production of *The Hero Rises Up*, which revealed to these playwrights just how much freedom bodies like the ICA allowed to the artist, and how libertarianism, 'if it trod too far out of line – could be chopped off by the neck by those whose public postures had always been so erect in its defence'.[17] It was also during 1968 that Arden and D'Arcy collaborated, for the first time, with a committed socialist group, Roland Muldoon's CAST (Cartoon Archetypal Slogan Theatre), to create *Harold Muggins is a Martyr* – the production of which occasioned a movement for greater unity and contact among left-wing artistic groups and individuals.[18]

As Arden himself wrote later, politically many things 'had come to a head' in 1968: besides the student–worker revolt in France, the brutal police attack at the Chicago Democratic Convention, the Soviet invasion of Czechoslovakia, and the massacre during the Mexico Olympics, there was 'the prohibition by Stormont unionism of a perfectly reasonable Civil Rights March in Derry, the incorrect accusation that Northern Irish Civil Rights was a front for the IRA, the savage attack on the marchers who had the nerve to defy the ban, and the inexorable slides of the largely-forgotten Irish problem into the maelstrom of blood and bitterness which to this day swirls wider and wider'.[19] Helped by the political developments that were overtaking Western Europe and North America, his political and artistic consciousness matured rapidly and, among other things, he came to recognise the fundamental correctness of Margaretta D'Arcy's staunchly political and passionately partisan view of things.

The main orientation of Arden's thinking at that time found an expression in his autobiographical radio play, *The Bagman, or The Impromptu of Muswell Hill*, where he openly investigated the relation between theatre and politics and articulated his growing recognition of the political potential of theatre.[20] The play also indicated that in the conflict between the privileged few and the disinherited masses the artist cannot be a mere onlooker but must align with one or the other. This already more committed, more openly partisan view of socio-political conflicts was further strengthened by Arden and D'Arcy's visit to India, where 'the war between the fed men and the hungry men, the clothed men and the naked men, the sheltered men and the exposed men, is being waged with great ferocity'.[21]

This visit made them 'more inclined to see the direct connection that the theatre should have with the struggles of everyday life – shall we say, more alienated from the professional theatre'.[22] *The Island of the Mighty* was written in the context of all these political and artistic experiences. It reflected a more confident political position deriving from the playwrights' greater familiarity with various forms of economic and cultural oppression, with the nature of imperialist domination of the Third World, and with various positions on the questions of revolutionary strategy and tactics. Painstakingly re-written from the earlier Arden drafts, its text testifies to the degree to which Arden and D'Arcy's dramaturgy had matured both artistically and politically. It combines theatrical fun and cognitive seriousness, and by using an emblematic form of presentation, signifies an indissoluble union of form and horizon. Such a dramaturgy could not be accommodated within the established British theatre, for it militated not only against its liberal ideology but also against the conventions, notions, and values through which that ideology operates in artistic production. As a result this work, which by any standard is one of the major twentieth-century plays in the English language, has yet to receive a proper staging.

Even before the controversial RSC production of the Arthurian trilogy, Arden and D'Arcy wrote *The Ballygombeen Bequest*. First produced in Belfast by a committed socialist theatre group, 7:84 Company, in the midst of a violent conflict there, the play reflected – even more sharply than *The Island* – the new subversively political cast of its authors' mind. Although its story depicts an absentee English landlord cheating a poor Irish family of tenant farmers of its inheritance, it is in fact a parable of Britain's imperialist domination and exploitation of Ireland. As Hunt has correctly observed, with this play Arden and D'Arcy had 'moved into a new dimension of political theatre', in which an openly Marxist position is couched in Arden's characteristically playful style strongly reminiscent of the music-hall.[23]

In *The Ballygombeen Bequest*, *The Island of the Mighty*, and the subsequent plays like *Vandaleur's Folly* and *The Non-Stop Connolly Show*, we see Arden, in his own words, 'at last affirming from his own hard experience the need for revolution and a socialistic society: and moreover convinced that his artistic independence and integrity will be strengthened rather than compromised by so *doctrinaire* a stance'.[24] It is this openly partisan, revolutionist stance of his and D'Arcy's recent work which the British theatre establishments and critics have found so unacceptable. Many critics – including some of those who had once hailed him as one of the most promising playwrights of the post-war period – now openly or tacitly regard him as a cultural *persona non grata* who has renounced 'dilemmas' and 'art' for the sake of 'dogmas' and 'propaganda'.[25]

Michael Bristol writes, 'The institutions of theatre affect forms of artistic production, of social interaction, and of the creation of meaning; by favouring certain styles of perception, representation, and understanding, institutional constraints determine how meaning will be created by the audience's experience of the text in performance.[26] Arden's dramaturgy with its collectivist and ludic (that is, non-illusionist) emphasis was clearly incompatible with the social as well as artistic complexion of the theatre where his plays were produced.' His drama required not only a new kind of audience but also a new kind of relationship with the audience. He had, from the beginning, written for a truly popular kind of theatre which serves the purpose of 'bringing men together in a kind of secular Eucharist, so that they can leave the building feeling that they are a society, not just a collection of odds and sods who have been coincidentally killing time for a couple of hours on a wet evening'.[27] Even his early plays revealed a powerful impulse to open out the conventional stage-space in order to connect it with the auditorium in a more fluid, more actively collaborative and dialogical, and therefore socially more meaningful, relationship. He tried to achieve this dramaturgically, by using conventions and devices (such as his favourite method of casting the spectators into the play – see for example, *The Waters of Babylon*, III; *The Happy Haven*, II.i; *The Island of the Mighty*, I.x) which are essentially those of the open, comic (historically plebeian) dramaturgy and stage, and are clearly in contradiction with the illusionism of the picture-frame stage. His preferences – as expressed in the prefatory notes and stage-directions in his plays – show a growth from what Brecht called the 'partial illusion' of the early plays to the complete non-illusionist or emblematic scenography of the late plays.[28] Throughout his career, he has sought to emancipate the scenography from proscenium restriction and to recover something of the openness and versatility of traditional popular staging.

Arden was aware that radical alterations in the make-up and function of the existing theatre were desirable but not immediately possible. With time, he came to recognise that such transformations would require changes in some fundamental economic and political relationships within the theatre as a public institution as well as in society at large. He and D'Arcy grew increasingly conscious of, and uneasy about, this tie-up between established cultural forms and institutions and political power. They also grew progressively more alert to the lack of freedom and unacceptable working conditions that such a system produced for the artist, particularly the playwright. It was against this state of affairs that they went on strike in 1972, withdrawing their labour from the professional metropolitan theatre.

They are still on strike.

Notes

1. Such an endeavour became necessary because the dominant forms of middle-class drama – with their preoccupation with the subjective–introspective standpoint of the individual (as reflected in a structural preponderance of the character, rather than the event), and their illusionist aesthetics (as evidenced in an often literal-minded insistence on the verisimilarity of speech, behaviour, and incidents) – have severely reduced the role and status of the theatre, both as an art form and as a social institution.

2. John Russell Taylor was the first to argue that Arden 'permits himself, in his treatment of the characters and situation, to be less influenced by moral preconception than any other writer in the British theatre today', and that his 'attitude to his creation is quite uncommitted'. See his *Anger and After* (Harmondsworth: Penguin, 1963) p. 84.

3. 'Telling a True Tale'. In Charles Marowitz *et al.* (eds) *The Encore Reader* (London: Methuen, 1965) p. 125. By building upon the old and forgotten traditions of plebeian culture, by trying to forge an indissoluble union of the issues presented and *how* they were presented, Arden was radically re-organising the dramaturgic structure of feeling. His choice, which was against the grain of the established middle-class theatre, signified a recognition (in strict congruence with modern criticism) that form is the key to meaning in culture.

4. *Ibid.*, p. 128.

5. Interview in *Plays and Players* 10 (1963) pp. 16–18.

6. Raymond Williams, *Resources of Hope* (London: Verso, 1989) p. 80.

7. In his preface to the play, Arden himself hints at this connection between Musgrave and the bourgeois heritage. The crucial significance of this connection is that, within a play modelled on the celebratory form of the Mummers' Play, it demonstrates how the popular cultural forms and traditions are, in Forsas-Scott's words, 'being quenched by a new order which turns the theatre into a place for arid speech-making and sermonising' (Helena Forsas-Scott, 'Life and Love and Serjeant Musgrave: An Approach to Arden's Plays', *Modern Drama* 26 [March 1983], p. 7). Confrontation between these two major socio-historical traditions (the plebeian, essentially carnivalesque tradition and the bourgeois puritanical one) is a recurrent motif of Arden's drama, and finds its most direct expression in his 1979 radio play *Pearl* (London: Methuen, 1979).

8. Peter Szondi, *Theory of the Modern Drama*, trans. Michael Hays (Minneapolis: University of Minnesota Press, 1987) p. 53.

9. It was out of this tradition that the styles of psychological Expressionism and, more recently, the Absurd arose. In these dramas the inarticulateness and incommunicability of human experience, as well as the impossibility of any meaningful relationship between people, are elevated to the level of a universal, metaphysical 'truth', and pauses and silences, rather than speech, are perceived to be more meaningful. This notion of the failure of communication between human beings, this haunting and agonising feeling of the utter inadequacy of speech and relationships, seems to be related to the general crisis and breakdown in the culture of individualism and liberalism in the twentieth century. That is perhaps why it is a common motif of a good deal of contemporary bourgeois literature.

10. For a fuller discussion of this aspect of Arden's dramaturgy, see my 'Society and History in Arden's Dramaturgy: The Supra-Individual Emphasis of His Agents', published in the May 1990 issue of *Theatre Journal*.

11. It is significant that the play begins with an agreement between Labour and Conservative factions on the choice of Feng as the new police chief, a gesture signifying their common interest in 'law and order', and ends with their common rejection of Butterthwaite and reconciliation with each other, which is highlighted in the metaphor of 'white-wash'. Blomax's direct narration in the last scene underscores this: 'You'll observe the general sense of bygones be bygones.' The whole trajectory in between confirms the basic unity of the two political parties, despite bitter electoral rivalries. The Epilogue, sung by 'all' who remain after Butterthwaite and his plebeian supporters have been forcibly removed from the stage, translates this unity into a striking audio-visual image.

12. This conflict between a reigning hegemony, asserting and reproducing itself in different ways, and the plebeian masses, who continually challenge and oppose it in a myriad ingenuous ways, is a persistent theme of Arden's drama. However, as already noted, what is new here is the expressly subversive class-bias.

13. Untitled piece in *Essays and Studies* (London: John Murray, 1977) p. 86.

14. In his preface to the play, Arden tells us that it was only after he had become sufficiently interested in the historical implications – in fact, in the 'apparent complete failure' – of the Charter and the problematic nature of its implications in liberal mythology that he could make sense of this theme.

15. For a detailed analysis of the trilogy, see my 'The Polarised Universe of *The Island of the Mighty*: the Dramaturgy of Arden and D'Arcy', *NTQ*-5 (February 1986) pp. 38–53.

16. See *Brecht on Theatre*, trans. John Willet (New York: Hill and Wang, 1964) p. 108.

17. *To Present the Pretence*, (London: Methuen, 1977) p. 83.

18. Cf. Catherine Itzin, *Stages in the Revolution* (London: Methuen, 1982) pp. 20–23.

19. Arden, *To Present the Pretence* (London: Methuen, 1977) p. 83.
20. Arden returns to this theme in his radio play *Pearl* (op. cit.), and again in his novel *Silence Among Weapons* (London: Methuen, 1982).
21. Arden's Preface to *Two Autobiographical Plays* (London: Methuen, 1971) p. 14.
22. Quoted by Ronald Hayman in radio talk titled 'The Conversion of John Arden', BBC Radio 3, 25 August 1980.
23. Albert Hunt, *Arden* (op. cit.) pp. 153 and 156.
24. Arden and D'Arcy, *To Present the Pretence* (op. cit.) pp. 157–58.
25. Interestingly, and quite logically, some liberal critics turned quite illiberal when faced with Arden's later activism and more direct involvement in political and communal forms of 'Alternative' theatre. Already, in 1969, Simon Trussler had lamented Arden's increasing entanglement in the more radical, more openly political forms of theatre, and praised, by contrast, the greater vitality and 'insidiousness of Arden's approach' in his earlier plays which 'defined not dogmas but dilemmas' ('Political Progress of a Paralysed Liberal: The Community Dramas of John Arden', *The Drama Review* 13 (1968–69) pp. 181–91.) In 1980, Ronald Hayman accused Arden of renouncing 'art and art values' in favour of 'community', declaring that 'Arden hasn't given up writing plays, he's just given up writing good ones.' ('The Conversion of John Arden', op. cit.) It is often whispered (and not always so discreetly) that this 'contamination' of his writing is the result of his collaboration with an intransigent Irish revolutionary, Margaretta D'Arcy. It is a measure of this prejudice that although Arden and D'Arcy are still writing plays of great artistic and cognitive merit, as evidenced in their recent nine-part radio series on early Christianity, *Whose is the Kingdom?* (London: Methuen, 1988), they are no longer written about except in occasional newspaper reviews.
26. Michael D. Bristol, *Carnival and Theatre* (London: Methuen, 1985) p. 3.
27. 'Correspondence', *Encore* 20 (May–June 1959) p. 42.
28. *Brecht on Theatre* (op. cit.) p. 219. The early dramaturgic preference for 'partial illusion', for keeping the property and sets to the necessary minimum and for re-shaping the stage space so as not to allow the proscenium arch to exercise an illusionistic effect is also found in *Serjeant Musgrave's Dance*, where Arden recommends stylised scenes and costumes and specifies that 'scenery must be sparing – only those pieces of architecture, furniture and properties actually used in the action need be present.' It was with *The Happy Haven*, his first play in collaboration with D'Arcy, that Arden got his first opportunity to see a play produced on a stage radically different from the conventional proscenium stage. The effect of this first experiment with the open stage can be seen clearly in the text of the play itself, where the stage is used, as Hunt points out, 'partly as a music-hall platform and partly as a lecture theatre, in which Copperthwaite demonstrates scientific experiments which are also magic conjuring tricks'. (See *Arden*, op. cit., p. 67). With its use of masks, games, songs, direct addresses, and elements of fantasy, the play endeavours to attain a form and style completely free from any illusionism.

9

Oh What a Lovely Post-modern War: Drama and the Falklands

DEREK PAGET

INTRODUCTION – THE 'DRAMA' OF THE FALKLANDS

Argentina, Argentina, what's it like to lose the war?
What's it like to lose the war?
(World Cup Football Chant 1982–1986. Tune: 'Bread of Heaven')

In 1982, if the British right is to be believed, the Lion roared once more over an obscure group of islands usually described as 'windswept', 'barren', and 'inhabited mainly by sheep'. The Falklands became the site of the war which put the 'great' back in 'Great Britain', and the 'united' back in 'United Kingdom'. That unfailing barometer of ultra-right-wing sentiment, the British Football Fan Abroad, was still celebrating this notion even when the England team was being defeated by Argentina (through a typically-dago dirty trick) in the World Cup of 1986. The so-called 'Falklands Factor' not only put Margaret Thatcher back in Downing Street the following year (and again in 1987), it also made the post-Falklands Conservative Party a very different animal from the pre-Falklands version. The war gave the party, if not 007's licence to kill, a licence to rule apparently indefinitely.

British culture, too, has been inflected post-1982 with the very Falklands Factor that it was partly complicit in creating; the Falklands Image-War was also a site of conflict in which an 'Old Britain' was resurrected and fused into a 'New Britain'. Through a ramshackle amalgam of nationalist rhetoric past and present, the New British ideology has by now inscribed itself into the lives of a whole generation. They have grown up with a history increasingly made up of 'Heritage', with lectures about a British 'economic revival',

154

and with constant invitations into the booby-trapped promise of the 'enterprise culture'. The Falklands Factor helped Thatcherism yomp its way into a credibility which can, and must, be opposed – for Thatcher's Britain became (to borrow from Ezra Pound) 'a botched civilisation . . . gone in the teeth'. Unfortunately this particular canine can still, as the music-hall joke has it, give you a very nasty suck.

The Falklands war seemed to come from nowhere both literally and metaphorically. First there was a small item of news buried towards the back of the Sunday papers in mid-March (when Argentinian scrap-metal dealers 'invaded' the deserted South Georgia); then the invasion of the rather less deserted Falklands themselves suddenly erupted into the news on 2 April 1982. In a Commons emergency session the following day, all the politicians who rose to speak seemed bent on outdoing each other in terms of a bellicose and xenophobic rhetoric. The morning's *Times* set the tone in a leader, referring to 'as perfect an example of unprovoked aggression and military expansion as the world has had to witness since the end of Adolf Hitler'; speakers from all sides of the House more than matched this appeal to historic democratic rectitude.

Labour Party leader Michael Foot told the government that they would have to 'prove by deeds – they will never be able to do it by words – that they are not responsible for the betrayal [of the Falkland Islanders]. Enoch Powell reminded Thatcher of her famous sobriquet, the 'Iron Lady'. 'In the next week or two,' he intoned, 'this House, the nation and the Right Honourable Lady herself will learn of what metal she is made.' In a moment now mythologised to the point of apotheosis, Thatcher herself is said to have nodded a grim but vigorous assent to this proposition. As Anthony Barnett has said, speakers from all sides of the House that day 'delivered the country into her hands'. This uncommon Commons consensus 'nationalised Thatcher's style of leadership' and , as a result, 'an Iron Britannia' was born.[1]

Few MPs were able to refuse the siren call to war: to be precise, thirty-three of them resisted the pressure of historical necessity and voted a month and a half after the crisis had begun against the use of force (20 May 1982). At the time, it was very difficult for anyone, in or out of Parliament, to marshal a coherent argument *against* Argentine 'aggression', still less to co-ordinate any sort of collective opposition to the wounded nationalism which flourished at that time. Tapping into a rich vein of knee-jerk jingoism, Thatcher's political project really took off at this point, perhaps even to her own surprise. By the time the Franks Report presented the results of its investigation into the causes of the war in January 1983, all evidence of government mismanagement and complacency had been elided into a triumphalism which reeked of Establishment self-congratulation.

In an episode of the 1988 Helena Kennedy–Peter Flannery TV series *Blind Justice*, a character described how it feels when a hegemony really exerts its power. 'There are moments,' he said,

> when you can actually *feel* the Monster roll its muscles under-neath your feet. And suddenly you've been moved. You're not standing where you thought you were.   (26 October 1988)

The feeling of 'not standing where you thought you were' was the essence of the Falklands feeling for many people on the left. Just like the Opposition in Parliament, opposition in general was 'bounced' by the sheer dramatic power of the Falklands as Event. The mediation of the war caused a huge simplification of the actual issues which was of ultimate benefit only to the collective that wields the real power in the UK. It was this social animal whose muscles we all felt move, and the media were part of the efficient articulation of the monster's anatomy.

It is still astonishingly difficult to argue against the myth which began to be constructed in 1982, and which has burgeoned in spite (because?) of the manifest mendacity of the government's account of the war. Despite the brave and painstaking attempts of people like Tam Dalyell and Clive Ponting, all that has been achieved is the raising of an element of *doubt* about some of the government's actions during the Falklands/Malvinas war. This has done very little to shake the notion created during the conflict that Thatcher is a Great War Leader. Cast at the time as a mixture of Boadicea and Churchill, it is difficult to believe that many people who accepted the casting then have changed their minds subsequently as a result of any 'true facts' revelations.

Thus it does not matter in the end how much one 'knows' about, say, the sinking of the *General Belgrano* on 2 May 1982 and its relation to the Peruvian peace proposals, since most attempts to argue the case against the Falklands war tend to founder against the very real strength of the constructed mythology of 'standing up to dictatorships', 'protecting the democratic rights of the islanders', and 'resisting unprovoked aggression'. The generalised verdict now is that the UK should be proud of its achievements in 1982. Validated during those months in 1982 was a self-image of 'Britishness' many of us had believed extinguished in the post-imperial twilight:

> Its resurrection ought to be a cause for concern for, behind the presumption that a British voice must speak out against violations of humanity elsewhere (which is welcome), lies the assertion that the Anglo-Saxon accent can and should arbitrate across all frontiers . . . its core is a presumption of national superiority.
>
> (Barnett, p. 33)

During the 1980s, this superior Anglo-Saxon accent sermonised from Gdansk about free trade unions, while at Cheltenham similar unions were in manifest chains. It pontificated upon human rights in the USSR, while passing Clause 28. The very advertisement which tried to persuade us to buy shares in the privatised British Steel in 1988 proclaimed, *'British Steel – British Strength'*. Such political legerdemain, such an hubristic advertising campaign, would have been unthinkable pre-Falklands. Almost inevitably, the domino-collapse of monolithic state Communism in Eastern Europe presented the same voice with a golden opportunity to celebrate 'the triumph of capitalism'. Street demonstrations were, of course, fine in Eastern Europe; when they were directed against the iniquitous poll tax in the UK in 1990, they quickly became 'riot and affray'. In such ways as these did Margaret Thatcher continue to capitalise on the first real enterprise of her 'enterprise culture'.

THE POST-MODERN WAR

> I remember writing my last letter home to my parents. It was a bit like one of those 1940s Richard Todd movies . . .
>
> (Robert Lawrence)[2]

The Falklands/Malvinas war which so strengthened Thatcher's hand was a 'post-modern' conflict, in which the image *preceded* the facts. The features of the post-modern war as exemplified by extant examples (Falklands '82, Grenada '83, Panama '89) are: they take

place in countries 'remote' from home both literally and metaphorically; they last a very short time and end in 'victory'; they
involve opposition to political systems readily constructed as unacceptable by home public opinion (the Argentinian Junta, the Gre-
nadan Marxists, the Panamanian 'drug baron' Noriega); they are
unlikely to provoke much opposition from the rest of the world;
they depend upon sophisticated intelligence and surveillance technology (such as spy satellite systems) which gives one side massive
advantages; they provide opportunities to 'road test' new weapons
technology (like infra-red rifle night-sights, the infamous Exocet,
and the Stealth fighter); and finally, their loss of life is, relatively-
speaking, small (and sustainable as far as home public opinion is
concerned).

But, most important of all for image management, post-modern
wars are both *intertextual* with, and *antithetical* to, other conflicts.
Cultural mediation of the Falklands 'drama' caused facts about the
war to be read through an opaque medium of Britishness originally validated at the Saturday emergency debate in Parliament,
but actually constructed in the films to which *Tumbledown* hero
Robert Lawrence draws attention. These films might include *The
Dam Busters* (1954) and *Yangtze Incident* (1957), both Richard Todd
epics, but Lawrence was doubtless thinking too of films like *In
Which We Serve* (1942) and *The Way to the Stars* (1945). The images
mobilised for the post-modern war are constructed mainly from
the collective cultural memory of an apparently unproblematical
and heroically 'successful' conflict (the Second World War), but
they must also be seen ultimately in relation to 'unsuccessful'
conflicts (Suez/Cyprus/Northern Ireland for the UK, Vietnam/El
Salvador/Nicaragua for the US).

The Times leader already quoted demonstrates how, from a very
early stage, the Falklands war was referred to quite routinely as the
Hitler war. By making Falklands accounts intertextual with cultural
myths associated with this war, a mass of quite readily-accepted
learned responses was made available. Intertextuality brought
about the Harrier's construction as the Spitfire of the day, although
it was the *weapon* (the Sidewinder missile) and not the aeroplane
which gave British pilots such an edge in combat over the Argentinian Mirages and Skyhawks. It enabled the wartime Bordeaux raid
(cf. the film *Cockleshell Heroes* – 1955) to be re-celebrated by the
Marines on Pebble Island, and the 'gallant defeat' of Arnhem to be
re-fought as victory by the Paras at Goose Green. It enabled the

government to field Ian MacDonald as their MoD spokesman giving nightly briefings to the media. His portentous manner and delivery were pure 1940s BBC; he was a 'Voice of Authority' who could be read as calm, reassuring and truthful.

There was a readily-accepted logic in Margaret Thatcher addressing the nation in Churchillian tones on 25 April, following the re-capture of South Georgia. Very few people needed to enquire at the time *why* they should be expected to 'Rejoice!' in this news; Leith and Grytviken were intertextual with Rome, or Paris, or any European city released from the heel of the Nazi jackboot. No matter that these were empty and rusting former whaling stations (which had never ever sustained any sort of permanent community) they were places to be 'liberated' for as long as it mattered – which was probably about the fifteen seconds it took to take in the news and *not* be astonished by the cheek of its manner of announcement. The gap between the signifier and the signified was successfully elided in the mediation, which *assumed* its right to be taken seriously.

The post-modern war is an intertextual war, then, with an accelerated image construction which matches the speed of the conflict. There is little time in which to take bearings on any of the real issues at stake, partly because everything happens so quickly. The post-modern war has the hallmarks of that most efficient of all modern communicators, the television advertisement. It is quick, superficially well-organised, difficult to ignore, and very expensive; it gets its points over without digression, and hits at a subliminal level which defeats rationality. Even if you reject it, you cannot ignore it; like the advertisement, the post-modern war is difficult to oppose, because opposition demands the kind of measured refutation so easily constructed as dull in comparison with its quick neatness, its 'commonsense' obviousness.

The success of the Falklands war made it self-validating, and the Falklanders became a convenient *synecdoche* for New Britishness. As a Part signifying the greater nationalistic Whole, the islands contrast vividly with another territory where a group of people also 'wish to remain British' – Northern Ireland. Here, the war stands in antithetical relationship to the post-modern war in almost every respect: unsuccessful, costly, apparently interminable, and difficult to 'sell' to the home public. Britishness, problematical in the context of Northern Ireland, was a simpler issue in the Falklands, which also exorcised the war which had haunted the

British establishment for nearly thirty years – the 1956 Suez *débâcle*. Post-modern wars, then, are always 'successful', especially in massaging the damaged egos of Establishments.

The post-modern war is also quickly forgotten in any detailed sense once its talismanic usefulness has been established. Interest in the Falklands 'crisis' has vanished, to be replaced by the legend/story/myth which subsequently sustained the Conservative Party in power. This legend could have been so different. If Argentine ordnance had been fused correctly, for example, other capital ships might have been sunk, many more lives lost. But how often does one read of such things? Brilliantly improvised the task force arrangements may have been, but they are not usually presented as 'lucky' in their outcome. Like Waterloo, a 'damn close-run thing' has been converted into a victory to be celebrated, in spite of the *Sheffield*, the *Belgrano*, the *Ardent*, and Bluff Cove.

The successful *Britishness* of the Falklands campaign has been the validated image, with the swaggering success of its heroically 'yomping' paratroops, the 'daring dawn raids' of its Royal Marines, and the Battle of Britain 'Few' reincarnated in its Harrier pilots. Away from the field, the service chiefs and the politicians of the War Cabinet have also been able to bask in positive images, no one more so than Thatcher herself. A just and successful war has been relatively easily established in the public mind as historical fact, and this carrying of the Image-War has secured more difficult political matters. By 3 July 1982, not three weeks after the conflict had ended, Margaret Thatcher was addressing a Conservative Party rally and claiming:

> Britain has found herself again in the South Atlantic and will not look back from the victory she has won.   (Barnett, p. 153)

The Falklands 'drama' created at the time by representations of the war has tended to swamp subsequent Falklands dramas, making it particularly difficult to create any space from which to *oppose* the Myth of Victory.

FALKLANDS DRAMAS – GETTING PAST THE CENSOR

> In the end, censorship relates more to the likely *impact* of a piece, in the public domain, than to its style.   (Albert Hunt)[3]

By now there is a considerable amount of cultural production on the Falklands available for discussion. There have been various 'straight documentary' accounts on television (often efforts to make plain the mind-wrenching 'reality' of modern warfare); exhibitions of paintings, drawings and photographs; books and other publications of various kinds. Then there has been the drama – stage plays, TV plays, and films about the war. Of all these, only the television plays have been controversial, precisely because of the means of their insertion into 'the public domain'.

There were no *films* about the Falklands before 1988; film finance hinges on the one-off creative 'package', and depends primarily on the American domestic market. Initially conceived as a film project, Charles Wood's tele-play *Tumbledown* failed because the Americans 'were not interested unless we came up with an overtly anti-war film or a Rambo-style kick-the-spics-for-a-shit film.'[4] No American distribution, no film – such is the (non-aesthetic) world of film economics. John Ellis has noted that the 'pressures of profitability' are different for TV and film, and that this impacts upon their 'forms of decision-making and planning'.[5] These 'pressures' partly account for the delay, and out of three films directly about the Falklands, two were funded through a kind of alternative film finance mechanism (combinations of the BFI and Channel 4).[6]

Each film has a relation to precise actualities, but this has not been *controversial* in the way it has been in television. If a time-lag was less evident with stage and TV plays, closeness to the event hardly made things easier. A more complex relationship with Falklands actuality (normally the preserve of the 'documentary') contributed to processes of covert and overt censorship in which the management of the Falklands myth can be clearly discerned. While the extent of the 'documentariness' of individual works can always be debated, it is not their 'accuracy', but their existence at all which is really significant. 'Documentary drama' represents a *problematic*, and not a tightly definable form; attempts at definition and description do not facilitate greater clarity, they simply continue to mark a site of conflict between discourses of 'factuality' and 'fictionality'. When fact and fiction do collide, there is a potentially turbulent moment which must be policed very carefully by the most trusted agents of the hegemony, and these moments tend to occur more often in television.[7] With Charles Wood's *Tumbledown* and Ian Curteis's *The Falklands Play*, there was a furore on the scale of *Death of a Princess* (1980) and *Who Bombed Birming-ham?* (1990).

It is perhaps significant, given later institutional pussy-footing, that there were plays on the Falklands as early as 1983. Don Shaw's *The Falklands Factor* was broadcast by the BBC on 26 April 1983, in other words even *before* the June General Election (it was, of course, the closeness of the 1987 election which was the BBC's ostensible reason for the postponement of *Tumbledown*). Based on Samuel Johnson's suddenly-apt eighteenth-century pamphlet 'Thoughts On The Late Transactions Respecting Falkland's Is-lands', this play gave an early warning of institutional paranoia. Basically a historical piece on Johnson's reaction to another Argen-tinian 'takeover' of the islands in 1770, the closing sequence mon-taged then-and-now cunningly. Donald Pleasance (as Johnson) spoke the latter's words in direct address close-up, while images from the very latest 'transaction' on the islands were superim-posed. The telling juxtaposition accused Thatcher very clearly as newsreel film of her emerging from 10 Downing Street accompanied these words:

> As war is the extremity of evil, it is surely the duty of those whose station entrusts them with the care of nations to avert it.

The then Director of Programmes, Brian Wenham, decided to cut this whole final sequence after the press showing. It was, he judged, likely to be far too 'distressing' for those whose loss was so recent.

The BBC was not alone in censoring under the guise of making 'compassionate' interventions; in May 1982 an episode of Central TV's historical series *I Remember Nelson* was withdrawn at the last moment, following news of the sinking of the *Sheffield*. The epi-sode in question dramatised the Battle of Trafalgar. It is through such decisions as these that the true nature of broadcast televi-sion's institutional paternalism expresses itself. The extent to which the wrong kind of intertextuality must be suppressed is also revealing (hard to use Nelsonian 'hearts of oak' rhetoric in the face of random strokes of modern technology).

The Falklands Factor was therefore transmitted as a simple cos-tume drama with historical connections if-you-cared-to-make-them. As a result of the institutional meddling, Shaw asked (un-successfully) for his name to be removed from the credits. If nothing else, the Catch-22 parameters were clearly established – you could talk about the Falklands war on television provided you kept your distance. The eighteenth century represented the right kind of distance; relevant, but comfortably remote. Nancy Banks-Smith remarked in The *Guardian* that the production team ought to have taken the act of censorship 'as a compliment, a proof of power'. 'Somebody' she went on to say,' is running scared' (27 April 1983). Intertextuality was only permissible, it seemed, with a Government Health Warning.

Maggie Wadey's *The Waiting War* was also transmitted in 1983 (6 July). Partly researched amongst the 'Navy Wives' of South Coast communities, the hour-long play followed three (fictionalised) *HMS Sheffield* wives through the evening on which the news of the destroyer's sinking broke. *The Waiting War* was a piece of standard tele-naturalism authorised by a 'True Story' rubric, and underwritten by a readily-identifiable (and easily-playable) dramatic tension – which of the wives would get the *really* bad news before the hour was up? In its way, this kind of dramatic project is not unlike the tele-journalism which seeks to be 'really there' at moments of acute crisis. As a microphone is thrust under the nose, a camera into the face, of the recently-bereaved, or the survivors of a disaster, TV makes a classic claim for its reason-to-be.

Capitalising (the word is deliberately chosen) on the individualistic desire to know more about psychological states without having to live through them may be worthy but it is, of course, totally uncontroversial – the broadcasting institution is rarely embarrassed by such things. The 'human drama' of *The Waiting War* formed a focus which enabled politics to be eschewed 'naturally'. This is not to say that the story was not very much worth the telling, groups such as service wives tend, after all, to be marginalised unless they are needed for public Services of Thanksgiving.[8] It is necessary, however, to point up the ways in which naturalism/ social realism of this type tends to serve the hegemony whatever its creators' intentions may be. Wadey's drama depended quite simply on a willingness to empathise with the wives' experience; no understanding of the context of the Falklands war was required beyond a very generalised one. It is really not very difficult to give assent to this kind of project.

THERE'LL ALWAYS BE AN IAN

I am not in the business of throwing together instant drama, just pour on water and stir.   (Ian Curteis)[9]

My next example, Ian Curteis's *The Falklands Play*, has never been screened *at all*, but certainly raised the temperature of the debate. Planning it as early as October 1982, Curteis hoped to repeat the success of his earlier tele-plays *Churchill and the Generals* and *Suez 1956* (both 1979). Although his reputation had been made by such transmutations of 'history' into 'drama', he appears, from his own published comments, to be sensitive about the whole concept of dramatising events from the recent past. He seems especially defensive about the accusation that he is a mere compiler of the despised 'drama-documentary', and not a 'real' writer:

> for a play one needs above all things to get to the human side of things. The historical playwright is not trying to put over the facts in an objective, drama-documentary sort of way, but to get into the characters' heads and hearts and emotions, to show them as real, all-round, vulnerable human beings, acting sometimes instinctively, sometimes illogically, responding to the strange, volatile inner music of real human relations. (p. 13)

The sweep of this is quite remarkable, suggesting that a kind of essential history (existing way above the level of mere factuality) is conveyed mystically by the writer's innate 'feel' for that 'inner music'.

Like getting a sight of the Emperor's New Clothes, you will, of course, recognise this mysterious tune when you hear it; it suffuses the following sequence, designed to show what a truly emotional heart beats beneath the metallic surface of the Iron Lady:

> [JOHN] NOTT (quietly): The *Sheffield*'s been hit. We think by an Exocet. There may be a lot of casualties.
>
> *The PM says nothing. Her hands clench and unclench, she arches her head back and the tears silently flood down her face.* (p. 178)

Thus ends sequence 171, montaged between two 'official' sequences (170 in the Cabinet Room, 172 in the House of Commons). In a similar vein, dialogue between Sir Nicholas Henderson and Sir

Anthony Parsons has them meditating in mid-Atlantic upon St Margaret of Finchley:

PARSONS: She's quite the most wonderful and quite the most impossible human being I've ever met. While she was talking, I kept on remembering 'Little man, little man, *must* is not a word to use to Princes'.

HENDERSON: You know, she's written scores of letters in her own hand, to the families of every single serviceman killed. She'll go on doing that as long as the fighting lasts.   (p. 182)

Thatcher as Henry V is a casting not only accepted by her English liegemen, apparently: it turns out that the *Argentinians* accept it too. Sequence 99 has their Foreign Minister (Costa-Mendez) saying,

She *knows* what the British people think and feel, and by instinct gives to it a voice – sometimes against all logic. It is a phenomenon more easy to recognise in history than when it is happening. And it is a woman's thing. *That* is the root of her battle spirit – not out of her, but out of that instinct.   (p. 126)

The apotheosis of Thatcher-as-individual legitimates her political handling of events, although these are irrevocably part of a collective experience. But Curteis is not interested in a differentiated history; from him the Great Leader is an authentic figure, and he seems to see his job as one of *iconisation* (rather like the Elizabethan dramatists he so admires).

He partly acknowledges this when he talks quite openly of his play dealing with 'some of the issues, and principles I care about most strongly' (p. 12). In the play, however, he avoids any suggestion of direct congruence between his own views and those of his dramatised Leader, by positioning himself instead outside the text as 'omniscient author'. (Part of his omniscience is constructed from the very facts he affects to despise – see p. 16, for example, where he talks of the 'simply colossal amount of raw material' he had to 'master'.) The congruence of their views can, however, be easily demonstrated through the following quotations: (a) is Curteis himself (from his Introduction); (b) is the 'PM', his 'dramatic' creation; and (c) is the real Margaret Thatcher:

(a) This was not shallow jingoism, but the dramatic rising to the surface once more of values and issues that we on these islands have cared about most profoundly down the centuries, and on which our civilised freedom rests.   (Curteis, p. 15)

(b) If we are wrong to fight now, then we were wrong to fight Hitler, we were wrong to fight the Kaiser, we were wrong to fight Napoleon, we were wrong to fight Philip of Spain – wrong to do anything but throw in the towel and crumple before the first brute force to come along, and abandon all the fine and good and splendid things Britain has given the world down the centuries, for a bleak, totalitarian desert!

(Curteis, p. 185)

(c) The lesson of the Falklands is that Britain has not changed and that this nation still has those sterling qualities which shine through our history. This generation can match their fathers and grandfathers in ability, in courage, and in resolution. We have not changed. When the damands of war and the dangers to our own people call us to arms – then we British are as we have always been – competent, courageous and resolute.   (Barnett, p. 150)

It is not easy to distinguish between any of these speeches at the level of either their politics or their clarion call to a unified 'history'.

Curteis's view of a 'fine and good and splendid' Britain is accompanied by a correspondingly condescending view of all things Argentinian. Montage sequence 8 'scene sets' Argentina for *The Falklands Play*:

Blare of tin trumpets, clatter of hooves, and the presidential procession swings into view in the crowded streets of Buenos Aires. Weedy cavalry in bright Ruritanian uniforms ride along side. It is indeed close to Comic Opera Land. The crowds cheer and throw streamers.   (p. 60)

This blend of patronage ('Comic Opera') and contempt ('weedy calvary') seems close to the kind of haughty view of Johnny Foreigner as satirised in Steven Berkoff's 1986 stage play *Sink the Belgrano!*:

Oh you most brave and valiant Englishmen
Who never shall, no never bear the yoke

Of shame or curdled pride beneath the boot
Of some o'erweening greasy foreign bloke.[10]

Unfortunately, this very view seems to pass for considered foreign policy in those circles which regard British superiority as unchallengeable.

In some ways, it is a matter for celebration that such a nakedly-triumphant version of the Falklands war should not have been transmitted on television; in another sense it is to be regretted. Transmission might have had the function of flushing out the right, and it might have been possible to expose the nature of the dominant ideology through such a pernicious 'faction'. The eventual justification for non-transmission (that *The Falklands Play* is quite simply inept, a bad play) is somewhat thin, as Curteis rightly claims. After all, it is not as if the BBC does not routinely transmit bad plays. Perhaps his play could be better described as withdrawn because *too obviously* intertextual, rather than bad.

By suppressing this play, the BBC fulfilled its institutional role as cultural watchdog. It recognised that *The Falklands Play* was 'out of synch' with the times. The real problem with the play was that it is a cultural dinosaur, its huge body surmounted by a small head with a tiny brain. The portentous body is pure 'Heritage Britain' (like the war movies which pretend that the USA and the USSR had nothing to do with Germany's defeat in the Second World War). The tiny brain cannot comprehend that the cultural environment which once permitted it to flourish no longer exists. The post-modern war cannot be acculturated through such an *old-fashioned* form. *The Falklands Play* was sacrificed for the prize of greater general credibility. Like the MoD functionary who told a journalist during the crisis that he was there 'to do a 1940 propaganda job', *The Falklands Play* could not be heard because it would give the game away.[11] Ian MacDonald just about remained credible, but The Falklands Play was obsolete – an embarrassment.

The new role of cultural production, of course, was to mediate *doubt* – just enough to defuse real opposition, just enough to preserve a creaking consensus (it does not, in the end, matter how creaking, so long as it could be *presented* as consensus). The permitted parameters of doubt are marked by Charles Wood's *Tumbledown*. Curteis's peeved pursuit of the BBC's famed 'Militant Tendency' ('left-wing agitators' like Bill Cotton and Brian Wenham) had the side-effect of loading *Tumbledown* with unintended political significance. The whole furore ironically indicated just how thin the institutional cement securing our cultural understanding of events like the Falklands war really is.

'TUMBLEDOWN' – LOOKING FOR NEW ENGLAND?

| [Surgeon]: | Sorry, old man, but I had to take the other leg off below the knee. I couldn't save it. You're really lucky to be in the world still. |
| [Douglas Bader]: | That's all right, sir . . . I'll get some longer legs. I always wanted to be taller. |

(see Paul Brickhill, *Reach for the Sky*,
Odhams Press: 1955, p. 55)

YOUNG DOCTOR:	You'll never walk – properly that is. You took your last real walk on the Falklands, Robert.
ROBERT:	That's what [the surgeon] said. Piss off!
YOUNG DOCTOR:	You'll have to learn to be nicer to doctors and nurses. You're going to see a lot of them.
ROBERT:	I said, piss off. (Wood, p. 45)

Originally inspired by a *Guardian* article in 1984, *Tumbledown* was actually ready for transmission by 1986, but was delayed until 1988 because, as Charles Wood says, it became 'the film the BBC put on instead of *The Falklands Play*' (p. ix). Although *Tumbledown* was conceived as, broadly speaking, *anti-war*, it is only *political* to a very limited extent. Looked at 'cold', as the author himself remarks,

> there is nothing new in *Tumbledown* . . . The central character is a soldier and hero of Empire – just when you thought it was safe to come out.   (p. xii)

Robert Lawrence concurs with this view, saying that,

> it was simply about soldiers and young men; the reasons why young men join armies and want to go to war, and the reality of the possible consequences of their ambitions.

(Lawrence, p. 165)

It was Ian Curteis who made *Tumbledown* politically 'hot'; he caused it to be refracted through the distorting lens of his own bitter disappointment, and his own right-wing views.

Whereas Curteis only got public-figure 'authorised versions' from all the people he talked to (for all his introductory marvellings at the accessibility of important people in the UK), Wood seems to have been more painstaking (and more focused) in his effort to understand his central character. Lawrence has all the unpleasant traits of his class – at times he seems to be quintessential 'Sloane Ranger', a *louche* stormtrooper in Thatcher's New Enterprise Army. But after his injury he rejects the role of genteel disablement, and vociferously demands individual rights occluded by post-war triumphalism (because 'inappropriate' to it). He is a palpable Edward Bond-style Ghost, returning to haunt his progenitor with elements of her very own individualistic philosophy. To that extent he represents, in *Tumbledown*, a critique of Thatcherism (if Thatcherism is understood as a radical transformation of old-fashioned Conservatism).

For Douglas Bader, the Second World War fighter 'ace' with the artificial legs, substitute Robert Lawrence, the Falklands war 'hero' with half his brain blown away; but for Bader's 'Old Britishness', read Lawrence's 'New Britishness'. *Tumbledown* offers the trope of the Wounded Hero re-written for our times. Lawrence's post-imperial significance (and his post-modern strength as a character in a play) is that his 'sacrifice' was *not* subsumed in Baderian stiff-upper-lip heroics; on the contrary, he caused a radical re-reading of Old Britishness by screaming and shouting his refusal of the old role. Behind the various objections to *Tumbledown* lurked dislike of *any* kind of opposition from within the Establishment itself. The post-modern hero disrupted the upper-class spectacle; this Falklands Actor would not stick to the script, and threatened to upstage the triumphalists.

The actual limits of any apparent extension of permitted attitudes in a society can become clear in cultural production. It is perfectly possible that *Tumbledown* would have caused relatively little difficulty and might have been subsumed, by the very act of broadcasting, into a 'how terrible' view of the war disabled – easily constructed through the empathy of naturalistic identification. This *Tumbledown* would have been like *The Waiting War*. Cultural production (especially on television, that most consensual of media) is very good at accommodating the apparently-unaccommodatable. Such a Bader-figure is, of course, unthinkable *before* the

1980s, but *only* such a figure could be believed in the 1980s. The whole issue might have been assimilable if it had not been for Curteis's intervention; he it was who caused *Tumbledown* to be seen as an anti-Thatcher play.

The rest followed, including the famous 12-second 'compassionate' cut:

> Ext. Night. Mt Tumbledown
> PETER FYSHE *is sitting behind a rock, shivering, looking incredibly young. He hisses at* ROBERT *as he goes past*:
> PETER FYSHE: Don't go on, Robert. It's awful. Don't let them make you. Shoot anyone who tries to make you . . .
> (ROBERT *glares at* PETER FYSHE, *who shuts up.* ROBERT *and his platoon go on.*)

The high profile the tele-play acquired ensured much stronger scrutiny, much more careful smoothing-out of potential controversy (like this picture of a 'cowardly' Guards officer). The section of text was cut because Fyshe's version of the incident 'differed from that of Mr Lawrence' – well, it would, wouldn't it?

In the event, Richard Eyre's visualisation of Wood's tele-play may also have weakened it as a carrier of non-individualistic meanings. The prevailing style of tele-naturalism is disrupted in two ways in the published text: there is a complex 'flash-forward' management of time; and there is the use of 'dream images' to mediate two views of warfare. The effect is to focus attention *backwards* from the 'isn't this fun!' moment (p. 80) in which Lawrence's end was his beginning. In this moment the new disabled Lawrence was constituted out of the old scion of the Establishment – it occurred when a sniper's bullet blew off the back of his head on Mount Tumbledown. Yet the audience always already 'know' about this moment right from the beginning (see the 'then' and 'now' montage pp. 5–8). In this *discontinuous* way, War as Adventure is collapsed into War as Horror.

Tumbledown's management of time is radical in terms of 'normal' TV drama, which tends to prefer *linear* (or chronological) plot development and the logic of the flashback. If the full sequence of recurring 'dream images' had been preserved, the narrative treatment of time might have been even more striking. There are basically two images: of 'Bergen Man', and of Robert in the prow of the troopship sailing to the Falklands. They balance each other, one being 'innocent' – expressive of Lawrence's revved-up *Boy's Own* eagerness to go to war, the other being 'experienced' – expressive of a stumbling brutishness which is the reality of Man at War. The innocence and experience paradigm is emphasised further by contrasting dawn/night settings.

Eyre's precise visualisations of Wood's ideas suggest either that he lacked resources, or that he was unable to see the Wood for the trees. In the text, the images are first described thus:

Surprise Cut to:
Ext. Dawn. Prow of a ship at sea
Robert is in the prow. The drums sound harsh, metallic and warning
The first snatches of a song are heard: 'I will go, I will go/When the
fighting is over/To the land of . . .' (p. 9)

Ext. Night. Falklands
The extraordinary figure of a Scots Guardsman (BERGEN MAN) *with*
high-piled bergen and his rifle across his body, a lumbering silhouette.
(p. 42)

The Dawn image is repeated five times in the early part of the text, and three further times late on. It is a marker for the hero's 'travelling hopefully' and high-mindedly towards battle. The Night, 'Bergen Man', image has ten repeats in the latter half of the published text. Not only were these images drastically cut down, they were conflated in a way which seems to go against the grain of Wood's writing.

Neither image seems intended to be properly naturalistic; just when we may feel that the grimmer Bergen Man has taken over the symbolic role, showing that to travel hopefully is indeed preferable to Lawrence's kind of arrival, the prow image appears in counterpoint to remind us of what drives a young man into battle. If the prow is the fresh-faced and hopeful ideal, Bergen Man (with its suggestion of missing-link bestiality) is the reality of war. While it *is* Robert on the prow, the textual Bergen Man is and is not Robert. He is more the *quintessential* Scots Guardsman, the whole of which even Robert is only a part. The moment when he and Robert are one is made very clear in the text:

Int. Night. Military Hospital, Robert's room
ROBERT gets out of bed, holds on to the bed and tries to walk . . .

Ext. Night. Falklands
. . . As does BERGEN MAN.   (p. 58)

This montage was one of several crucial sequences cut from the TV production (including *both* the reprised prow images from the climactic final section).

What was also lost in production even when these images *were* used was, to coin a phrase, the 'thing-ness' of Bergen Man. In the text, it seems clear that he is a kind of de-humanised hulk, and his provenance is given in one of Robert's speeches (also cut in the television version):

> When we were packing to go to the Falklands, one thing after another, more and more to go into our packs, hilarious, on to our backs, stuffed into our packs, everything in and still more to go in, so that we were loaded like pack mules. Towering up on our backs, huge loads that exhausted you after a mile. Fall down, you couldn't get up without help. Those bloody bergens, they're still finding something else to stuff in them . . .   (p. 61)

Doubtless everyone involved in the TV production was under pressure to reduce the original 'feature film' length of Wood's script to manageable TV proportions, but what is deemed worth cutting is always revealing.

In general, the power of 'collision montage' was rejected in favour of a superficially 'cleaner' narrative drive, with minimal disruption from the non-naturalistic 'images of war' originally provided by Wood. The potential of Bergen Man was weakened further by a simple (and again naturalistic) identification of *Lawrence himself* with the shadowy figure of the script. In the TV sequences, Colin Firth (playing Lawrence) was also given the kind of halo-effect which idealised when it should have contextualised. An image which could have disrupted the naturalism of *Tumbledown* in a manner undreamed of by the likes of Ian Curteis was exchanged for a relatively-unproblematic naturalistic identification with the main character. The denial of a means for 'generalising out' from Robert's experience severely weakened *Tumbledown*, and contributed to making it controversial only up to its point of production. Subsequently the turbulence around it has been very slight indeed. It put the Falklands back on the agenda, but it was 'licensed' to do this precisely because it was not especially dangerous.

THEATRICAL FALKLANDS

THE PHILOSOPHER: The spectator isn't going to learn anything from having an incident just happen.   (Bertolt Brecht)[12]

The theatre has one ready-made technique for treating immediate
events in an overtly political way – factually-based, non-naturalistic documentary theatre in the European tradition established by the likes of Piscator and Brecht. The first production of
Theatre Workshop's *Oh What a Lovely War!* in 1963 provided a kind
of 'gate' through which this form entered British theatre, and
post-1968 it has been most evident on the 'Alternative' circuit. The
very event-specificity of the form (not to speak of its technical
complexity, collective tradition, and oppositional left-wing history)
has tended to militate against its construction as 'art' by those
empowered to make such judgements. Art, it seems, must be
'recollected in tranquillity' away from the hurly-burly of political
events, and put in the control of special individuals (on whom
special rights are conferred via copyright laws). As a result, this is a
marginalised form, and documentary plays rarely get published.
Of the four stage plays I shall discuss, the Royal Court's 1983
documentary *Falkland Sound/Voces de Malvinas* is the only one unpublished.

Documentary theatre has been recently extended to include
largely or exclusively tape-recorded material as part of the documentary base. The 'real words' of 'ordinary people' give dramatic
shape to this 'Verbatim Theatre', usually via classic 'epic theatre'
techniques of rapid transformations of time, place, and character.
The 'provisional' nature of all documentary plays makes them
vulnerable, but these recent examples have tended even more
towards the local and 'disposable' (rather than the universal and
'permanent').[13] Even when excerpts of the partially-verbatim *Falkland Sound* were televised in 1984, the context was a 'newsworthy'
local performance in Plymouth (to an audience who had themselves been caught up in the war) rather than a 'normal' transmission of a play.

Falkland Sound balanced taped material with letters from a Falk-
lands naval officer, Lt David Tinker, killed in an Exocet attack on
HMS Glamorgan. In the second half of the play (the 'Voces de
Malvinas' section), five 'voices' contextualised the single 'voice'
(Tinker's) of the first half. The play attempted to put an individual

experience in a precise historical context through its use of documentary material. Taking its cues from Tinker, the play analysed the whole conflict as (in the words of one of the second act characters) 'the blip at the end of the radar screen of Imperial history'.

The five 'voices' of the second half belonged to people involved in the war but not the fighting, who were therefore well-placed to put the sacrifice of lives so starkly portrayed in the 'Falkland Sound' section in a political and historical perspective. They were, of course, representative of a much wider constituency who provided the verbatim base. The whole play, research and all, was compiled during May–June 1983 by a small cast working with Louise Page as writer/editor. Everyone concerned,

> was surprised by the honesty with which people talked to us [in interview], not only about their opinions of the war, but also the details of their lives which lead them to hold those opinions.
> (Royal Court publicity document)

This 'surprise' at the articulateness of 'ordinary' people is something that strikes most collectors of verbatim material; as much as anything else, it perhaps demonstrates the hermetically-sealed nature of the theatre world. It is very regrettable that no verbatim play has been published, for detailed study of such texts would reveal much that is needlessly mystified about the nature of dramatic discourse.

Falkland Sound/Voces de Malvinas used a minimalist 'epic' staging technique, which gave the closing moments of the first act a studiedly Brechtian (yet very English) moment. The actor representing Tinker got up from the chair in which he had been sitting throughout the act, and moved to the back of the set. Standing against a quintessentially English country house window, and isolated by a single spot, he recited the names of those killed aboard the *Glamorgan* (including, of course, David Tinker's) in direct address. At the conclusion of this litany, the spot faded and the back-lighting from the window left only a silhouette. It was a moment when the facts alone were eloquent enough – rationality and feeling were balanced dialectically in a moment both moving *and* informative.

In the second half, actors simply addressed the audience directly from a static arc of spot-lit chairs (with the window now showing a bleak Falklands landscape). The fugue of voices was a counterpoint to the *Tumbledown*-like first half, in which the Establishment figure of David Tinker gave vent to more and more criticism of the posturing of the leaders who had sent him and thousands like him to the South Atlantic. This culminated in a remarkable letter of 28 May 1982 which began with Tinker, a serving RN officer, saying,

> I cannot think of a single war in Britain's history which has been so pointless.

Like Robert Lawrence, he had learned to refuse his alloted role in the Falklands drama, but unlike *Tumbledown*, the audience for *Falkland Sound* were given an opportunity to *situate* Tinker's growing disillusion politically.

Three other mappings of theatrical Falklands are to be found in Tony Marchant's 1983 *Welcome Home*, Nick Perry's 1985 *Arrivederci Millwall*, and Steven Berkoff's 1986 *Sink the Belgrano!*[14] All originate, like *Falkland Sound*, in the Alternative network: *Welcome Home* was toured by Paines Plough in 1983, *Arrivederci Millwall* was produced at the Albany Empire in 1985, and *Sink the Belgrano!* at the Half Moon in 1986. Subsequently, the 'afterlife' of all the plays was enhanced by publication. All three plays are political in their different demonstrations of the *suture* of British capitalist hegemony. Stitched up in this is a foul-mouthed world-view which has a significant appeal across key class formations in British society. The rapprochement between the conservative lower classes and the Conservative Party in power can be seen in their mutual valorisation of the Anglo-Saxon accent, and the Anglo-Saxon view of the world. The accent may be differently modulated for different purposes, but it is equally strident. To quote Anthony Barnett again,

> In so far as decision makers are really the masters of events, they act and react in a vulgar and personal fashion. In so far as they make up their minds in discussion with close associates, these exchanges are livid with the crapulous feelings of those whose lives are dominated by the struggle for power. Yet even in confidential documents, let alone public speeches, their motives are presented in the finest prose they can achieve. (p. 134)

The plays are all 'livid' with such 'crapulous feeling', and illuminate

the real nature of the energy behind the nationalistic righteousness of New Britishness. They convincingly link Yobbery and
Thatcherism.

In Berkoff's *Sink the Belgrano!* (based on the 1984 investigative
study *The Sinking of the Belgrano* by Arthur Gavshon and Desmond
Rice) we have an essentially 'Spitting Image' Thatcher, 'Maggot
Scratcher', who fumes on her first entrance,

> Those bloody junta bloody swine . . .!
> How dare they, how simply do they bloody dare
> When we've been so damned good to them
> Never complained when their death squads
> Got rid of opposition in mass graves . . .
> Nor publicly showed our disgust at torture
> For those that disobeyed (since naturally we
> Wish to trade) and now those greasy Argy wogs
> Show their thanks by stealing our sweet
> Precious lands. Call out the Fleet, get planes
> And tanks, I love to have a crisis on my hands.   (p. 4)[15]

Like a kind of skinhead Betjeman, Berkoff specialises in a doggerel
poetry of the four-letter word which is used to express ideas as
British as holidays in Ibiza or Costa del Mar. The lower-class sailors
of a nuclear submarine use language on this same continuum, so to
speak. Sailor 3 tells an 'oppo' who objects to the idea of a war over
the Falklands,

> Then fuck off this boat you cunt
> Don't fucking winge, you got no guts
> A soldier's life's obey the Queen
> The thinking's done by Whitehall nuts
> We know there's right and wrong on both
> But basically we trust our state
> You must believe in England's green
> And pleasant or fucking emigrate.   (p. 10)

Both Berkoff and Perry are self-conscious in their intertextuality –
Berkoff gives us a mock-Shakespearian drama (his *Henry V*-type
Chorus calling, not for 'a muse of fire' but for 'a brace of Exocets').
Perry's is a crypto-Bondian drama (though when *Arrivederci Millwall*
was televised in early 1990 it had significantly lost most of its

Bondian literariness and symbolism). He dovetails parliamentary and yobbish discourse by counterpointing words from the 3 April 1982 emergency debate:

> British sovereign territory has been invaded by a foreign power . . . In the end in life it is self-reliance and only self-reliance that counts. The time for weasel words has ended. (pp. 38–9)

with the story of a European Cup Final:

> And when the Villa fans started singing 'Rule, Britannia' I could feel the hairs standing up on me cobblers, I was that proud.

The interclass suture is made visible in this macho-male, neo-Imperialist stance. It is traced further in a dream-sequence in which the narrator-hero Billy 'celebrates' the Triumph of the Hooligans at the 1982 World Cup:

> You should of seen us. You should of seen us. We wasn't Millwall no more. We wasn't Liverpool or Man Ewe, West Ham or Chelsea. We was an army that day, a fucking army. We was England. (p. 87)

In *Arrivederci Millwall*, the equation of football hooliganism and the Falklands war proposes the solution that both are peculiarly English types of violent behaviour – but only one is politically sanctioned (and therefore respectable).

In *Welcome Home*, Tony Marchant offers a full-blown naturalism in which the latter type of violent behaviour is critiqued through the words and actions of a detachment of paratroopers, coffin-bearers for a colleague killed in the Falklands. Their leader Corporal Sharp articulates New Britishness:

> Every name on [the roll of honour] is a reminder of just how much this country is prepared to stand up for what it believes in and defend its territory. In our case, forty-four blokes who gave the paras an even better reputation than before, who lost their lives making fucking greasy tinpot dictators see that no piece of Britain is there for the taking. (pp. 23–4)

The emotive situation leads Marchant to comment on warfare as a *function of masculinity*. One of the paras, Polo, is already on the verge of mental collapse as a result of PTS (post-traumatic stress – what used to be called shell-shock). At his final crack-up, the taunts of Sharp and Walters (designed to shame him back into macho line) fail and it is left to the doubter of the group, Goldie, to offer comfort:

> Yeah – he's crying. And not only that – he's trembling, like a little dog who's been left out in the cold and there's snot on his fuckin' chin. And I'm hugging him cos . . . cos . . . I want to . . . cos he might need it. I know I do sometimes.   (p. 28)

The equation of masculinity with violence tends to code emotion and tenderness as breakdown; *Welcome Home*, like many 'Vet Films', is a 'Male Weepie' before it is an analysis of a specific conflict. There is a reliance on an *intensity*, which derives from the idea that soldiers see things ordinary mortals never will see.[16]

In *Gotcha!*, his analysis of the role of the media in the Falklands war, Robert Harris notes that the sheer speed of the crisis gave the whole experience this very intensity, which 'briefly illuminated aspects of British society *usually hidden from view*' (p. 152 – my emphasis). One can conclude that cultural production about the Falklands war faithfully carried out a project of pushing some deleted events, ideas and feelings back into the light, of illuminating one or two dark corners of the dominant triumphalism. This was a valuable job of political opposition to the attempt to create a unitary, 'unruptured', history of the conflict; but it was a job done in isolation both from a coherent politics of *real* opposition and from any desire on the part of drama-makers to situate their dramas politically. It is ironic that Ian Curteis's 'Great Woman of History' soap-opera *The Falklands Play* might well have provoked more turbulence – simply by presenting uncensored the authentic self-congratulatory odour of Thatcherian righteousness.

Notes

1. Anthony Barnett, *Iron Britannia: why Parliament waged the Falklands War* (Allison and Bushy: 1982) p. 20.
2. John and Robert Lawrence, *When the Fighting is Over: Tumbledown* (London: Bloomsbury, 1988) p. 15.

3. Letter from Albert Hunt to the author, 7 May 1987.
4. Charles Wood, *Tumbledown* (Harmondsworth: Penguin, 1987) p. xiii.
5. John Ellis, *Visible Fictions: cinema, television, video* (London: Routledge, 1985) p. 182.
6. The three 'Falklands films' are: *Veronico Cruz* (1988) directed by an Argentine, Miguel Pereira; Paul Greengrass's *Resurrected* (1989); and *For Queen and Country* (1989) directed by Martin Stellman).
7. See my book *True Stories?: documentary drama on radio, screen and stage* (Manchester: Manchester University Press, 1990) for a fuller theoretical discussion of 'documentary drama'.
8. In 1988, the touring company Transfer Theatre also explored the experience of service wives in their play *Cut the Girls' Talk! This is War*, a basically 'verbatim' documentary play (see also Note 13).
9. Ian Curteis, *The Falklands Play* (London: Hutchinson, 1987) p. 11.
10. Steven Berkoff, *Sink the Belgrano!* (London: Faber, 1987) p. 3.
11. See Robert Harris, *Gotcha! The Media, The Government and the Falklands Crisis* (London: Faber, 1983) p. 69.
12. Bertolt Brecht, *The Messingkauf Dialogues*, trans. John Willett (London: Methuen, 1985) p. 32.
13. For further details, see my article 'Verbatim Theatre: oral history and the documentary method', *New Theatre Quarterly*, 3, 12 (1987) pp. 317–336.
14. Tony Marchant, *Welcome Home* (London: Methuen, 1983); Nick Perry, *Arrivederci Millwall* (London: Faber, 1987); Steven Berkoff, op. cit.
15. Thatcher, of course, actually said this last line when addressing the Scottish Conservative Party conference on 14 May 1982.
16. The Falklands films *Resurrected* and *For Queen and Country* share these characteristics with *Welcome Home*.

10

Playing Soldiers: The Politics of Casting in *Tumbledown* and *Born on the Fourth of July*

VAL TAYLOR

I felt like a burden was lifted, that I was passing all this on to Tom. I knew he was about to go to Vietnam, to the dark side in his own way.

> (Ron Kovic, *Empire* March 1990, p. 39)

We ended up emotional Siamese twins really . . . I started having the most appalling dreams, some of them as if I was Robert, doing the things that Robert was doing.

> (Colin Firth, *Wogan*, BBC1, 27 May 1988)

You're a lot like him, only better. And worse. He was a natural heroic son of a bitch.

> (Commander Mike Metcalf, *Top Gun*, 1986)

That scene is real. It's happening. You're there. In person.

> (Tom Cruise, *Time Out* 31 Jan–7 Feb 1990, p. 16)

You never fought that war. You weren't even there, man!

> (Charlie, *Born on the Fourth of July*, 1989)

Militarism from twelve to half-past four. Little boys all dressed up and playing soldiers.

> (Tommy Judd, *Another Country*, 1984)

A conundrum: is it possible for a fiction film to take as its subject the personal experiences of a real-life soldier as combatant in and casualty of a recent controversial and politically influential military campaign and its domestic after-effects, and for that film not to be construed as political comment upon both that campaign and its instigators, the film-makers' publicly-expressed intentions notwithstanding? The answer, in the specific cases of the BBC film

Tumbledown, transmitted in May 1988, and Universal Pictures' feature film *Born on the Fourth of July* (1989), would seem to be no, if the critical debate occasioned on both sides of the Atlantic is anything to go by. That debate pivots, of course, around two closely-related issues: the proprietary claim to 'truth' made by all concerned, film-makers and opponents alike; and the choice of medium: fictional film narrative.

For Robert Lawrence, whose experiences as a disabled veteran of the Falklands war form the basis of both *Tumbledown* and a subsequent autobiography, truth was not, as the old adage runs, a casualty of war but of political expediency, visible to him in the discrepancy between his own experience of the conflict and its personal aftermath, and government-manipulated campaign reports. *Tumbledown* constitutes Lawrence's version, 'the truth as I saw it through my eyes, from my personal level';[1] a version nonetheless hotly contested by some fellow combatants, and other commentators. For journalist John Pilger, veteran reporter of the Vietnam war, truth is an almost inevitable casualty of Hollywood cinema when the subject is the US involvement in South-East Asia;[2] yet for disabled Vietnam veteran Ron Kovic, subject and co-author of *Born on the Fourth of July* – based on his 1976 autobiographical novel – that film constitutes an accurate account of the conflict and its domestic consequences for returning veterans. But, whilst Kovic himself re-asserts the unexaggerated authenticity of the Dantesque Bronx Veterans' Hospital scenes, fellow Vietnam veteran, co-author and director of *Born*, Oliver Stone has – reportedly – had to apologise to the New York police for the hostile depiction of them in scenes at the Syracuse University anti-war demonstration. Truth, in all these instances, appears to be an elusive commodity.

The source of much critical anger resides in the use of fictional film narrative as the medium of expression. An alert Tom Cruise, leading actor in *Born*, makes an intriguing oblique reference to this in an interview with Robert Scheer: *'It's as true a story as ever told* about the effects of the Vietnam war on America – and on the times America lived through.'[3] For Charles Wood, writer of *Tumbledown*, that might seem to resonate with his feeling that what matters is not the (arguable) authenticity of the narrative's details, but rather its capacity to engender belief in both teller and audience. It seems that both Cruise and Wood are articulating a post-modern perspective, from which the critical debate becomes an unresolvable – and misplaced – conflict between an attempted government meta-narrative and multiple dissident micro-narratives. From this point of view, it is less the tale itself that counts than the teller and the skill of the telling.

It is at this precise juncture that the motivations of the film-makers attract discussion: do they intend to offer specific political comment through the micro-narrative, or not? In the case of *Tumbledown* signals were mixed. The BBC, singed by the blazing row ensuing from Alan Bleasdale's *The Monocled Mutineer* (also produced by *Tumbledown* producer Richard Broke), denied any intentional political comment; Charles Wood, in the published screenplay of *Tumbledown*, professes to have avoided any political stance; yet director Richard Eyre, also director of *The Ploughman's Lunch*, another Falklands micro-narrative with very definite politi-cal signification, has declared forthrightly his belief that *Tumble-down* is both political and partisan by design. *Born* offers no such equivocation: it is avowedly polemical, the screen Kovic's howl of anti-government rhetoric at the Miami Republican Convention – 'The government is a bunch of corrupt thieves, rapists and rob-bers!'[4] – echoing precisely that of the 'self-professed anarchist' Oliver Stone: 'The vandals are at the gate . . . We have a fascist security state running this country . . . If I were George Bush, I would shoot myself.'[5]

Born's publicly-declared intention is no less than the awakening of the individual citizen to active democratic participation, particu-larly targeted at the young. Tom Cruise, again, makes this clear:

> It's a film that tells us we can't just blindly trust the leaders of this country, that *we ourselves must search and find out where we stand and what we believe in*.[6]

Kovic's own possible future Democratic Congressional candidacy attests to the film's capacity to persuade: *Born* is, in that sense, agit-prop. Robert Lawrence's intentions in 'correcting' the British government meta-narrative of the Falklands war stands in an interesting relationship to the *Born* team's, and to Richard Broke's disavowals that *Tumbledown* offers any more than the vaguely political generalisation that the actuality of war is awful. In a televised interview with Terry Wogan, Lawrence declared

I fought for democracy, and every person in this country has a right to know the realities . . . so that *they can actually use their vote properly and know what they're doing*.[7]

reinforcing the exhortation of *Tumbledown*'s leading actor Colin Firth, in the same interview, to 'Have your opinion, but take responsibility for your opinion. Go and fight the war, but take responsibility for it . . . Don't hold opinions on the cheap.'

Born's targets are specific: Kennedy, Johnson, Nixon – and by extension, also Reagan and Bush. *Tumbledown*, whilst not overtly anti-Thatcher or anti-Conservative – Lawrence declares his own politics to be right of centre, and that he agreed with the military response to the Argentine occupation of the Falklands – nonetheless appears to offer the distinct possibility of a subversive challenge to the hegemony of the ruling élite. As Richard Eyre is no doubt very well aware, it is probably very difficult to contradict a would-be meta-narrative so central to a particular political ideology without also challenging both that ideology and the would-be meta-narrator.

Both *Born* and *Tumbledown* are thus revealed as highly political dramas, albeit one more overt than the other; and broadly similar in target, in that they both address the democratic deep structure of both British and American society. But similarities extend way beyond this. A still deeper structure is reflected by both films, revealed by the centring of the narratives upon the single figure of a soldier, crippled in combat, suffering rejection upon his return, before finally re-integrating into the 'non-combatant' social environment. The stereotype of the soldier stands at the confluence of the many discourses of a patriarchal system, embodying simultaneously the apparent moral contradictions of the hero and the killer; the archetypal repository of 'masculinity' – strong, courageous, macho, aggressive, physically and sexually dominant, traits which are held naturally to accrue to the male in a patriarchy. By dint of his role within the workings of the discourses of patriotism and nationalism, the soldier reflects and validates the conservative Establishment it is his function to protect and preserve; but he also constitutes a potentially disruptive threat to it, by the very nature of the actions it employs him to undertake in combat and their moral ambiguity. He is both insider and outsider at once, and this is most fully apparent when he is known to have 'seen action'. In centring upon crippled, dissident soldiers, *Born* and *Tumbledown* interrogate that stereotype, and by so doing also lay bare the patriarchal roots of the system which generates it.

Structurally the two films share many parallels; hardly surprising given the remarkable similarity in their respective stories. Each man comes from a Services family, though Kovic's father and uncle were not the career-military men that John Lawrence seems to have been; nonetheless, there is a clear sense of both Kovic and Lawrence following a male family tradition. Barely out of his teens, each man willingly sought the battlefront, which he mentally constructed in terms of the romanticised cinema imagery of his childhood: John Wayne /Audie Murphy in Kovic's case, Richard Todd /John Wayne in Lawrence's. Each was disastrously and permanently wounded by sniper fire in battle, resulting in hemiplegia and partial incontinence (Lawrence), or total below-the-chest paralysis and sexual impotence (Kovic). On returning home, each suffered bureaucratic and social indifference and/or hostility, triggering an aggressive, almost sociopathic response in its victims. The two men part company only at this late point: Kovic having been politically radicalised and activated by his experiences, Lawrence seemingly less so.

Both films employ first person narration, involving the use of flashbacks and fantasy. In *Tumbledown* this structure is highly complex, involving both flashback and flash-forwards within an overall framework of 'Robert's' narration to 'George Stubbs', the fictional version of Charles Wood. This framework is broken for the climactic sequence of the battle on Mount Tumbledown, culminating in Robert's wounding. Structurally this occurs after Robert and Hugh Mackessac have left the Stubbs house, which would seem to indicate its taking place after the end of Robert's narration: a kind of marking off of the central event from Robert's point of view, from which everything else has, apparently, been seen. *Born* uses a simpler linear narrative structure, but begins with a flashback to 'young Ron's' (Bryan Larkin) childhood wargames in Sally's Woods, whilst Tom Cruise ('Ron') narrates in voice-over. The sequence ends prophetically with young Ron 'killed' by a surprise attack: prophetic and also symbolic, for in one sense that version of Ron does die in Vietnam. Though the explicit framework of narration disappears after this point, the source novel's alternation of first and third person voices has conventionally been established. It is also traceable in the dominant use of low-angle (that is, wheelchair height) point-of-view shots, and in the use of slow-motion / monochrome / montage, signalling interiority. As with *Tumbledown*, there is a clear sense of a story being told; in *Tumbledown*, at one remove, to George Stubbs; in *Born*, directly to the audience.

The central figure is also isolated in relation to other characters, none of whom share his precise perspective. This is made clear through parallel scenes and characters. Both families seem unable to comprehend fully the psychic anguish of Ron and Robert; in *Born*, that estrangement is total, and extremely expressed. Both men's closest relationships seem to be with fellow veterans also physically or psychologically marked by war; for Robert, it is Hugh Mackessac, for Ron, both Timmy Burns and Charlie in Mexico. And yet neither's relationships seem to offer much comfort or relief; for, by the nature of their shared traumas, the friends cannot connect beyond an implied acknowledgement of shared pain. Female friends fail both men, romantically and sexually: Sophie, after sleeping with the injured Robert as an experiment, rejects him; Donna, though a key figure in Ron's political awakening, ignores his tentative declaration of love – and implied sexual plea – leaving him symbolically and literally stalled at the kerb in his wheelchair while she runs up a flight of steps to a political meeting on the Syracuse campus. In Mexico, Maria Elena, the whore to whom Ron loses his virginity cruelly disabuses him of his romantic aspirations when she stands revealed, upon his next visit to her, as the prostitute she is; to her, he is clearly no more than another trick.

This sense of isolation is deepened by scenes echoed in both films. Ceremonial occasions, such as the Falklands Memorial Service, at which Robert, marooned at the back in his wheelchair, is simultaneously patronised and marginalised; or the Memorial Day Parade at which Ron is lionised but terrified by firecrackers all too reminiscent of rifle-fire, and dries during his address to the crowd, are markers of the increasing social estrangement of each man. Only the viewer sees what is happening – often sees it expressly from Robert's and Ron's viewpoint – and sees his response; and by so doing is expressly urged to sympathise, to share his growing anger and therefore to approve his movement from passive suffering to active confrontation.

It is at this point that the critical significance of the role of the actors playing Robert and Ron emerges, for there are dangers inherent in such a structure, and particular requirements imposed by the political focusing of the narratives. The inherent danger is that the concentration on a single figure may risk him being seen as unique, and therefore of limited political importance; and in the appeal to audience empathy, which could obviate any further political and intellectual exploration. From the political perspective, it is crucial that Ron and Robert be seen as representative rather than singular, and that emotional triggers should also release intellectual consideration of their immediate socio-political circumstances and context. There is a further requirement which carries immense political meaning, concerning the nature of the two central figures' politicisation. (Whilst acknowledging the limitations of Lawrence's political shift, I think the term holds.) For each, the route was empirical rather than theoretical; theory, in the form of both government propaganda and patriotic cinema texts, was repeatedly shown to be false by exposure to direct personal experience. This represents an active rather than a passive process; and one that, from a political point of view, needs to be promoted, even idealised, by each film, for it is the perceived dangers of democratic passivity which are being addressed.

However, neither film takes the form of a *lehrstück* – the audience cannot take part in the action and thereby learn – and thus there is a risk that the films will simply replicate the effect of the hero-narratives they seek to interrogate. Although in this instance the content will be more ideologically acceptable, from the film-makers' point of view, nevertheless it is still being received in the same passive manner. But, as the theory which underpins 'epic theatre' suggests, it is possible to challenge that notion of passivity through the construction of the narrative and the manner of its transmission; and in this form of drama, the actor is crucial in importance. Once again it seems that, as with the post-modern perspective, the political message depends upon the telling of the tale, and therefore upon the chief 'teller', the actor.

It seems therefore that the two central performers – in *Tumbledown* Colin Firth, in *Born* Tom Cruise – have to function in a particularly complex fashion if the political dimension is to be fully realised. For them, the playing of the role needs to go beyond a simple re-enactment of Kovic's and Lawrence's experiences into the creation of a parallel experience of their own; thus rendering Kovic and Lawrence special but not unique. That parallel experience has to be transmitted – in the Stanislavskian sense – with sufficient clarity and intensity for the audience to be able to empathise; but it must also be continuously alienated so as to promote intellectual engagement. Cruise and Firth must function, in other words, as *doppelgängers* for Kovic and Lawrence; in photographic terms, as a kind of double exposure through which the original is still – and simultaneously – visible.

Performance analysis has pointed to the significance of casting within the sign systems of drama, drawing attention to the tension existing between an actor's real-life existence and his/her iconic function within the drama. Attention has also been paid to the erotic nature of the actor/audience relationship, and to the potential for signification in the actor's own erotic magnetism.[8] Richard Dyer, in *Stars*, has argued for the possibility of the star actor functioning as an ideological vehicle, or within an ideological context. In *Born* and *Tumbledown* both this erotic base and ideological function are traceable; in *Born*, very clearly. This is due in part to the difference in medium – feature film as opposed to television – but chiefly to the more overt political targeting of the American film. In terms of the medium, the economics of film demanded that the role of Ron be played by a star actor with proven box office appeal; and Cruise, with box office receipts of over one billion dollars from his four most recent films, more than fitted Universal Pictures' bill. In Firth's case, given the nature of BBC funding through the licence fee, no such imperative arose, freeing Richard Eyre to employ other criteria in casting.

One of the commonest criteria in casting is physical type, based upon familiar, culturally-specific stereotypes. From *Tumbledown*'s point of view, where the stereotype of the soldier comes under intense scrutiny, the possibilities of interrogation through physical typing seem potentially productive; and indeed this was a significant factor in Eyre's casting of Firth. Describing Firth's appearance as 'conventional English good looks, a copybook hero',[9] Eyre clearly alludes to a deliberate intertextuality between Robert and the romantic soldier-heroes of 1940s cinema; in particular, there are faint echoes, in Firth's looks, of Kenneth More, whose role as the wounded airman Douglas Bader in *Reach for the Sky* is an obvious and powerful reference point for Robert. Equally clear is that this intertextuality takes precedence over any attempt to replicate the real Robert Lawrence's looks: 'Robert' is to be viewed as distinct from Robert Lawrence himself, thus underlining the representative nature of the central dramatic figure.

On the other hand interviews given around the time of transmission of *Tumbledown* in 1988 by both Firth and Lawrence together – and subsequent interviews given by Firth in promotion of later work – throw up similarities in personality between the two men. Though hailing from somewhat different social, educational and probably also political backgrounds, the two share a brisk, coolly-articulated approach to the performance of their respective jobs. Yet there is also more than a hint of ambivalence towards the glamorous stereotype of both actor and soldier, traceable in the intensity of their respective absorption in the role. There are, too, in Firth's interviews, hints of a parallel mixture of emotional vulnerability – occasioned by that intense absorption – buried anger, and combative self-assertion that Lawrence also projects, and which is fundamental to the character of 'Robert'. In the *Wogan* interview cited earlier, the confrontational nature of Firth's 'Have your opinion' challenge is balanced by his at times halting attempt to articulate the personal impact upon him of playing 'Robert' and working closely with Lawrence:

> It became almost like something psychic after a while . . . I started having the most appalling dreams, some of them as if I were Robert, doing the things that Robert was doing . . . It was the beginning of something for me.[10]

In describing his relationship with Lawrence, who acted as both consultant and coach to Firth on *Tumbledown*, in terms of 'emotional Siamese twins', Firth seems to be alluding to an almost symbiotic type of partnership, very near the *doppelgänger* discussed earlier. At the same time, the variation in physical appearance so clearly visible in joint interviews served to re-state the separation between them thus helping to alienate the role of 'Robert' from both men. Such interviews, and pre- and post-transmission publicity photographs of the two together on set served to promote the 'double exposure' effect. But it is clear that both Eyre and Wood intended to operate the character of Robert on an extended plane of reference, beyond a simple identification with the real-life Lawrence. The use of two non-naturalistic devices, the twin 'blue' images of Robert: in the prow of a ship echoing the sort of poses struck by Jack Hawkins in *The Cruel Sea*, and what Wood refers to in the screenplay as 'Bergen Man', a soldier piled high with towering Bergen backpack, staggering through combat fire and smoke, signal this. These are clearly designed to cross-refer, offering on the one hand the standard cinematic stereotype so potent in recruiting and promotion of the military life; and on the other a disturbingly animalistic, quasi-primeval image hinting at atavistic roots of violent behaviour. The two are mutually interrogative, and jointly extend the portrait of Robert beyond simple imitation into complex critique. In Wood's text, it is not clear who the figure of 'Bergen Man' is meant to be; in Eyre's text, it is visibly Colin Firth. Some commentators have suggested that this identification of Firth / Robert /Bergen Man is reductive in effect. I disagree: I would suggest that it is actually of critical importance that the two meta-dramatic images should both be grounded in Robert. By creating a triangular intertextuality between these three fictional figures, the character of Robert is repeatedly ironised and critiqued; whilst he, placed in the main narrative within precise socio-political and economic contexts, continually interrogates and responds to those two – supposed – opposites, revealing their common base. That this is Eyre's purpose in signalling Firth's presence as Bergen Man is suggested further to me by the manner in which he, and Wood, repeatedly offer glimpses of a less palatable 'Robert'; for example, in Robert's association with the skinhead Prothero, his general yobbish behaviour both pre- and post-injury – aggressive, rude, abusive – and most particularly coalescing in the stabbing of the fallen Argentine soldier on Mount Tumbledown. It is for this reason that I believe the final sequence is 'marked off' from Robert's narration, as discussed earlier. Firth's embodiment in physical terms of the conventional 'hero' stereotype is thus of key significance.

For Oliver Stone, the casting of Tom Cruise had less to do with considerations of physical type and more to do with a perceived congruence between Cruise and Ron Kovic. Stone has expressly drawn attention in interviews publicising *Born*, to the fact that both men originate from working-class white Catholic East Coast American backgrounds, and to parallel personality traits: 'They were both obsessed with excellence – perhaps too much so.'[11] Kovic underlines the extreme level of identification between himself and Cruise, which transcended even his initial doubts about the actor's professional capabilities:

. . . even if he isn't that strong, at least . . . the message . . . will get out . . . When I first met Cruise, he was very much a mirror image of myself when I went to Vietnam in '65 . . . Cruise understood.[12]

Critically, this circumstantial likeness is constructed as an important vehicle for a total emotional identification between them,
leading Kovic to assert 'I truly believe he actually becomes me.'
This begins to sound very much like Firth's description of
'emotional twinning', which Cruise himself also underlines: 'Kovic
really opened up to me. . . . It was very emotional. I felt an
immediate understanding looking at this man, talking with this
man.'[13] Cruise has stated, for example in the already quoted article
by Robert Scheer, that it was this sense of close personal identification which impelled him to take on the role. Revealingly, he
describes his response not in intellectual but in physical terms: 'I
could feel this script in my balls.'[14]

For Stone there was also another consideration in the casting of
Cruise, which in fact bears no relationship to Kovic at all:

> I saw this kid who has everything . . . And I wondered what
> would happen if tragedy strikes, if fortune denies him . . .
> 'What would happen to Tom Cruise if something goes wrong?'[15]

It was Cruise's celebrity status that Stone sought, for complex
political reasons unrelated to box office returns. Cruise's public
persona is invariably stereotyped in the media as 'the all-American
boy': handsome, clean-cut, clean-living, decent, honourable, sexy,
straight and hugely successful. He is often cited as representative
of the Reaganite Me generation, and has been acknowledged as a
role-model for American youth both by the White House (in 1985,
for his transcendance of his dyslexia) and by American teenagers
themselves, male and female. Above all, Cruise seems, at least on
the surface, to embody the archetypal American Dream achiever; a
living vindication of the American capitalist democratic system.
But intriguingly for Stone, beneath the perfect façade Cruise
offered hints of 'a crack in his background, some kind of un-
happiness',[16] an allusion to childhood domestic traumas, suggesting a potentially exploitable emotional vulnerability. And further,
in Cruise's own repeated aggressive challenges to media stereo-
typing of him – perceived by him, probably correctly, as attempts
to control and contain his personal and professional mobility –
there seemed a clear possibility of creating through Cruise himself,
rather than solely through the character of 'Ron', an intensely
resonant political exploration.

There are echoes here of the use of Firth to interrogate the soldier stereotype beyond its incarnation in Robert Lawrence. But unlike that usage, which makes its points through a complex system of cross-references between Firth's physical closeness to the film stereotype and the cited ironic images built into the narrative structure, *Born* makes its political point powerfully through one simple image alone: the visible suffering of Tom Cruise himself. Stone, with Kovic's assistance and that of military and political consultants and advisors such as Abbie Hoffman, set out to take Cruise through a gruelling physical and emotional endurance test: a deliberately constructed parallel to Kovic's own experiences. 'To the dark side', in Ron Kovic's phrase; a giveaway allusion to the *Star Wars* saga which both bridged and reflected the early Reagan years. This implied linking of Cruise with Luke Skywalker, country-boy hero of the space trilogy, is far from accidental; it invites a reading of Cruise, and of the Vietnam war – the 'struggle against the evil Empire' – in mythic terms. That Cruise is being projected in such terms is underlined also by Stone's description of him as 'Homeric',[17] inviting identification with Achilles and Aeneas. Such labels and allusions condensing around Cruise then map directly onto Ron, with whom Cruise is so closely associated, elevating Ron's status also: not a debunking of conventional hero-mythology, but a refocusing. In that sense, unlike *Tumbledown*, there is no sustained ironic debate.

Both actors in performance capture with great realism the effects of physical pain and emotional anguish suffered by their characters. In Cruise's case, this is taken to an extreme degree: gouts of blood spurt from his mouth as he falls, spinal cord severed by a Vietcong rifle bullet; in the workout room at the Veterans' Hospital, as he overdoes his attempts to walk with calipers and crutches and snaps a thighbone, the shattered bone is seen through the skin, jagged and bloody. Throughout, Cruise is subjected to extreme physical stressing, visible in the exhaustion in his face as he propels the heavy wheelchair; in his face, suffused with blood as he screams and vents his primal rage at family and friends; audible in his voice, alternately thin, piercing and high-pitched, or breathy and sobbing, throat rarely relaxed (a signal that emotional intensity is taking over from pure technique); but visible most clearly and consistently in the hauntedness of his eyes and mouth, to which Stone's camera repeatedly returns again and again in close-ups. Indeed, it is through Cruise's eyes, mouth and face that *Born* is to be understood. And, notwithstanding the brilliance of Cruise's performance as a sustained piece of acting, the audience is never once allowed to become unaware of the fact that it is Cruise, the American icon, who is enduring all. This is somewhat different from *Tumbledown*, where Firth's highly skilled performance serves to create a believable Robert; in *Born*, Stone simultaneously promotes both Ron and Tom Cruise as victims.

One of the ways in which this is achieved is by means of a different kind of intertextuality: not between other hero-narratives, but between other Cruise films, in particular, I would suggest, Cruise's two other military films *Taps* (1981) and *Top Gun* (1986). A similar intertextual exercise is available for Colin Firth also, through his roles in *Another Country* (1984) and *A Month in the Country* (1987), in which he also plays a soldier. In *Another Country*, a film adapted from Julian Mitchell's stage play, Firth plays Tommy Judd, schoolboy Marxist at a thinly-disguised pre-war Eton. His closest friend is Guy Bennett, a character modelled on the spy Guy Burgess. The narrative demonstrates the conditions under which spies like Burgess, Maclean, Philby and Blunt were made; the fictional Eton functioning as a microcosm of the class-bedevilled, sadistic, sexually repressive and hypocritical contemporary British society. The homosexual Bennett (whom Firth also played in the stage version) is alienated from the insular clique of The Gods, the tiny group of highly privileged prefects to whom he aspires. Judd, on the other hand, rejects his background, espousing proletarian dress, *Das Kapital* and Marxist–Leninism; he is an anomic character,[18] entirely outside, and hostile to, the prevailing ideology. He is particularly scathing about the officer-class mentality which is being drilled into the boys – literally – through the Officer Training Corps, which he refuses to enter. He refers to the drilling, for competitive purposes ('the Jacker Pot'), as 'little boys all dressed up and playing soldiers'. Which, of course, is precisely what they are.

In 1987, in *A Month in the Country*, scripted by Simon Gray (another writer, like Wood, to explore the military and colonial mentality) from a J. L. Carr novel, Firth played Birkin, a traumatised veteran of the First World War. The narrative follows Birkin to Yorkshire – he seems to be a southerner, by his well-to-do Home Counties accent – where he is engaged to uncover and restore a religious fresco on the wall of a church. He meets a fellow veteran, Moon, an archaeologist (Kenneth Branagh) similarly psychologically scarred by his experiences in battle, and by his homosexuality.

Birkin is similarly emotionally estranged, his wife having run off with another man; angry and embittered towards what he sees as religious cant, he is slowly and partially restored by the friendliness of the Yorkshire village community. However, the sight of a terminally ill child with tuberculosis once again unleashes all the unexpressed grief and pain of his military service. In a central scene with Moon in the supposed sanctuary of a pub, the two men finally exchange a little information about the horrors of their experiences; it is delicate, oblique, low-key – underplayed beautifully by both Firth and Branagh. The sense of grief and suppressed rage is strong; both men, but particularly Birkin, once again seem to be anomic, totally outside the prevailing social norm, aware of its stupidity. But whereas in *Another Country* the roots of Judd's anomie were political and ideological, in *A Month in the Country* Birkin's has been triggered by his war service. Of course, from a Marxist perspective, the concept of anomie is suspect as it rests upon a psychological base rather than upon a challenge to the dominant power structure, so it is perhaps a little awkward to apply it to Judd; however, there is in Judd a residual emotional romanticism, discernible in his attachment to Bennett, and his eventual fate as casualty of the Spanish Civil War, which I think makes it possible to employ the term.

The intertextual possibilities between these two films and *Tumbledown* are numerous. In all three cases, Firth plays an isolated individual, isolated either by dint of personal politics (Judd) which find especial resonance in relation to militarism, or as a direct result of having embraced militarism and suffered the consequences. In each case, the Firth character is in opposition to the dominant ideology, or to some aspect of it; and in each case he is also its victim. Judd is too young to oppose it beyond the confines of the school, and is persuaded by Bennett to a degree of collaboration with it; on seeing its destructive effect upon Bennett at first hand, Judd's course for the battlefront in Spain is set from that moment on. Birkin's service in the trenches, to which he no doubt went voluntarily, as did so many men in the 1914–18 war, has, it seems, emotionally destroyed him, and there is no comfortable sense of healing closure at the end of the film. In that, it seems to presage *Tumbledown*, where 'Robert' is not merely psychically but also physically maimed; for 'Robert', there is to be no physical healing, and though *Tumbledown* has been described as part of the healing process for Robert Lawrence himself, it is not clear at the end of the film exactly how healed we are to assume 'Robert' is.

If those two earlier films of Colin Firth's can be used to develop, by means of intertextual cross-referencing, the political dimension in *Tumbledown*, it must be acknowledged that such cross-referring is unlikely to be widespread. Firth's status is not such that the majority of *Tumbledown*'s viewing public would necessarily be aware of those earlier roles. It is much more likely that for the majority Firth would constitute something of an unknown quantity, and that the more obvious intertextual references would be between it and *Reach for the Sky*, called up not only by 'Robert's' injury, but by the explicit hinting of the opening credit sequence, as the Panther car bowls through the green fields of a Camelot-like England, to the strains of Waltonesque music. In the case of *Born on the Fourth of July*, the intertextuality between Cruise's other films and this one would be very much to the forefront of a cinema audience's mind; and in particular, it would be *Top Gun* (1986) that sprang to mind.

Top Gun has, since its release, attracted its full share of critical opposition. Its narrative centres upon a young navy pilot, Lieutenant Pete 'Maverick' Mitchell, son of a disgraced Vietnam pilot – the strikingly-named 'Duke' Mitchell – and his quest for acceptance and the honour of winning the Top Gun trophy at the Miramar, California, combat training school. In the course of the narrative unfolding, Maverick (Cruise) wins, loses and regains the love of a female astro-physicist who is also a Top Gun trainer; discovers the truth about his father's heroic and self-sacrificing final mission 'over the wrong line on a map' in South-East Asia; loses his crew partner 'Goose' in an aerial accident for which he suffers feelings of guilt; and finally redeems himself in actual combat with an unnamed enemy (but which flies Russian MiG-28s) above the Indian Ocean, before relinquishing active service to become a Top Gun trainer himself, alongside his father-substitute, Commander Mike Metcalf ('Viper'); having finally proved himself, like his father, to be a 'natural, heroic son of a bitch'.

Criticism of *Top Gun* has centred upon its identification as a paean to Reaganite New Patriotism, and reviled it as a right-wing navy recruitment commercial. There is no doubt that director Tony Scott's advertising background produces a succession of glossily attractive images which fairly drool over the multi-million dollar hardware, in particular the F-14 Tomcat; and over the lean, tanned, frequently undressed and perspiring bodies of its macho cast, projecting a view of military service as sexy and fun. And indeed, the US Navy was quick to see its recruiting potential, lending Paramount producers Simpson and Bruckheimer technical assistance and the necessary planes and pilots; and then setting up recruiting booths in the foyers of cinemas where the film was showing, resulting in a quadrupling of the usual numbers of enlistments. And most of all, *Top Gun* has been cited as the kind of film which projects, in contemporary terms, just as lethal an image of militarism as the John Wayne movies which caught young Ron Kovic; its aerial dogfight sequences do bear an uncanny resemblance to computer games (and in a kind of loop effect, *Top Gun* is now actually a video game itself). But there is another way to read *Top Gun*, a way which offers interesting intertextualities for *Born*.

Tom Cruise has always insisted that the political reading of *Top Gun* is misplaced, and that its real source is another set of films altogether: 'I saw the movie as *Star Wars* with real aircraft.'[19] Looked at from this perspective, intriguing markers rise to the surface: the range of names, based around call-signs – Maverick, Goose, Iceman, Hollywood, Wolfman, Viper, Jester – begin to strip away the realism and conjure up the names of *Star Wars*: Skywalker, Han Solo, Chewbacca, Obi-Wan Kenobi, Darth Vader, Moff Tarkin and so on. 'Duke' Mitchell – of course echoing John Wayne – the 'villain' father unknown to his adult son who hero-worships his dimly-recalled memory, but who is later revealed as a hero at the moment of death, very precisely mirrors the Dark Lord of the Sith Darth Vader, whose kinship to Luke Skywalker was revealed as he lay dying, in *The Return of the Jedi* (1983), having been hinted at in *The Empire Strikes Back*. Mike Metcalf moves into the role of mentor Obi-Wan Kenobi, Luke's Jedi trainer; and the *Top Gun* crews begin to look very much like the forces of the Rebellion, with the unnamed MiG pilots representing the Empire (as Ronald Reagan himself pointed out). Similarities run much deeper: *Top Gun* shares certain narrative similarities, and structurally contains many scenes which mirror scenes in *Star Wars* – compare, for example, the whole final sequence from Maverick and Iceman's return to the USS Enterprise (!) to the congratulatory hugging on deck, with the sequence in *Star Wars* from the briefing to the congratulatory hugging between Luke and his friend and rival Han Solo.

Seen from this perspective, *Top Gun* confers upon Cruise, in the Skywalker role, the mythic-hero status discussed previously; and offers an explanatory link to Kovic's remark about taking Cruise to 'the dark side' in the course of *Born on the Fourth of July*. It thus allows Cruise to be read as mythic outside the context of *Born*, that is in a prefiguring sense: Maverick/Luke prefiguring Ron/Tom/ Luke. This extends the other reading of *Top Gun* in relation to *Born*, in which the right-wing Maverick comments upon the seventeen-year-old 'Kennedy boy' of *Born*'s early pre-Vietnam sequence; and in which the maimed and impotent Ron confronts and ironises the beautiful, promiscuous Maverick. In both directions the political resonance is strong: *Top Gun* sits continually in the background of *Born*, and the vital presence of Tom Cruise in both renders both texts meaningful precisely through this keen intertextual linkage. But there is another film of Cruise's also sitting in the background of *Born*, and that is *Taps*, his first major role, in 1981. Like *Top Gun*, *Taps* seems to offer prefiguration and political resonance to *Born*.

In *Taps*, Cruise is Cadet Captain David Shawn, student at the symbolically-named Bunker Hill Military Academy, run by George C. Scott (General Patton in *Patton*, 1969). Shawn is an iron-pumping 'natural leader', a punchy young baby soldier also in love with the hardware of militarism and its uses. The narrative turns upon the shock decision to close the Academy for development as commercial real estate, and the cadets' military defence of their beloved school and its ideals of honour and duty inculcated in them by Scott (their spiritual father figure). The siege laid to the Academy by the National Guard ends in tragedy, triggered by Cruise's Shawn finally tipping over into the psychopathic madness which has been incipient throughout the film and opening fire on the 'enemy'. Shawn is seen, seconds before the National Guard blow him and Cadet-Major Morland (Tim Hutton) to kingdom come, in an orgiastic spraying of rifle and machine gun bullets, laughing 'It's beautiful, man!'. The orgasmic nature of the moment is played very clearly by Cruise. Earlier, as the siege was just beginning, Shawn escalated the situation by firing his M16 in the nearby town, to scare off local thugs bent on attacking supply trucks bound for Bunker Hill: an action called immediately into question by the film's moral conscience, Sean Penn.

Once again there are obvious links between *Taps* and *Born*. The youthful Shawn is roughly the same age as 'Ron' in the pre-Vietnam scenes, and there are many echoes in the way 'Ron' regurgitates Kennedy administration anti-Communist propaganda, and Shawn's complete espousal of Scott's honour-and-duty creed. But Shawn is quite clearly less bound up with the theory than with the military practice: it is he, rather than Morland, who is the real 'death-lover' in Colonel Kirby's description. In this, he sheds an interesting light upon 'Ron's' behaviour in combat, getting up after being shot in the heel, re-loading and firing, yelling 'Come on Charlie motherfucker!' seconds before taking the sniper bullet. The two sequences, Shawn's death and Ron's wounding are disturbingly alike, offering a view of Ron informed by the psychotic craziness of Shawn; there is but a hair's breadth between them. But despite his viciousness, Shawn can also be read as a victim of the ideology which also traps Ron. Critical reaction to *Taps* identified its allegorical nature, pointing to its discussion of the rise of Reaganite patriotism. It thus cross-refers also to the political dimension of *Top Gun*, and the two films together extend the political resonance of *Born* to embrace Reagan and Bush, as well as Kennedy and Nixon. In order for this continual process to take place, Tom Cruise's placing within the three central roles has to occur.

It is clear that the presence of Tom Cruise, and to a lesser extent Colin Firth also, in the central roles of *Born on the Fourth of July* and *Tumbledown* add to the political reading of the two films; their presence extends and develops the significance beyond the confines of the narratives. But there is one respect in which their presence does not assist, and that is in the context of patriarchy. Both films might, through their central characters, have been able to develop a far more deeply searching political exploration of the roots of the damaging and socially destructive doctrines in the deep structures of such a system. But this does not happen; ultimately, both films address only symptoms rather than root causes, touching upon the myth of the hero and the stereotype of the soldier, and the specific political ideologies in which these flourish, without ever locating those in the discourses of masculinity. As ever, it is Tom Cruise who hints at that possible investigation,[20] but by virtue of both his and Firth's perfect embodiment of precisely those characteristics which are deemed quintessentially masculine, in their screen personae, the route is closed off. Ironically, if Cruise's own discussions of masculinity are anything to go by, he would have been more than capable of carrying such a provocative and far-reaching debate.

Notes

1. *Wogan*, BBC-1, 27 May 1988.
2. J. Pilger, *Weekend Guardian*, 24–25 February 1990, pp. 12–15.
3. R. Scheer, 'Playboy Interview', *Playboy*, January 1990, p. 56.
4. *Born on the Fourth of July* (Universal Pictures, 1989).
5. E. Dutka, 'What would happen to Tom Cruise if . . .', *Empire*, March 1990, p. 38.
6. Scheer, op. cit., p. 56.
7. *Wogan*, op. cit.
8. M. Esslin, *The Field of Drama*, (London: Methuen, 1988), pp. 59–60.
9. Telephone interview with Val Taylor, 29 March 1990.
10. *Wogan*, op. cit.
11. R. Scheer, 'Born on the Third of July', *Premiere*, February 1990, p. 53.
12. Scheer, *Premiere*, op. cit., p. 53.
13. P. Chutkow, 'Soldier of Misfortune', *Time Out*, 31 January–7 February 1990, p. 16.
14. Scheer, *Playboy*, op. cit., p. 39.
15. Dutka, *Empire*, op. cit., p. 39.
16. Chutkow, *Time Out*, op. cit., p. 16.
17. J. Kornbluth, 'Fortune Smiles', *Elle*, May 1989, p. 54.
18. R. Dyer, *Stars* (London: British Film Intitute, 1986) p. 59.
19. *Premiere*, November 1989, p. 98.
20. Scheer, *Playboy*, op. cit., p. 58.

Acknowledgements

Special thanks to Geraldine Moloney, United International Pictures, London.
Thanks to: Ian Carre, Yorkshire Television; Richard Eyre, Royal National Theatre; Jeremy Ridgman and Felicity Lander, Roehampton Institute of Higher Education.

Further Reading: Vietnam

G. Adair, *Hollywood's Vietnam* (London: Heinemann, 1989).
M. Baker (ed.), *Nam* (London: Arrow Books, 1978).
T. Christensen, *Reel Politics: American Political Movies From Birth of a Nation to Platoon* (London: Basil Blackwell, 1987).
M. Herr, *Dispatches* (London: Picador, 1978).
S. Karnow, *Vietnam: A History* (London: Penguin, 1984).
M. Klein, 'Historical Memory: Film and the Vietnam Era', in *Red Letters* RL22, March 1988, pp. 21–34.
R. Kovic, *Born on the Fourth of July* (London: Pocket Books, 1976).
R. J. Lifton, *Home From the War: Vietnam Veterans neither Victims nor*

Executioner, (London: Wildwood House, 1974).

T. O'Brien, *If I Die in a Combat Zone* (London: Granada, 1980).

T. Page, *Tim Page's Nam* (London: Thames and Hudson, 1984).

A. Santoli, *Everything We Had* (New York: Ballantine, 1982).

N. Sheehan, *A Bright Shining Lie* (London: Jonathan Cape, 1989).

G. O. Taylor (ed.), 'The Vietnam War and Postmodern Memory', *Genre* XXI, 4 (Winter 1988) University of Oklahoma Press.

J. Walsh and J. Aulich (eds), *Vietnam Images: War and Representation* (London: Macmillan, 1989).

11

Conspiracy and Consensus: Television Drama and the Case of *A Very British Coup*

JEREMY RIDGMAN

. . . it's impossible to be paranoid nowadays because there are so many conspiracies about: and so paranoia has lost its meaning. If you don't think there is a conspiracy you're really terribly naive. And after what we've learnt about the intelligence services just recently, plainly there are conspiracies going on all over the place.

Ken Loach's comment during shooting for his film *Hidden Agenda*[1] testifies to a vital strand in the popular consciousness, one which wove its way unmistakably into British film and television drama during the 1980s. Well before the allegations of a secret shoot to kill policy in Ulster (the subject of Loach's film), before the revelations of *Spycatcher*, before Ponting, Tisdall and Massiter, British screen fictions had begun to reflect unease about the secret machinations of the state. Early forays at the turn of the decade into the Second World War legacy of black propaganda and secret intelligence in David Hare's *Licking Hitler* and Ian McEwan's *The Imitation Game*, and the underworld of municipal corruption, international crime and IRA terrorism in *The Long Good Friday*, paved the way for a cluster of films in the mid-1980s, all reflecting apprehension about the covert and increasingly authoritarian nature of centralised power in Britain. 1985 alone saw the release of the feature film *Defence of the Realm*, the BBC serial *The Detective* – which dealt with the unofficial growth of a national police force – and (also from the BBC) the television adaptation of Robert McCrum's novel *In the Secret State*, a tale of the collusion between government, multinational corporations and private databases in the illicit surveillance of the ordinary citizen. In the same year, perhaps the most fêted television drama of the decade, the BBC serial *Edge of Darkness*, probed the dark triple alliance between Whitehall, a secretive nuclear industry and the new American entrepreneurial and technological ideology of the 'high frontier'.

Later examples of the form were to include the serial *Rules of Engagement*, set during secret preparations for the aftermath of an impending nuclear attack, and, as well as *Hidden Agenda*, two contrasting dramatic treatments of the shoot to kill question – *1996*, G. F. Newman's fictionalised projection of the Stalker investigations into a violent dystopia of political unrest and police execution squads, and Peter Kosminsky's drama-documentary for Yorkshire Television, *Shoot to Kill*. However, it is the three-part serial *A Very British Coup*, adapted for Channel 4 by Alan Plater from the novel by Labour MP Chris Mullin and directed by Mick Jackson, which perhaps epitomises this genre of conspiracy screen thrillers and which certainly marks the furthest extent of its penetration into the implications of the state within the state.[2] While all these films and dramas engage at some level with specific symptoms of the increasingly anti-democratic power of centralised institutions of the state, *A Very British Coup* confronts what in popular terms might be regarded as the most fundamental of political questions; who runs the country? The answer provided by this apocalyptic fable of treason and de-stabilisation is unequivocal: power resides in an unofficial alliance between the financial institutions, the media industry, the economic and military forces of the USA and, above all, the privileged upper echelons of the civil service.

This surge of conspiracy fictions can possibly be seen as a response to tangible developments in the politics of the right, particularly those that seem to characterise the early years of Thatcherism. The threat of a national police force, the clamp-down on trade unionism, the harassment of the BBC and the surveillance of dissident, particularly anti-nuclear, activists; all evolved out of an identifiable ideology of the 'enemy within', cultivated and sustained through the particular confrontations of the miners' strike, GCHQ, Greenham Common and the Falklands war. Like a number of these other films, *A Very British Coup* is set in the near future (1989 in the novel, the early '90s in the adaptation) but its roots go deeper than the objective consolidation of the state under the Thatcher administration. The primary reference points of Mullin's novel lie on the one hand in the belief that the left were situated to take control within the Labour Party and, on the other, in the lingering suspicion that events behind the last days of the Wilson administration may not have been all they seemed. According to Mullin, the idea for the novel came from a conversation during a train journey, sometime in the late 1970s, in which he and three party colleagues speculated about whether a radical Labour government would ever be allowed to remain in power.[3] The novel was published in 1982 and the film option taken out by the production company, Skreba films, the following year, but it was not until script development was well under way that Peter Wright's confirmation of the attempted de-stabilisation, however inefficient, of the Wilson administration by MI5, began to emerge. As one of the producers, Sally Hibbin, would later point out, the original script 'was in a way quite gentle, and as the Wright allegations emerged we realised that the reality was much harder and tougher than our story. We then had to make it all sharper.'[4]

In fact, Alan Plater's script for the serial, while it adds specificity to a number of historical references, is largely concerned with developing the imaginative scope of the fantasy underpinning the dramatic scenario. Each of the three episodes centres on one of the key confrontations between the newly elected Perkins and the forces of the Establishment – a bank crisis, an engineered strike in the power industry and (the main plank in the government's radical programme) the initiation of multi-lateral nuclear disarmament and negotiations to remove American military bases from British soil. However, it is in the final dénouement that a crucial re-shaping of the narrative takes place. Instead of a gradual collapse of morale in the administration – brought about, in Mullin's scenario, by an accident in the nuclear power industry – we have a triumphantly stage-managed public relations stunt as Perkins has the first Polaris warhead dismantled in full view of the nation's television cameras: and a meek retreat into 'ill health' gives way to a dramatic show-down, the eventual outcome of which is to be both more extreme and more ambiguous. Confronted by the head of the security forces, Sir Percy Browne, with forged statements from bank accounts in Geneva, showing him to be in the pay of Moscow – an allusion to the smearing of Labour minister Ted Short in 1974 – Perkins decides to call his blackmailers' bluff. In one last media 'coup', he appears on television, substituting for the pre-scripted resignation announcement his own account of the plots against him and, promising a public enquiry into the allegations, he calls a general election. Finally, as election day dawns, the World Service news warns of an impending statement from Buckingham Palace 'expected to clarify the constitutional situation' and, in the closing image, the shadow of helicopters falls over a polling station: the screen goes to black, sound is cut and, after a few seconds pause, the credits roll.

This ending is open only in so far as it dares the spectator not to believe the worst. From the fleeting shot over uniformed shoulders during Perkins' victory speech in the first episode to the more emphatic juxtaposition of Percy's final, icy plea 'Who will free me from this turbulent priest?' with an image of the generals impassively watching the speech to the nation, and not least in the slow-motion image of exploding petrol bombs that accompany the opening titles, there have been portents of the military solution that the novel deliberately avoids. Indeed, the comparison with the overthrow of Allende in 1973, which in the novel serves to indicate the bloodlessness of Perkins' downfall, is conveyed here in the more coded form of a news item on an earthquake in Chile; guarded ambiguity combined with apocalyptic premonition.

In its balancing of intrigue with counter-intrigue and its movement towards the dark dystopia of the final episode, this adaptation is a very different sort of political thriller from the original. The detailed literalism of Mullin's writing is rejected for a fast moving, melodramatic and tautly edited narrative, in which the audience themselves are often required to supply the connective tissue of the plot. The distilled scenario also concentrates on a tighter and less schematic group of characterisations. Perkins himself, foregrounded from the opening shot as the principal dramatic subject, is tougher and more astute than his prototype, his sense of humour an important element in the utopian exhilaration of the first episode but also as a strategy in the tactical manoeuvres of the developing scenario. The forces ranged against him also undergo a transformation. Mullin's Establishment archetypes, plotting together from the sequestered luxury of the Athenaeum, are replaced by a more diverse set of power-brokers, figures with little apparently in common but communicating by a discretely coded system of leaks, hints and delegated responsibility. Sir Percy Browne's passionate opposition to Perkins is balanced by a respect for the foe and distaste for the measures to which he is driven – a patrician sensibility heightened by the contrast with his fanatically zealous assistant, Fiennes. This adversarial relationship, which reaches its climax in the final face-to-face confrontation over the forged bank statements, gradually acquires a mythic dimension, a sense of combatants inheriting an ancient struggle that stretches back through generations, as both men recognise, 'yea, even unto the Middle Ages.'

The newspaper owner, George Fison, on the other hand, is a more recognisably contemporary figure and his active presence throughout the drama a considerable development upon the hastily sketched press baron of Mullin's opening chapter. The owner of a cable television network as well as newspapers, he is also an active journalist, making guest appearances on current affairs programmes and, more significantly, leading the campaign against Perkins with his own headlines and editorials. For a central, dynamic element in the adaptation of *A Very British Coup* – a function both of the transfer to television and of the explosion in information technology that has taken place even since the book was first written – lies in the foregrounding of the politics of the media itself.

In its transposition to the medium of television, the title of Mullin's fiction appears to acquire a particular self-reflexive irony. Seen in terms of the politics of cultural intervention, the broadcasting of a popular serial presenting a radical critique of the fundamentally anti-democratic nature of power in Britain might well be regarded as a coup in its own right. Indeed, the same metaphor is to be found in Catherine Itzin's description of Trevor Griffiths' eleven-part television drama *Bill Brand* as an 'interventionist coup'.[5] Transmitted by Thames Television in 1976, this serial dealt with the conflict between the radical socialism of a young labour MP and the contradictions in the struggle for parliamentary power. In the penultimate episode, which centres on the battle for the leadership of a post-Wilson Labour government, the forces of reaction are exerted not through any objective conspiracy but effortlessly and anonymously through the belief within the party that a left-wing candidate would simply not receive the call from Buckingham Palace. The conspiracy scenario, in other words, is pre-empted by ideology: 'Power,' as Brand himself observes, 'indeed.'

There is clearly a considerable distance between the critique of Labourism that runs through much of the work of Griffiths, Loach and Garnett's *Days of Hope* (even the early Potter play *Vote, Vote, Vote for Nigel Barton*) and a series which begins by celebrating the arrival at 10 Downing Street of a working-class socialist some time in the early 1990s. Indeed, the radical tradition in television drama (such as it exists) has been largely concerned with the polemical and historical interrogation of what Graham Murdock refers to as 'the twin legacies of Stalinism and social democracy', and in its New Left scepticism has tended towards a mode of critical and historical realism very different from the epic futurism of texts such as *A Very British Coup*. The charismatic characterisation of a Perkins may be seen as something of an antidote to these more familiar representations of betrayal and compromise. An oblique acknowledgement of this inheritance occurs when, alone for the first time amid the august splendour of the cabinet room, Perkins talks of the 'odd whiff of betrayal', but it is left to his opponent, in the final confrontation, to drive home the historical analysis. 'You're a bad dream,' declares Sir Percy. 'I could always comfort myself that socialism would never work because it has always been in the hands of bungling incompetents, trimmers, compromisers. But you, Mr Prime Minister, could destroy everything I've ever believed in.'

Behind the comparison with *Bill Brand*, however, lies a more fundamental political question of television drama as an area of radical cultural practice. The idea of such a text as an 'interventionist coup' has its roots in what Griffiths himself refers to as 'strategic penetration'[6] – a conscious project whereby the socialist playwright engages not only with established or familiar modes of representation (mainly forms of popular realism) but with the dominant cultural institutions themselves as a means of creating meaning for the widest possible audience. Ultimately, this interventionism is concerned not only with the issue of a mass audience but with contesting the cultural hegemony at its strongest point. Thus, at the heart of the theory lies the very commitment to television itself, as opposed to the more marginal site of theatre, a commitment which in the inevitable dialectic between opposition and accommodation may entail a certain redefinition of the functions of the writer and an involvement in areas of production such as casting, rehearsal, even negotiations over scheduling. Key examples of such strategic practice are to be found in John McGrath's involvement during the 1960s with the early *Z Cars*, in the wide range of Griffiths' writing for television during the 1970s, from single plays to serials and adaptations, and in the long-standing collaboration between the writer Jim Allen and the producer Tony Garnett and director Ken Loach, which culminated in 1976 with *Days of Hope*.

How valid is the model of radical interventionism for assessing the political nature, a decade later, of a project such as *A Very British Coup*? This particular serial is the product of a period of enormous change in the organisation and expectations of television drama and of the medium in general. At one level, the complex process by which a serial such as this reaches the screen, particularly in the context of the relationship between Channel 4 and an independent film company such as Skreba Films, differentiates it from any idea of identifiable strategic practice. The notion at the centre of interventionism – that of the entrist author (who may be the writer or the producer), motivated by a political commitment and engaged in a strategic struggle on behalf of an inherently 'progressive' text – seems peculiarly inappropriate to such a situation.

Moreover, the retreat during the 1980s of writers such as Griffiths, Hare and Allen and the departure of Tony Garnett for film-making in America would appear to suggest an environment increasingly intolerant of the politically subversive work. Compared with the theoretical debates of the 1970s, more recent discussions of television drama in general have been dominated by fears of attrition rather than assimilation and few commentators would have dissociated themselves in 1990 from the nagging pessimism behind a National Film Theatre retrospective of 'quality' television in the 1980s – plaintively titled 'Goodbye to All This?' – nor from the prognosis which placed 'experimental, expensive or controversial drama' alongside investigative journalism, children's programmes and avant-garde comedy as one of the genres most vulnerable to the cost-effective imperatives of a broadcasting industry moving towards commercial de-regulation.[7] Nor can we ignore the extent to which the institutionalised retreat from the politically contentious in drama production has been induced by a climate of fear and self-censorship directly attributable to the ascendancy of the New Right. This, of course, is not simply a question of political content but of perceptions concerning the position of television itself, and particularly public broadcasting, within the wider ideological framework. 'How do you think it would look if just as Margaret Thatcher was about to be elected, we were stupid enough to record a play which featured a twelve-inch penis in a bottle?' David Hare recalls being asked by a BBC executive following the banning of Ian McEwan's *Solid Geometry* two days before it was due to be recorded:[8] and the delay in transmission of *Tumbledown* occasioned by the 1987 General Election tells its own story.

At the heart of the perceived vulnerability of television drama to the economic and political pressures of the 1980s has lain the precarious fate of the single play. Critical discussion at the beginning of the decade is marked by disquiet not only at tangible cut-backs in volume and quality in this field but at such identifiable shifts in emphasis as the dropping of the title 'Play for Today' and the new emphasis on film and co-production. For, despite the impact of serials such as *Days of Hope* and *Bill Brand*, the single play has occupied a privileged place in the critical canon of television drama. By the essential a-typicality of its relationship with the flow of the medium as a whole, its position, as the critic and one-time producer W. Stephen Gilbert puts it, 'outside the consensus', the single or one-off play has often been perceived as the principal bearer of the progressive or radical impulse in television.[9] Unfettered by the demands of continuity, format or familiarity of style and, above all, by the need to maintain a large audience, the single drama emerges blessed with the unique power to disturb and challenge, a shock, as it were, to the system represented by the medium as a whole.

The contradictions within this critical view are several, but at the centre lies the problem of intervention as the guarantee to a progressive discourse. As Stephen Gilbert admits, one of the signs of the freedom exercised by the single play is the creative access offered to individuals working outside the broadcasting institutions, particularly writers. For, paradoxically, the tradition of controversial work has often been fostered on the back of a paternalistic cultural ideology, particularly within the BBC – an attitude, partly inherited from the theatrical culture out of which the promotion of television originally grew; in short, the 'play', manifestly the work of a 'playwright', can be regarded as transcending the ephemerality of the medium and achieving the status of a work of dramatic literature or even 'art'. At the same time, the liberal tolerance of the authorial voice may act as a form of ideological containment, a means of privatising what may well be a very public text. As Ros Coward has argued, the elevation of Dennis

Potter to the position of the nation's 'greatest' television writer, and the accompanying critical obsession with the autobiographical basis of his work, may not be without a hidden agenda, much of it to do with masking the truly radical aspects of his work.[10]

It may be, then, but a short step from elevating the single play to a privileged position outside the consensus to having to acknowledge its cultural marginality and its inherent susceptibility to various forms of closure and recuperation. Furthermore, it must be recognised that the unique impact of any single play is increasingly eroded by the expanding volume and variety of dramatic fiction on television in general. In the late 1950s and early 1960s, the power of the play as a discrete dramatic event was considerably enhanced by the concentration of resources and attention into only two channels and by the comparative novelty of the medium itself. Ken Loach's observation that when a play went out 'half the nation watched' is no great exaggeration:[11] the 1958–59 season of ABC's Armchair Theatre comprised a remarkable forty-eight productions, with an average audience of eleven million, and this long before the distribution of television sets had reached saturation point.[12] In fact, this is precisely the figure quoted by Trevor Griffiths in identifying the unusually high ratings for his play *Through the Night* in 1975[13] and half a million *more* than the audience for the extensively publicised *Tumbledown* in 1988. The viewing figures for *Tumbledown* were far in excess of what would be expected for a one-off drama in the late 1980s and were later cited as proof of the 'oxygen of publicity' that had been provided by the pre-transmission campaign of vilification in the press: by contrast, Alan Bennett's series of monodramas, *Talking Heads*, had averaged four million viewers in the same Tuesday slot.[14]

During the 1980s, on both the creative and the critical fronts, the perceived association between the single play and the idea of a 'serious' or 'progressive' drama has steadily broken down. Clearly, this development has been greatly determined by economic and organisational considerations as companies have sought to rationalise resources in a world increasingly dominated by the imperatives of co-production and international sales, but it has also been shaped by producers and executives such as Margaret Matheson, Kenith Trodd, Michael Wearing and Jonathan Powell who have inherited from their own directing and editorial work in the 1970s a commitment to the dramatic and narrative sophistication of the serial form. That commitment is also demonstrated in the interventionist transition of writers like Griffiths and Potter from single plays to serials like *Bill Brand* and *Pennies from Heaven* as they consciously engaged with the stylistic and narrative dimensions of the extended form as a means of offering a more complex social and political argument. These early serials, and the highly inventive *Rock Follies*, stand out against the dominant genres of volume drama in the 1970s – the historical biography and the classical literary adaptation, with their shared fascination in the high production values and nostalgic glow of the costumed past. The block-busting *Brideshead Revisited* and *Jewel in the Crown* mark the watershed in a tradition that by the early 1980s had begun to price itself out of the market.

The remarkable popular impact of *Boys from the Blackstuff* in 1982 signalled the beginning of a steady development of the serial as a site for challenging new work. In particular, the serial began to inherit the mantle of indigenous, social contemporaneity which since the seminal *Cathy Come Home* had been the property of the single play. Serials such as *Edge of Darkness*, *The Singing Detective*, *The Monocled Mutineer*, *Blind Justice*, *The Life and Loves of a She-Devil*, *The Real Eddie English*, *Oranges Are Not the Only Fruit* and, of course, *A Very British Coup* have all been at the cutting edge of television's social, sexual and political discourse.

Embodied in this canon is a convergence between the traditionally polarised fields of 'art' television and 'popular' genre or format based production. Yet to recognise that convergence is, as James Donald has pointed out, to begin to beg questions about the critical privileging of any body of work within the television output.[15] In contrast with the formalist discussions of the 1970s, more recent work in cultural studies has evolved around a recognition of the polysemic nature of the television text – its openness to a variety of socially and ideologically determined readings. This emphasis on the spectator and the experience of television reduces the primacy accorded to the individual text itself and throws into question the validity of defining any one drama as inherently progressive. In respect of a serial which manifestly offers itself, by generic definition, as 'political', Terry Eagleton's caveat seems particularly appropriate: 'As far as "literature" goes, political is as political does: novels are political as much by virtue of their effects as by their themes, and the former cannot be "read off" the latter.'[16] A judgement of the possible effects of *A Very British Coup* must take into account not only its appropriation of a particular popular literary genre, but also its place in the popular discourse of television itself and the broader context within which television drama or fiction is mediated and received.

Michael Denning, in a recent study of the spy thriller, explains how this particular genre of popular political fiction has operated within the broad project identified by Lukács's account of the modernist novel, that of 'magically' reconciling 'individual experience with an increasingly reified and incomprehensible social order.'[17] One of the specific functions of the spy as a fictional character has been to provide a link between the actions of the ordinary individual and the broad historical movements of the twentieth century. 'The secret *agent* returns *agency* to a world which seems less and less the product of human action.' Denning also identifies more recent changes to the formula of the thriller, in *Day of the Jackal* and *Eye of the Needle*, which either build supposedly documented historical narratives on a counterfactual premise or insert an invented history into the fabric of documented events – 'secret histories', inspired by and drawing upon what John Sutherland calls 'the eradicable popular belief that the *real* facts of history are never given.'

As one of a small number of left-wing novels within this genre, Mullin's novel clearly contains two political projects. The first is broadly based in the appropriation and subversion of a popular literary genre traditionally dominated by the right-wing ideologies of imperialism, class and the Cold War. Thus, the inversion of a conventional narrative of treason and betrayal acts not only against the real 'enemy within' but against the nationalist assumptions at work within the ideology of the genre as a whole. The second aim, identifiable with Denning's model of the 'secret history', lies in a mode of predictive journalism, merging factual research and historical conjecture with an adventure narrative to endorse a contemporary structure of feeling concerning politics as a hidden agenda – what Mick Jackson identifies as the 'vague anxiety' about the state in the 1980s; 'a feeling deep down that things are spiralling out of control, that the rules of the game have been changed. It is an inarticulate, unexpressed feeling, but it is definitely there. Films like *A Very British Coup, Defence of the Realm* and *Edge of Darkness* help to legitimise such feelings.'[18]

In the dramatised and popular form of a television serial, the metaphor of agency embodied in characterisation resonates particularly loudly. From the triumphal opening of the victory journey from Sheffield to the final blackout, this political romance may implicitly endorse the ascendancy of socialist values, but the explicit concern of the narrative is less with socialism itself than with the extent to which the very realities of politics as a process have been obscured by the dark, cabalistic forces of reaction. Harry Perkins, particularly as re-drawn by Plater and realised in Ray McAnally's performance, serves to restore human agency to our perception of politics. Part man of the people, part hero in the mythic battle between the forces of light and dark, between truth and deceit, he is at the centre of the serial's popular and theatrical purpose.

The opposition between Perkins and the forces ranged against him is deeply embedded in the highly foregrounded stylisation of Jackson's film making. The expressionist lighting and camera angles of *film noir*, typically associated with the screen thriller and increasingly pastiched in the television commercials of the 1980s, are crucial to the 'look' of the serial, particularly in the depictions of the shadowy underworld of Sir Percy and Fiennes, the latter typically depicted framed by the darkness of his office, his face bathed in the sulphurous glow of his computer. This unashamedly literal symbolism also extends beyond the associative level of visual texture into key denotative areas of the narrative. The televised dismantling of the nuclear warhead is bathed in brilliant white light, the glare of huge film lamps a crucial component in the ecstatic theatricality of the event. By contrast, the final coup is marked by a blackout, which extends beyond the end of the narrative and into the final credits, which roll, quite literally, to the sound of someone – perhaps Perkins himself – whistling in the dark.

The association between this strand in the serial's imagery and the values invested in the characterisation of Perkins is at its most evident during the power crisis section of the narrative, significantly at the centre of the tripartite structure. 'Perkins' Darkest Hour' trumpets Fison's tabloid headline, as the lights go out across the nation, cabinet meetings begin to fall apart in acrimony and Perkins, accompanied at a discreet distance by his bodyguard, walks the city streets in a night of doubt and despair. A subjective flashback to the heady celebrations at the Sheffield station – superimposed over his close-up – and a lamp-lit encounter with his trusting local newsagent, Mr Patel, as he finds himself back in the

neighbourhood of his old London flat, emphasise the elision between political crisis and personal test of faith that is written into
this hour of darkness.

Images abound which continually reinforce this identification
between the integrity and strength of Perkins as a character and
the values associated with his politics. The shaving mug inherited
from his grandfather, the election campaign mug from which he
drinks his tea, the compulsive nocturnal game of darts are part of
an iconography which yokes working-class inheritance with personal idiosyncrasy yet without any ironically implied sense of
affectation. Running through the serial is the constant presence of
the Mozart C Minor Mass, and in particular the exuberant and
aptly titled Credo, which provides both an accompaniment to the
more triumphalist moments of the action and a *leitmotif* for Perkins
himself. 'When a man's weary of Mozart, he's weary of life,' he
breezily advises one of the more conspiratorial Downing Street
mandarins on overhearing the tail end of his conversation – one of
the many small, quick-witted theatrical coups which mark his path
through the drama: a coded demonstration for the benefit of the
unfortunate civil servant of his keen ear for the unguarded aside
and, for the spectator, sudden confirmation of the association
between the score and Perkins the political and humanist man.

It may be argued that the dramatic mileage invested in the
character of Perkins implicitly upholds a conservative ideology of
politics as definable by strong and charismatic leadership. Democracy may be at stake, but it is never seen at work. Cabinet meetings
are predominantly shot from Perkins' point of view and Parliament
itself is no more than a couple of voice-over extracts from Question
Time. Crowds cheer Perkins on his way to victory but are seen no
more. Indeed, in the closing credits the only names to appear
under 'The People' are key acquaintances of Perkins himself; his
mother, the faithful Patel, and the former mistress and middle-
class intellectual, Helen. It has been generally argued that the
political intention of narrative television drama is potentially
undermined by the conservatism of a form which encourages
identification with a central protagonist. The danger, as David
Edgar describes it in discussing *Bill Brand*, 'is that by the end of
eleven episodes, the audience is identifying with Brand exclusively
as the pivot of the story (my hero right or wrong), and sympathis-
ing with his views and actions only insofar as it is necessary to a
satisfactory dramatic experience . . . The audience is prepared to

share Brand's socialism for the duration of the play, but no longer.'[19]

The assumptions about the predictability and simplicity of audience response that underlie this formalist critique have been much discussed. What such an argument would fail to recognise in the case of *A Very British Coup* is the extent to which the essential politics of the narrative are those embodied in the dramatic and theatrical values of the serial as a whole. Unlike the tradition to which *Bill Brand* and much of Edgar's own political theatre belong, *A Very British Coup* is not a polemical work but a visionary, cautionary and celebratory one. The comedy which runs through the serial may be a tactical weapon in Perkins' armoury, but it is also an essential ingredient in the theatricality of the text's foregrounded style. The upbeat humour that characterises Perkins' ascendancy – the first episode ends with the joke of his own headline for the assembled reporters, 'Perkins Saved by Kremlin Gold', and the second with a parting shot to the American ambassador, 'Have a nice day?' – and fleeting visual 'gags' such as the image of Fison floating into sight in his swimming pool, foregrounded by a Mickey Mouse model, or Fiennes' wince of horror at the media spectacle of the nuclear disarming, is part of the element of participation offered by the spectacle of the serial itself, a dimension underwritten by the emphasis on changing fortunes and victories won and lost across the narrative as a whole.

A second participatory dimension lies in the narrative method itself. If the political thriller as a genre is predicated on the idea of politics itself as a secret process, a hermetic world out of reach of human agency, that sense is intensified in the transposition of the narrative of *A Very British Coup* to the medium of the screen. The explanations, descriptions and expository dialogues of the novel give way to a codified system of fleeting hints, looks and glancing fragments of conversation. Although not in itself a mystery story, this film narrative nevertheless foregrounds what Denning, employing the terminology of A. J. Greimas, refers to as the cognitive dimension of narrative ('what do I know?') over the pragmatic dimension ('what happens?').[20] The spectator is constantly required to decode the narrative from an intricately textured web of jump-cuts, uncontextualised shots and unresolved sequences of action.

Information – access to it, the technological proliferation and eradication of it – is at the heart of the scenario. Amid the familiar iconography of surveillance – the disembodied tape-recorder whirring into action, the telephoto cameras and binoculars, the bug in the ceiling – the computer screen occupies pride of place. Visual display units glow, cursors blink and data spills from files called up at the touch of a button. Certain events, a tumbling stock market or the elimination of an advisor, are even narrated by means of a matched shot of information appearing – or disappearing – on a computer screen. This emphasis on the power of information technology in the politics of secrecy is foregrounded in a key sequence during the power crisis when Perkins' press secretary and confidant uses the darts scoreboard to chalk up a diagram of the conspiracy against the government. This sequence, quite literally, is at the heart of the scenario, and its emblematic quality in terms of class difference and resistance is obvious, the stark contrast between the hand-drawn diagram and the sophisticated split-second technology of Fiennes' computer underscored by the echoes on the soundtrack of the electronic *musique concrète* associated throughout with the half scenes of secret intrigue.

The concentration on the power of the screen to shape and influence the political scenario extends to the overwhelming presence throughout the serial of television itself. Cameras follow Perkins to the door of 10 Downing Street as they do to the funeral of the Foreign Secretary's wife and his hold on power varies in proportion to his control of the initiative in the daily press briefings. But it is in the television studio that advantages are lost and won. Perkin's progress is charted through interviews, news items and commentaries, each media event overseen from the gallery by the same production crew, a sort of Greek chorus of the professionally detached – spectators to the action itself, momentarily fired into enthusiasm by the challenge of the nuclear warhead spectacular but frozen into a crisis of liberal conscience by the unprecedented order to 'fade to black'.

It is in the recurrent visual presence of television within the frame, and in the image of spectatorship as a dominant activity, that the power of the medium is most fully dramatised. A key motif, from beginning to end, is the television screen itself, framed in a variety of settings and watched by a range of characters. Sometimes this screen within the screen may be no more than the surface of the projected image, blown up into a close-up so extreme that colour and definition take on surrealistic proportions. Images may be ironic – the disembodied detail of a politician's mouth, or a disjunction between sound and vision – or they may serve to propel the narrative itself. At key moments in the scenario, however, both functions begin to merge. The end of the power strike and Perkins' return to public favour is marked by a bizarre, channel-hopping montage of images from the nation's restored television output (one which itself contains a screen within the image!). But it is in the three critical media 'events' of Perkins' regime – the election, the nuclear disarming and the final address to the nation – that the assimilation of television into the narrative is at its most complex. By the end of he warhead sequence, as the screen is filled with the animated image of doves released into a blue-black sky, we cannot be certain if what we are watching is Perkins' spectacle or an elaborate fantasy sequence that has been built out of it. A similar pattern emerges in the final speech to the nation. Of the sixty-four shots that make up this four-minute sequence, just under half are explicitly televisual in their framing – shots of Perkins on studio monitors or past cameras, shots of the abandoned autocue or shots of the broadcast itself beamed into the TV sets of watchers in the world outside, the whole sequence intercut with the unmediated close-up itself, as screen and frame merge to produce what is effectively a direct address to the audience itself.

There are elements of this experimental foregrounding of the conventions of television in earlier work by Plater, in particular his series *Trinity Tales* and *The Blacktoft Diaries*, but the shifting of spectatorial perspective and the transgression of the diagetic boundaries of the image and the narrative in *A Very British Coup*, given added dimension by the foregrounded stylisation of Jackson's film making, steers the serial into important but problematic areas of self-reflexivity. We are close here to Malcolm Bradbury's notion of television drama as 'a form for exploring not so much the naturalistic face of society [as] the modes by which we fictionalise it and ourselves into existence . . . penetrating the nature and the ambiguity of its own signs.'[21] Certainly there are echoes of the screen work of writers much admired by Bradbury in this respect, such as David Hare's *Licking Hitler* and Ian McEwan's *The Ploughman's Lunch*, both concerned with the relationship between broadcasting, propaganda and the public and private lie. The media-saturated world of *A Very British Coup* launches us into more ambiguous territory in which the process of politics is itself perhaps ultimately consumed not only by the forces of conspiracy but by the hyper-reality of the media themselves. Perhaps it is only in a particular mode of spectatorship – the active, imaginative participation in the narrative process itself – that the seeds of resistance to this bleak scenario are to be found.

Notes

1. *The Late Show*, BBC-2, April 1990. *Hidden Agenda* went on to win the Jury Prize at the Cannes Film Festival, to the consternation of several journalists present, who considered the film to be 'unBritish'.
2. *A Very British Coup*. All quotations are from the transmitted version.
3. See D. Perretta, 'Coup de Grace', *Time Out*, 15–22 June 1988, p. 47. The other travellers were Peter Hain, Stuart Holland and Tony Banks.
4. J. Petley, 'A Very Pretty British Coup', *Sight and Sound*, 57, 2 (Spring 1988), p. 96.
5. C. Itzin, *Stages in the Revolution: political theatre in Britain since 1968* (London: Eyre Methuen, 1980) p. 168.
6. See N. Andrews, 'Trevor and Bill: on putting politics before News at Ten', *The Leveller*, November 1976, pp. 12–13.
7. National Film Theatre programme, March 1990, p. 14.
8. D. Hare *et al.*, *Ah! Mischief: The Writer in Television* (London: Faber and Faber, 1982) p. 41.
9. W. Stephen Gilbert, 'The TV Play: Outside the Consensus', *Screen Education*, Summer 1985, 35, pp. 35–44.
10. R. Coward, 'Dennis Potter and the question of the television author', *Critical Quarterly*, 29, 1, p. 83.
11. *The Late Show*.
12. See G. Murdock, 'Radical drama, radical theatre', *Media, Culture and Society*, 1980, 2, p. 157.
13. T. Griffiths, Preface to *Through the Night and Such Impossibilities* (London: Faber and Faber, 1977).
14. *Guardian*, 13 June 1988, p. 23.
15. Editorial, *Screen Education*, pp. 1–2.
16. T. Eagleton, 'Towards a Critique of Political Fiction', *Meanjin*, 3, 1980, p. 383.
17. M. Denning, *Cover Stories: Narrative and Ideology in the British Spy Thriller* (London: RKP, 1987) p. 14.
18. Petley, p. 97.
19. D. Edgar, 'On political theatre: part two', *Socialist Review*, May 1978, pp. 35–38.
20. Denning, p. 125.
21. M. Bradbury, Introduction to *The After Dinner Game* (London: Hutchinson, 1982) pp. 18–19.

Index

INDEX

skip captain of a team who also decides strategy during the game

sponsor to support an organization or sport by giving money or other assistance

stamina ability to keep going for long periods of time without tiring too much, particularly while taking part in sport

strategy planning how to go about something, for example winning a game of curling

sweeping when players move their brushes back and forth in front of a moving stone in order to change its direction or make it go further

synthetic human-made, using chemicals

tactic action or technique used to achieve a desired goal

tee *see* button

volunteer do something you don't have to, usually without expecting to be paid

FIND OUT MORE

Books

Curling, Etcetera, Bob Weeks (John Wiley and Sons, 2008)

Ice Hockey and Curling (Winter Olympic Sports), Robin Johnson (Crabtree, 2009)

The Story of the Olympics, Richard Brassey (Orion, 2011)

The Winter Olympics, Nick Hunter (Raintree, 2013)

Websites

www.englishcurling.org.uk
Learn more about the curling scene in England on the English Curling Association's website.

news.bbc.co.uk/sport1/hi/other_sports/winter_sports/4464752.stm
This web page has a basic guide to curling, including video guides from Eve Muirhead.

www.olympic.org/curling
The official Olympic website has a section on curling.

www.royalcaledoniancurlingclub.org
The Royal Caledonian Curling Club is the governing body of Scotland. It has a Try Curling programme to introduce new players to the sport.

www.welshcurling.org.uk
Visit the Welsh Curling Association's website.

www.worldcurling.org
This is the website of the World Curling Federation.

Topics to research

- Find out how a sport goes from being a demonstration sport to an official Olympic one.
- Learn about which exercises are best for different aspects of curling.
- Research the history of curling, particularly in your own country.

Have a go!

Curling may not be a particularly well known sport, but since its inclusion in the 1998 Winter Olympics more and more people have become interested in the game. Numbers of people playing, watching live, and watching on television have increased all over the world. Curling is a fantastic and challenging sport to take up. Why not have a go yourself?

No Way!

Even the Simpsons have curled! In one episode of The Simpsons, Homer and Marge became part of a mixed doubles team that represented the United States in the Olympics. The episode was shown on television in the United States during the 2010 Winter Olympics.

Children can curl too! Ask your parents or a carer to take you to a local club and see how much fun it is to join in.

QUIZ

How much do you know about curling?
Test yourself with these questions.

1. Which member of a team does not usually sweep?

a) vice-skip

b) lead

c) skip

2. Which women's team has won the Olympics twice?

a) Canada

b) Sweden

c) Great Britain

3. How many countries play wheelchair curling?

a) 15

b) 24

c) 45

4. What is the 'stone of destiny'?

a) The last stone delivered by Great Britain when winning the Olympics in 2002

b) A well-known curler's engagement ring

c) The oldest curling stone

5. What's the maximum width of a curling sheet?

a) 10 metres

b) 5 metres

c) 200 centimetres

6. What type of material is often used on the bottom of a curling shoe?

a) Wood

b) Copper

c) Teflon

7. Who helped to develop the free guard zone rule?

a) Homer Simpson

b) Cassie Johnson

c) Russ Howard

8. What is pebbling?

a) Spraying the surface of the ice with hot water before a game

b) Throwing pebbles onto the ice to try to trip up the opposition

c) A victory dance done by any team that wins a major competition

7–8 correct answers: Clearly you know your stuff when it comes to curling! Perhaps you could be competing for medals in the future.

4–6 correct answers: Not bad. Try to join a club in your area and get some practice in.

1–3 correct answers: There is so much to learn about curling. Try to watch some on television or on the internet, and see if you can learn more about it. You might find you want to play!

GLOSSARY

Brier annual Canadian men's curling championship

button small circle at the centre of the house; also known as the tee. The main object of curling is to get the stones as close to the button as possible.

curling sheet area of ice where the game of curling is played

demonstration sport sport played at the Olympics before it is officially accepted as an Olympic sport. No medals are given out for demonstration sports.

end period of time during which each player throws two stones. Games have either eight or ten ends. An end is similar to an innings in cricket.

free guard zone area at the playing end between the hog line and the tee line, but not including the house

governing body group that ensures everyone plays a sport to the same rules and standards around the world

guard stone that is placed so that it protects another stone in the house

hack foothold at the end of the ice from which players push off when delivering a stone

hog line line that goes across the width of the curling sheet. Players must release the stone before they reach this line.

house area within the circles at each end of the curling sheet

Paralympic relating to the Paralympics, an international competition for disabled athletes that takes place every four years

pebbling method of preparing the ice for a curling game, in which water is sprayed onto the ice in order to reduce friction between the stone and the ice

rink curling team, or the name of the place where curling is played (ice rink)

round robin competition format in which each team plays every other team once

sheet *see* curling sheet

Olympic gold medal winners

Women
1998 Canada
2002 Great Britain
2006 Sweden
2010 Sweden

Men
1924 Great Britain
1998 Switzerland
2002 Norway
2006 Canada
2010 Canada

Paralympics

Wheelchair curling made its first appearance at the 2006 **Paralympic** Winter Games in Turin, Italy. Teams have four people and must include men and women. No sweeping is allowed in wheelchair curling. Delivery of the stones can be done by using an extender cue, a type of stick. In 2010, ten teams competed in Vancouver, Canada. Canada won the gold medal in 2006 and 2010.

Canada's men celebrate after receiving their gold medals at the 2010 Winter Olympics in Vancouver, Canada.

The World Championships

The top 12 curling nations come together once a year to compete in the World Curling Championships. The men's tournament was first played in 1959 and was well established by the time the women's event started in 1979. Few spectators went to the women's event, so from 1989 to 2004 the two tournaments were held together. Since 2005, the men's and women's events have been held separately. This is because it was felt that the women's game now had a decent following, and it also allows major curling events to be taken to more places.

NO WAY!

In 1968, Air Canada **sponsored** the world championship and called it the Air Canada Silver Broom. What was the prize given to the winners? A silver broom!

The 2012 World Men's Curling Championships took place in Switzerland. In this match, Scotland's are playing Canada.

The format

The format of the World Championships is the same as the Olympics – round robin followed by the play-offs – but with two extra teams. More than 30 countries try to get a place at the Championships, so teams have to play regional championships to determine who gets the available places. Europe gets eight places, North America two places, and the Pacific region (including Australia, China, and Japan) two places.

NAIL-BITING MOMENT!

The Women's World Championship final of 2006 was one of the closest matches ever. The US had only 50 seconds left on the clock to make the last delivery. The shot had to be rushed and left Sweden with a good chance to win. The winner of the gold medal was … Sweden!

Curling is so popular in Canada there are even postage stamps celebrating it!

Canada
postes / postage
8

The World Wheelchair Curling Championships

Switzerland and Sweden were the first countries to try wheelchair curling in 2000. The first World Wheelchair Curling Championship took place in Switzerland in 2002. The home nation won. The Championship now takes place every year except the year when the Paralympic Winter Games happen.

Tom Killin releases a stone during a match between Great Britain and the United States at the 2006 Winter Paralympic Games in Turin, Italy.

Other tournaments

An annual Junior World Championship has been played since 1975 for men, and 1988 for women. There are 10 teams and players must be under the age of 21. More recently, a Senior World Championship has been set up for the over-50s, as well as a Mixed Doubles World Championship in which one man and one woman plays on each team. The European Championship is played once a year between 37 curling nations. Sweden is dominant in the women's game, while Scotland has won the most men's championships.

NO WAY!

The 2005 Brier, held in Edmonton, Canada, was attended by 281,985 people.

National championships

The Four Nations is a tournament played every year by England, Scotland, Wales, and Ireland. Each team also plays each other in separate tournaments. Qualification for major tournaments is based on how the Scottish team does, but at these major tournaments a Great Britain team plays.

Japan's women's team competes at the World Junior Curling Championships in Scotland in 2011.

WATCHING CURLING

Curling has become more and more popular since its entrance into the Olympic Games. Watching curling is something many people now do, either by going to matches or watching on television.

Curling live

Going to see matches locally and at major championships is a pastime enjoyed by millions of people. The total number of spectators at Canadian men's tournaments regularly hits 200,000. There is nothing like going to a live sporting event and hearing everyone cheering for their team and celebrating success.

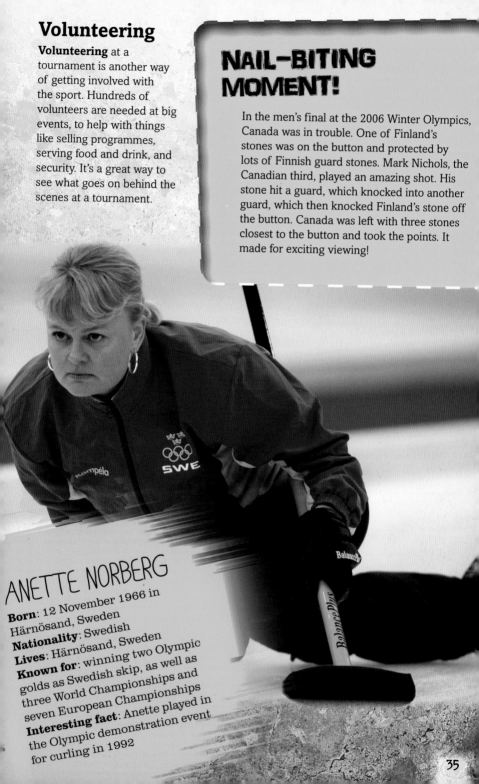

Volunteering

Volunteering at a tournament is another way of getting involved with the sport. Hundreds of volunteers are needed at big events, to help with things like selling programmes, serving food and drink, and security. It's a great way to see what goes on behind the scenes at a tournament.

NAIL-BITING MOMENT!

In the men's final at the 2006 Winter Olympics, Canada was in trouble. One of Finland's stones was on the button and protected by lots of Finnish guard stones. Mark Nichols, the Canadian third, played an amazing shot. His stone hit a guard, which knocked into another guard, which then knocked Finland's stone off the button. Canada was left with three stones closest to the button and took the points. It made for exciting viewing!

ANETTE NORBERG

Born: 12 November 1966 in Härnösand, Sweden
Nationality: Swedish
Lives: Härnösand, Sweden
Known for: winning two Olympic golds as Swedish skip, as well as three World Championships and seven European Championships
Interesting fact: Anette played in the Olympic demonstration event for curling in 1992

Built for television

An American curling commentator, Don Chevrier, once suggested that curling was 'built for television'. This is because there is space for cameras at either end of the sheet and the players wear microphones so that viewers can hear what they talk about during the team meetings between ends. Not only does the team's strategy get discussed, but listening in on all the stress and tension of playing in a major tournament can help to make the game more exciting for the viewer.

There are often several curling sheets in a curling arena. Here, several teams compete alongside each other at the 2010 Winter Olympics in Vancouver, Canada.

NO WAY!

Curling was not a well-known sport in the UK before the 2002 Winter Olympics. However, when Rhona Martin sent down the 'stone of destiny' (as it became known in the media) the nation celebrated. As Great Britain beat Switzerland, over six million people were watching on television – and it was past midnight!

Big viewing figures

Curling has become one of the most popular televised Winter Games sports, particularly in North America. Millions also watch in one of the newer curling nations, China. In Canada, even the finals of the men's and women's national championships were watched by over a million people.

Curling can be an exciting game to watch as the tension rises.

NAIL-BITING MOMENT!

In the Women's Olympic final in 2010, Canada and Sweden were playing a tense close match. Canada skip Cheryl Bernard's last stone of the 10th end failed to curl as much as she wanted, and the Swedish skip, Anette Norberg, was able to force an extra end. Bernard's last throw in the 11th end overcurled, and left one Swedish stone still in play. The Swedes celebrated – they had beaten Canada 7–6 to win the gold.

CURLING IS FOR EVERYONE

Curling is a game that can be played by anyone, from children to the elderly. Age is not important, because neither speed nor a lot of physical strength is essential. There are lighter stones for children to use. There are no inequalities – curling can be played by men and women on the same team (mixed). Age is not even an issue at international level. Eve Muirhead was made Great Britain's skip at the age of just 19, while Russ Howard was 50 when he helped Canada win gold in 2006.

As long as you're reasonably fit, your age shouldn't stop you from enjoying curling.

"I was surprised [at being made skip], but if you're good enough you're old enough."

– Eve Muirhead

EVE MUIRHEAD

Born: 22 April 1990 in Perth, Scotland

Nationality: Scottish

Lives: Blair Atholl, Perthshire, Scotland

Known for: Four-time world junior women's champion and skip of Great Britain in the 2010 Winter Olympics

Interesting fact: Eve is also excellent at playing the bagpipes, having performed in four World Championships!

Curling for disabled athletes

There are teams for wheelchair curling, people who are visually impaired, and those who are hearing impaired. Wheelchair curling is usually played by mixed teams. There are currently 24 countries taking part in wheelchair curling. Players who take part in wheelchair curling have lower body impairments and usually need wheelchairs for everyday life. Visually impaired curling might sound difficult, if not impossible, but it is a fast-growing version of the game. Hearing impaired curling is also becoming more common with a World Championships already set up.

Could curling be the game for you?

In the United Kingdom, curling is most popular in Scotland. There are more than 13,000 members of their governing body, the Royal Caledonian Curling Club. While international competitors train hard and have high levels of fitness, people playing casually at local clubs can decide how much they want to put into the sport. There is a Try Curling programme in Scotland, which allows people who have never played to give the game a go. There is also a scholarship called Winning Students for Scottish athletes, allowing them to study and curl.

Curling is a sport that is usually played indoors on ice rinks. However, sometimes it can take place outside in front of spectacular scenery.

Curling facilities in England and Wales are not as easy to find, but the English and Welsh Curling Associations' websites will have helpful information (see page 46). Open days for curling allow people to try the game for the first time.

Each team has a set of stones of the same colour. In major championships, the colours used are usually red and yellow.

Adapting

The position of stones in the house may change after every stone is delivered, so plans have to be adapted all the time to suit the situation. This involves quick thinking and decision making. For example, one of the things a skip might need to consider is what if the next shot is missed? What could be the consequences? The ice also has an effect on how stones move, so that too can affect strategy. All kinds of tactics that are not always obvious to the spectators may come into play.

THE SPIRIT OF CURLING

Curling has a reputation of sportsmanship, perhaps more than any other sport. There is a handshake before and after a game, and players wish each other 'Good curling'. If there is any breaking of rules, curlers usually own up. For example, if a player touches one of the opposition's stones as it is in motion (known as burning the stone), they are expected to declare this to the officials. Respect for fellow curlers is a very important part of the game.

"Curlers never knowingly break a rule of the game, nor disrespect any of its traditions ... the spirit of curling demands good sportsmanship, kindly feeling, and honourable conduct."

– Part of the WCF rules of curling document

Sportsmanship awards

Both men and women have the opportunity to win a sportsmanship award at the World Championships. For the men, the award is called the Collie Campbell Award. The women's version is known as the Frances Brodie Award. These awards are voted for by the players in the tournament. There are also awards made in the junior and wheelchair curling championships.

> "Curlers do not need an umpire or a referee or rules. They govern themselves as gentlemen."
>
> – Collie Campbell, former president of the International Curling Federation

RUSS HOWARD

Born: 19 February 1956 in Ontario, Canada

Nationality: Canadian

Job: When he isn't curling, Russ works in real estate, does some commentating, and also coaches in Switzerland

Known for: 2006 Winter Olympic gold medal winner and developer of the Moncton rule (now called the free guard zone rule, one of the main rules now used in international competition)

Interesting fact: Russ is the oldest Canadian ever to win an Olympic gold medal

FITNESS AND MENTAL STRENGTH

Perhaps the most important way for a player to improve their skills is to practise, but there are other things that can have an effect on how well they play.

Fitness

Fitness wasn't always seen as essential to the sport of curling – in fact, there was a view that it was only played by old, overweight people! However, these days most professional curlers are very fit. Pre-season training is now standard. Curling matches last about two hours, and in major tournaments more than one game can be played in a day. This means that **stamina** – being able to keep playing at a high level for a long time – is also important.

If players want to make a success of curling, they have to train hard. Gym work is just part of the training they do every day.

It's all in the mind

Players often talk about mental preparation being important for winning matches, but what does this mean? Thinking positively, being confident, staying relaxed, being motivated, and wanting to win are some of the things that top players do to stay at the top. Trying to get inside the mind of your opponents can help too.

"A team that is fit and has done its mental preparations probably has an edge on other teams."

– Shannon Kleibrink, skip for Canada at the 2006 Winter Olympics

"It used to be a hobby. It's nice to be able to say that we're athletes now. We train just as hard as other sports do. We live, sleep, eat, and breathe curling."

– Jackie Lockhart, GB curling team member, 2009

CHAMPIONSHIPS AND TOURNAMENTS

There are a number of different international competitions for curling as well as national tournaments and local leagues and events.

Sweden celebrates after beating Canada in the 2010 Winter Olympics.

The Winter Olympics

The Winter Olympics comes around once every four years, and is the main tournament for most players. There are two separate tournaments – one for women and one for men. In major championships like the Olympics, teams can have a fifth player known as an alternate. The players can be swapped from game to game, but not within a game.

Teams can get points for Olympic qualification from World Championships in the two years running up to Olympic year. The seven top teams qualify for the Olympics and are joined by the host team. A further two teams will qualify for the Olympics by topping the table at an Olympic Qualification Event held the year before the Olympics.

Olympic sport

Curling has been an official Olympic
sport since 1998, but its first
appearance (for men only) came in
the Winter Games at Chamonix
in France, in 1924. Curling was
considered to be a **demonstration
sport** at the 1924 games, which
meant the winners were not officially
recognized. However, over 80 years
later, in 2006, the IOC confirmed
curling as an official event, and
the medals awarded in 1924 were
given official status. The gold medal
winner? Great Britain.

NAIL–BITING MOMENT!

In the 2010 Winter
Olympics, the USA team
lost three matches in a row
on the very last shot of the
game. Unlucky!

The format of Olympic curling

At the Olympics, ten teams play a **round robin** format, so each team plays every other team once. The top four teams go into the quarter finals. The winner of a game between the first- and second-placed teams goes straight into the final, while the loser goes to the semi-final. They are joined by the winner of the match between the third- and fourth-placed teams. The winner of the semi-final meets the team that went through automatically to the final.

RHONA MARTIN

Born: 12 October 1966 in Irvine, Scotland

Nationality: Scottish

Job: works as an elite coach with the Scottish Institute of Sport and was a TV commentator during the 2010 Winter Olympics

Known for: skip of Great Britain team who won the 2002 Winter Olympics, Great Britain's first Winter Olympics gold medal in 18 years

Interesting fact: Rhona carried the Olympic torch through Glasgow in June 2012

THOMAS ULSRUD

Born: 21 October 1971 in
Oslo, Norway
Nationality: Norwegian
Started curling: 1981
Known for: being skip for
Norway; winner of silver medal at
2010 Winter Olympics
Interesting fact: Became well
known at the 2010 Winter
Olympics for wearing the loudest
trousers you've ever seen!

HOW TO PLAY

To deliver a stone, a player holds it close to their toes, pushes off from the hack, slides forward, and then releases the stone. At this point, a player can use the handle to make the stone curl clockwise (known as an in-turn) or anti-clockwise (known as an out-turn). The stone must be released before it crosses the hog line. It must then cross the far hog line in order to be in play.

The three main shots are:

- **The draw** – this gets a stone into the house
- **The guard** – this places a stone at the front of the house to protect the stone nearest the tee (the one that will score a point) from the opposition's stones
- **The hit** – this removes one or more of your opponent's stones from play

When delivering a stone, a player has to be careful not to put too much force into the release or the stone may not go in the required direction.

Sweeping

Sweeping the ice in front of the stone helps to control how far the stone travels, and also the direction it moves in. Sweeping melts the ice slightly, allowing the stone to travel further and straighter. All team members can sweep between the tee lines, but beyond the tee line, only one player is allowed to sweep.

NO WAY!

Good, experienced players can help the stone to move a further 1.5–1.8 metres by sweeping. That's about the height of an adult.

Strategy

Strategy – deciding what shot to play – is very important in the game of curling. At the start of a match, teams flip a coin to see who gets last stone advantage. This is when a team gets to deliver the final stone of an end, which is known as the hammer. Whichever team scores in an end then takes the first stone in the next end. Strategy for an end is usually based on whether or not the team has last stone advantage. Earlier stones can set up what hopefully can be finished off with the final delivery – although it depends on the other team, of course!

The skip usually stands behind the tee so he or she can determine what the best path for the next stone will be. When the skip is delivering the stone, the vice-skip takes this role. While the skip makes the final decision about the placement of a stone, team discussions occur before each end, and often before each shot.

The US team discuss **tactics** at a match against China during the 2010 Winter Olympics.